TRADE, INCOME LEVELS, AND DEPENDENCE

D1477568

STUDIES IN
INTERNATIONAL ECONOMICS

Editors

JAGDISH N. BHAGWATI
JOHN S. CHIPMAN

Volume 8

NORTH-HOLLAND
AMSTERDAM · NEW YORK · OXFORD

TRADE, INCOME LEVELS, AND DEPENDENCE

MICHAEL MICHAELY
The Hebrew University of Jerusalem

1984

NORTH-HOLLAND
AMSTERDAM · NEW YORK · OXFORD

ISBN: 0 444 867716

Published by:
ELSEVIER SCIENCE PUBLISHERS B.V.
P.O. Box 1991
1000 BZ Amsterdam
The Netherlands

Sole distributors for the U.S.A. and Canada:
ELSEVIER SCIENCE PUBLISHING COMPANY INC.
52, Vanderbilt Avenue
New York, N.Y. 10017
U.S.A.

Library of Congress Cataloging in Publication Data

Michaely, Michael.
   Trade, income levels, and dependence.

   (Studies in international economics ; v. 8)
   Includes bibliographical references and index.
   1. Commerce. 2. Income. 3. Dependency. I. Title.
II. Series: Studies in international economics (Amsterdam,
Netherlands) ; v. 8.
HF1411.M485 1984   382'.01   84-5951
ISBN 0-444-86771-6

PRINTED IN THE NETHERLANDS

INTRODUCTION TO THE SERIES

This series is intended to embrace all aspects of international economic analysis: theoretical empirical and econometric. It will equally encompass contributions to pure and monetary theory.

The series will include the publication of collected essays, conference proceedings of exceptional professional quality and interest, and edited volumes addressed to specific phenomena of importance in the analysis of international economics. It will particularly encourage, however, the publication of hitherto unpublished studies which represent fresh and valuable contributions to the analysis of international economic problems.

The *Journal of International Economics* now provides an excellent outlet for original scientific work in international economics in article length form. For pamphlet length contributions, the different series published by the *International Finance Section* at Princeton have long been of exceptional value, even though they have not generally extended beyond international monetary issues. It is the hope of the editors that the launching of this series, *Studies in International Economics*, will now fill the lacuna in the systematic publication of monograph and volume length research output of international economists, and succeed in doing so consistently with the high quality that the promotion of scientific study of international economic issues requires.

THE EDITORS

CONTENTS

PART II. INCOME LEVELS AND TRADE PATTERNS

ACKNOWLEDGEMENTS

This study was started when I was a Fellow of the Leonard Davis Institute of International Relations at the Hebrew University of Jerusalem, during 1975–77. Much of the work presented in the second part of the study was done during my visits to the Institute of International Economic Studies at the University of Stockholm in the summers of 1977, 1978 and 1980; whereas the first part, as well as the book as a whole, was completed during my tenure as Visiting Scholar at the Hoover Institution, Stanford University in 1981–82. I am deeply grateful to these institutions. I also wish to acknowledge the continuous financial support for the project from the Aron and Michael Chilewich Chair in International Trade at the Hebrew University.

Partial findings of the project were often reported in conferences and seminars in Australia, England, Israel, Sweden and the United States. I was fortunate to receive on these occasions comments, suggestions and criticism from which I have greatly benefited. Of particular help has been the constructive advice offered by Gary C. Hufbauer and by Alexander J. Yeats. Helpful suggestions have also been made by an anonymous referee of the series of *Studies in International Economics*.

I am most heavily indebted to Matti Gutraich, who has shouldered all throughout the heavy load of compilation and manipulation of the data. His contribution to the project has been major. I am also indebted to Mary Berg, Eva Jondal, Parameswar Nandakumar and Christina Peck for further statistical assistance, and to Susan Hammond for her expert handling of the typing of many drafts as well as of the final manuscript of the study.

Much of the material in chapters 6 and 7 of this book appeared, under the title "Income Levels and the Structure of Trade", in the volume on *The World Economic Order: Past and Prospects*, published by the Macmillan Press in 1981. Similarly, the subject matter of chapter 10 was mostly contained in a paper on "The Income Level of Exports and Tariff Discrimination", which appeared in the special volume on *Issues in International Economics*, published by The Oriel Press. Permission for reproduction from these publishing houses is gratefully acknowledged.

PREFACE

This is a study of attributes of size and structure of foreign trade and their implications for several major issues of concern for national and international economic policies. The study is divided into two parts: "Trade Dependence: Concepts and Measurements"; and "Income Levels and Trade Patterns".

The first part is designed as a contribution to the theory and measurement of economic dependence; specifically, the dependence of nations on their foreign trade. It is an issue that has occupied a major position in politics, as well as in economics, for generations; but about which precious little in the way of systematic work has been carried out – a scarcity particularly pronounced where quantitative aspects of the analysis are concerned. Hirschman's (1945) pioneering study of some aspects of trade dependence has remained, some forty years later, in almost splendid isolation. While it would be illusory to expect *all* components of dependence to be potentially subject to quantitative description, I believe that much could be done in the way of conceptual clarification and of devising methods for empirical work on the issue. This is the essence of the first part of the study.

The second part starts not with an issue, but with a *tool*. A simple index of income level of trade is proposed, with the aid of which many issues of international trade theory and policy may be investigated more effectively than otherwise. Several such issues – the testing of alternative trade theories, the pattern of product cycles, the terms-of-trade between poor and rich, and the possible existence of discrimination in commercial policies – are indeed analyzed by the application of the proposed tool.

Each of the two parts of the study is constructed as an integrated and systematic discussion, within which the analyses of issues follow on from each other and depend on each other. The two separate parts, on the other hand, are self-contained, and could be handled independently. They are, however, similar in nature, beyond the fact that the data requirements for the two parts to a large extent overlap. Many of the basic issues and concerns, in particular a focus on the relationships of trade levels and trade structure to income levels and stages of development, are shared by both. Even more important, the study as a whole follows the same fundamental analytic approach. It searches to define and clarify concepts and methods, and to offer empirical illustrations. These components are highly interdependent. It is impossible to justify or, to the contrary, to deny the validity of a contemplated empirical verification, without an appreciation of the conceptual problem. In turn, it would be of very limited use to offer a conceptual analysis which would then be irrelevant for practical application and for the derivation of empirical inferences. As a rule, the measurement actually carried out is in this study meant only partly to suggest substantive, specific conclusions, rules, or patterns; it is meant more to demonstrate the concreteness and relevance of the conceptual issues, and the practical applicability of the methods and measures proposed in the study. In other words, this is viewed primarily not as a study which seeks to provide answers to issues but as an investigation of concepts and methods.

Yet, an indication of some specific, concrete findings may perhaps be in order at the outset. Thus, for instance, the study of indexes of trade dependence shows that the impression of Japan as the least dependent, or least open, of the developed economies may be misleading. This impression is gained from the observation of trade ratios; but appropriate qualifications of this index would change substantially the overall view. Similarly, still in the case of Japan, the perception that the country's degree of dependence has not changed much in the post-war period is due to the use of a given set of prices. The use of an alternative set – just as legitimate – would show a remarkable increase of openness. In the study of income levels, the adoption of conceptual approaches proposed in this analysis reveals that the terms of trade of the poor nations in their trade with the rich have *improved*, in the postwar period – contrary to conventional wisdom. A somewhat different application shows that no discrimination against the trade of the poor nations is apparent in the pattern of commercial policies followed by their rich partners. These, and similar conclusions, are inferences which illustrate the significance of the conceptual analysis proposed in this study.

A word about data. The nature of the study dictated the use of uniformly classified data pertaining to a very large number of goods and of countries – ideally, most often, to all countries and goods. This restricted the sources of data to international (mostly, United Nations) publications, excluding country-specific or unpublished sources (except on a few occasions, where the nature of the investigation required some other, specific information). The conceptual discussion and the methods of measurement devised and applied in the study are relevant in principle to international trade in goods and *services*. Since the required data on services are either inaccessible or absent altogether, and could not feasibly be assembled or constructed, the empirical content of the study is restricted to the trade in *goods*. This is obviously a deficiency; but not a fatal one, due to the fact that in the large majority of countries, and in the world as a whole, trade in goods constitutes the major component of international trade transactions.

Work on the study has been carried out over a stretch of a few years – partly, at least, due to the time-consuming process of the extensive manipulation of a very large body of data. Very often, it was deemed preferable to select for the empirical illustration data for the most recent years for which they were available. Since various segments of the study were undertaken at varying points of time, this has meant a shifting basis for the "most recent" data. Thus, no uniformity exists in the time coverage of the data in different parts of the study. Since, however, no conclusions of the study depend on a general evaluation which relies on some integration or incorporation of *all* the measurements offered in the study, this lack of uniformity would be immaterial for the purposes of the study.

The first five chapters of the book present the first part of the study, the investigation of dependence on trade; whereas the following five chapters submit the analysis of the second part – the study of the income level of trade flows. In addition, appendix A summarizes, for convenience of reference, the indexes developed and used in the study; and appendix B presents the Standard International Trade Classification – the basic scheme which serves for most of the study – so that the full description of goods could be dispensed with in the individual tables throughout the book.

PART I

TRADE DEPENDENCE: CONCEPTS AND MEASUREMENT

CHAPTER 1

INTRODUCTION: DEPENDENCE – CONCEPTS AND APPROACH

This chapter will set the stage for the study of dependence on foreign trade which will be undertaken in the next four chapters. It will define and delineate the subject matter of the study, and describe the approach which the study follows. To a large extent, this will be done through a process of elimination: A variety of possible concepts, or procedures, will be briefly surveyed, narrowing it then down to the concepts and procedures actually adopted in the present study.

1. Dependence: An all-inclusive concept

Dependence of one nation on others has been the focus of a vast amount of studies in the post-war years, although mostly in socio-political analyses rather than in strictly "economic" literature. It has constituted a major element in the analysis of "North–South" relationships, in particular in the contributions of the "Dependency School" in Latin America. It is interpreted in a multitude of ways and is assigned a plethora of meanings.

Very often, readings of the concept of "dependence" are far-reaching, in one sense or another. Thus, to some writers the concept suggests not a description of an actual dependence of one society on another, but a summary of certain attributes of the society itself (presumably, because most attributes potentially give rise to "dependence" in a stricter sense). For instance, an "underdeveloped" economy or a nonindustrialized one, or a society with a given class structure, or one with "inadequate" leadership, may be termed "dependent".

In another interpretation, "inequality" implies "dependence". Some may interpret this inequality in a very wide sense, so that the existence of poor nations alongside the rich indicates dependence of the former. To others, dependence would not be defined by inequality of stock ownership, but must relate to some flow relationships between participating countries, such as "unequal exchange" of goods and services in trade among countries.

Often, "dependence" would cover all aspects of social life: Effects of one nation on the other's cultural perceptions, social norms, social stratification, or foreign and domestic policies in all spheres. It may mean particular class alliances; specifically, the support of a "capitalist" class in the "periphery" (i.e. "dependent") nation by its counterpart in the "center". On other occasions, "dependence" is reserved for the description of purely "economic" relationships.

Being definitions, none of the interpretations given to the concept of "dependence" is either logically right or wrong. Some are clearly stated, while others may be confused and vague. Some are of a more operational nature, while others may be devoid of operational usefulness (the more so, one suspects, the more inclusive and ambitious the interpretation). Some are closer to the understanding of the term "dependence" in daily usage, while others may appropriate the term for phenomena which are quite removed from it. But in the main, the adoption of one interpretation of the concept or another must be a function of the subject matter in which one is primarily interested.

In the present study, only purely economic relationships and effects are of concern. That is, only "economic dependence" (dependence on and of economic variables) will be a topic of study. Moreover, it is still narrower; it is not "economic dependence" in general but that dependence which is attached to a certain segment of economic relationships among nations. Before, however, attention is restricted to this aspect alone, a brief mention of other forms of economic dependence may be in order.

2. Forms of economic dependence

Strict "economic" dependence may be grouped under five major headings:

(a) Dependence on trade in goods and (non-factor) services. The domestic economy uses, for consumption and investment, goods and services imported from the outside world; simultaneously (although, of course, not necessarily to the same extent), it sells to foreign countries part of the goods and services which it produces. This leads in rather obvious ways to a dependence of the home country on the outside world; and it is this dependence with which the present study will be occupied.

(b) Dependence on foreign capital and on capital income. The import of capital from the outside world leads to a dependence in a variety of ways. The channels and forms of dependence will be determined by, among other things, the nature of the capital exporter (e.g. a foreign government or a private-sector agent); by the claims established – a transfer on capital account will differ from an unrequited transfer and, when it is the former, a direct investment will differ from a long-term transfer, or from a short-term lending; and by similar considerations. The dependence associated with capital imports would be due, first, to the fact that part of the resources used in the importing economy – whether for consumption or investment, private or government – is provided (through an import *surplus*) by the outside world. More specifically, the rate of growth of the home economy may depend on other nations, through the impact of the foreign capital on the amount of resources available for investment; or the government sector may depend on them, if foreign capital serves, directly or indirectly, to finance government expenditures. The accumulation of capital transfers over time would also lead (if they are not of the unrequited nature) to a *stock* dependence; part of the nation's productive resources would be owned by the outside world. For the capital-exporting country, on the other hand, the ownership of claims on the outside world leads to the receipt of remuneration for capital services (dividend or interest payment), which makes the country dependent on these receipts to provide part of the resources which it, in turn, uses for consumption or investment.

(c) Dependence on foreign labor and on labor income. This form of dependence is, in a sense, a cross between the two aforementioned channels. Like the use of foreign capital, the employment of foreign labor implies that part of the economy's production of goods and services is made possible by the provision of a productive factor from the outside world. Unlike capital transfers, on the other hand, and in similarity to the use of some imported goods and (non-factor) services, the use of foreign labor involves the direct employment, or physical incorporation, of a foreign-provided element. And, again in similarity with the situation of capital transfers, the labor-exporting country depends on the outside world for the employment of part of its productive resource; and on the income derived from the rest of the world as payment for the factor's services to provide part of the resources used by the home economy for consumption and investment.

(d) Dependence on transfers of technology. Foreign technology may be embodied in a good or a factor, and thus may be imported to the home economy through them. Thus, some foreign skilled labor may be valued for its possession of certain technology, which is thus imported through labor rather than for other reasons; and some imported good – a tool or a piece of equipment – may embody a technology which is specifically owned by the foreign producer. Other elements of technological knowledge may be transferred directly (such as, say, by the sale of information or the sharing of patents), rather than be embodied in other factors and transacted through them. Be it as it may, transfers of technology are probably sufficiently important in the present-day world to merit a special mention and consideration.

(e) Macroeconomic influences. This final category differs from the rest in that it is really an *aspect* of all the others, rather than the result of a separate set of factors. Yet, again, its overwhelming importance deserves, perhaps, a grouping under a separate heading. From the exports and imports of goods and services, long-term and (primarily) short-term capital movements (and accompanying changes in money, interest rates and exchange rates) or changes in the size of imported or exported labor force, macroeconomic effects on employment, production and prices would follow.

As stated earlier, this study will be confined to just those aspects of economic dependence which are associated with the transactions listed under the first heading; namely, to the dependence on the outside world created by trade with it in goods and services. For reasons noted in the preface, the empirical work will even ignore trade in services, although this component would be part and parcel of the conceptual analysis. Dependence originating from transfers of capital, of labor and of technology, will remain beyond the confines of the study.[1] Macroeconomic impacts of changes in foreign trade, on the other hand, although rarely mentioned or analyzed in any detail, will form an integral part of the subject matter throughout this discussion.

3. "Dependence", "inter-dependence" and "power"

The term "dependence" is interpreted in a variety of ways with regard not only to the extent of relationships which it covers, but also to the nature of such relationships. It is important to define the meaning in which it will be used in the present context; and, no less important, to make clear which are the definitions which will *not* be applied here.

A state of "dependence", for an individual or for a nation, implies of course that in one way or another the position of the agent concerned, and its activities, depend on the position and actions of others. But in some definitions, *mutual* situations of dependence are considered before a state of "dependence" is declared. Just as the home unit depends on others, so do the others depend on it – although, obviously, not generally to the same extent. Sometimes, any mutual dependence would be referred to as "interdependence". But other applications of the concept would reserve the latter term for the definition of a situation of mutual dependence in which the extent of dependence in both directions (between the home unit and foreign units, whether *in toto* or particular foreign units under consideration), is *equal*. Only *inequality* (or "asymmetry") in the extent of mutual dependencies would, by this interpretation, be defined as a situation of "dependence". The latter would thus be a "net" concept, and could not be mutual; either the home unit is "dependent" on others' or the others are "dependent" on it, or, in the limiting case of equality in relations, no "dependence" exists at all – the home unit and the foreigners are "interdependent".

Related to these distinctions is the concept of "power". "Power" stands for the extent to which a given unit is able, whether actively or potentially, to affect the position of others and manipulate their activities. It may, again, be understood

---

[1] A partial analysis of dependence on capital transfers may be found in my paper on the topic (1981).

either as a "gross" or as a "net" concept; that is, either as considering just a one-sided relationship or as also subtracting from it the opposite relationship, namely, the ability of others to affect the home unit's position and manipulate its own activities.[2] "Power" is thus closely associated with the concepts of "dependence" which were just discussed; one is the precise reverse of the other. "Power" is the "dependence" of *others* on the home unit. If "net" concepts are used, a state of "dependence" on others is one in which the home unit has "power", and vice versa.

In the present study, "dependence" is understood strictly as a "*gross*" concept; it is confined to the dependence of the home country on others, ignoring the opposite relationship altogether. As such, it does not refer at all to the nation's "power". A certain phenomenon, or an attribute of the economy, would be understood here to lead to "dependence" (or to more of it), if, looking *one-sidedly* at the relationship of the nation with others, it contributes to the nation's dependence. The very same phenomenon, or attribute, may grant the nation more "power", by making others dependent on it; but this will be overlooked.

This interpretation of "dependence" may be regarded as restrictive. It might certainly have been useful and fruitful to examine mutual, two-sided relationships, and to arrive perhaps at some "net" concepts. But economy of means dictates the limitation of the field of view to a narrower range. It is only to be hoped that the realization that the concept of "dependence" as it is adopted in the present study is clearly "gross", would help to avoid confusion in the interpretation of the study's findings.

4. Dependence: Components of vulnerability

While the extent of relations of dependence, and the point of view of looking at them, have been discussed thus far, it has not yet been made clear what a relationship of "dependence" actually means. Once more, a variety of interpretations could be read into the term; hence, it is important to define as precisely as possible the sense in which the concept is used here.

"Dependence" is understood in the present study as *vulnerability*. An agent is "dependent" on some phenomenon (or position, or act), if it is vulnerable to its complete disappearance or to disturbances in it; and the more severe the vulnerability, the heavier the dependence. In the concrete subject matter treated here, a nation is "dependent" on others via its foreign trade to the extent that it is vulnerable to the disruption of its trade – either its complete elimination or the partial disturbances of its trade flows.

Vulnerability is a function of two components. One is the *extent of the damage* that would occur should the disruption of the phenomenon on which the agent is

[2] For a discussion and definition of "power" of nations and its components, see Knorr (1975).

dependent take place; the other is the *likelihood* of such an event, that is, of the disruption actually occurring. Dependence is thus a product of a multiplicand and a multiplier. The larger either of the two components is – given the other – the larger is the vulnerability and the higher the degree of dependence, as this concept is used here.

An analogy will perhaps serve to clarify the issue. The extent of dependence may be considered as the equivalent of the size of an insurance premium, paid in order to secure benefits should a certain event occur. The size of the premium will be a function of two elements; the size of the benefit payments expected should the event occur and the probability of such occurrence. The larger either of the two elements is, the higher the premium payment. The type of the event, and with it the benefit payments – the extent of the damage – may be defined in a unique way, in which case one specific probability would be attached to it. A car, for instance, may be either stolen or not, with a single probability assigned to the event; if stolen, a definite sum of benefits – the agreed value of the car – would be paid. Likewise, when life is insured, a given probability is attached to the loss of life and a unique, predetermined size of benefits would be called for in the event of death. But the insurance premium may also refer to a continuum of potential damages and ensuing benefits: A car could suffer one extent or another of damage from a collision; or a loss of earning power may take place to one extent or another. In such cases, a continuum of probabilities is attached to the continuum of potential events, and damages involved in them; and the premium payment is the sum total – the "index" so to speak – which expresses the aggregate of multiplications of all these events by their probabilities.

In the same way dependence, or vulnerability, would usually refer to the product of such continuums. In the concrete case of dependence on trade, again, disruption of trade flows may range all the way from a minor disturbance to a complete cut-off of the flow. Any such disruption would involve a certain damage and each extent of disturbance carries its probability. The higher the total product of all these events and their probabilities, the deeper the vulnerability of the economy, and the larger the extent of its dependence on foreign trade.

In the analysis that will follow, the "multiplicand" – the extent of damage expected from interruptions of trade flows – will be designated, for the concrete subject matter, as the degree of "*openness*" of the economy. The "multiplier" – the probabilities of disruptions actually taking place – will be referred to as the degree of "*susceptibility*" of the trade flows. The dependence of an economy on foreign trade is thus defined as a function of the degree of openness of the economy, and the degree of susceptibility of its trade flows. The first two chapters of this part of the study will deal with issues concerning the concept and measurement of the degree of openness; whereas the following two chapters will handle, in a similar way, the degree of susceptibility.

5. Dependence on foreign nations

Normally, international trade is not conducted by the "home country" with foreign "countries; it is rather an exchange transacted between many economic agents in the home country with just as many agents in foreign countries, all of whom are motivated in their production and trade by the wish to maximize profits rather than by a desire to attain some "national" goals. Yet such trade differs from domestic trade; hence giving rise, conceivably, to the issue of dependence through trade on the outside world. The sources of such differences are only too well known to deserve any extensive exposition here; indeed, these are the sources which justify not only the study of dependence, but the specific study of international trade as a separate category of the discipline of economics. In brief, these may be summarized by observing that foreign countries – each of them separately – are distinct units in which certain developments may give rise to positions and to changes which affect, in a fashion relevant to the home country, the aggregate of the multitude of economic agents residing in the foreign country. These may be "autonomous" developments; or changes which result from general economic policies; or, still, changes due to foreign policies specifically applied to international transactions; or, even more narrowly focused, interruptions which are due to foreign policies aimed specifically at the home country.

It is the latter possibility which, probably more than any other, gives rise to the wide attention that has always been paid to the issue of the dependence which must be associated with the existence of a country's foreign trade: the potential of a foreign country to use a variety of policies to affect the home country's trade with it – whether economic policies or military measures, leading to anything from a minor interruption to a complete cut-off – provides the foreign country with a clout which may be used to lead the home country in a direction its residents perceive as contradicting their individual or common interests. For mainly this reason, "dependence" on foreign trade has always been considered a "price", to be paid (if considered worth it) for the benefits yielded by specialization.

In the present study, indicators of "dependence" will usually be pointed out without necessarily specifying whether the susceptibility of foreign-trade flows is the product of specific policies of the foreign nation aimed at the home country, or of the other potential sources of disturbances of foreign-trade flows. Often, though, an indicator of dependence may be clearly related more to one source than to others and this will be evident from its analysis.

While a discussion of the issue of dependence thus justifies – indeed, almost dictates – references to the trade flows of "countries", care should be taken to avoid a misleading impression which may arise from short-hand descriptions. Terms such as "country A conducts its trade with", or even "country A has a monopoly in the trade of", and so on, will be used here freely and abundantly. But it should always be borne in mind that actual trade is most often conducted not by the "country", but by a relatively small agent in it; and that while government policies participate in shaping up private considerations, it is still the latter which by and large give rise to the existing trade flows.

6. The approach of the study

The present study of dependence is conducted overwhelmingly along one definite path; it is designed to discuss, often devise, *operational* indicators of the extent of dependence on foreign trade; that is, indicators which are subject, in principle at least, to *measurement*. Not much attention will be paid to the analysis of mechanisms through which trade flows lead to dependence; these will be by and large taken for granted, and will be mentioned in a merely summary fashion, to introduce the appropriate indicators. The emphasis will be, throughout, on the attempt to search for measures by which the extent of dependence could operationally be established.

Once an indicator is presented, an actual measurement related to it will most often be carried out. This will be done for a very large number of countries, on many occasions practically all the world's political entities. Thus, actual quantitative estimates of the indicators of the various components of dependence on trade flows will be provided.

A disclaimer should, however, be inserted at this point. While it is the dependence of *countries* which forms the subject matter of this study, the measurements suggested here may, at best, serve to *illuminate* the positions of individual countries. No overall index of the dependence of countries' trade is suggested here, to incorporate within it the estimates of the separate indicators for each country; nor do I believe that any such meaningful index could be devised. The analogy used earlier, with the size of a premium payment as the ultimate, overall index of the risk involved in an insurance coverage, could not be complete. There, weights are indeed assigned to various considerations, or components, and eventualities; and the product of the "multiplicand" and the "multiplier" is indeed used to arrive at the overall "index". No similar scheme could, I suspect, be devised which would serve in an operational way to yield a single index of dependence on trade (or, most probably, of any other form of dependence); none, therefore, is attempted here.

Thus, while separate indicators may serve to throw light on the positions of individual countries, no overall, aggregative estimates for countries are provided; nor, therefore, does this study contain any substantive discussion of the dependence of individual nations. Instead, the concrete findings derived in the study when separate indicators are estimated are applied, very often, in an attempt to reveal typical *patterns* of dependence. International, multi-country studies may best serve to indicate common attributes shared by countries which exhibit similar phenomena, or which share similar events. In this way, the present study's findings are often used to examine attributes of countries which share a similar degree of dependence on trade, as it is indicated by one estimated element or another. It is this, along with the development of appropriate concepts and measurement, which is the intended contribution of this study.

CHAPTER 2

THE OPENNESS OF ECONOMIES: GAINS FROM TRADE AND SIZE OF TRADE

1. Relationship of openness to the size of trade

As has been stated in the introduction (ch. 1), the term "openness" will stand here for the "multiplicand" component of the degree to which the existence of foreign-trade transactions makes an economy vulnerable, or "dependent". Thus, the degree of openness is meant to represent the extent of potential damage which may be inflicted on the economy through disturbances of its foreign-trade flows.

The potential damage associated with the existence of some phenomenon – due to the possible interruption of this existence – is the difference, in relation to some denominator, between the economy's position with and without the existence of this phenomenon. It is the impact of adding this phenomenon to a world in which it does not exist; or, conversely, of eliminating it from a situation in which it does exist. The importance of trade, and the degree of "openness" of an economy, is thus the impact on an economy of adding international trade transactions (as they are actually observed) to a closed economy; or, conversely, of eliminating trade transactions and reverting to a closed-economy situation. In principle, these two comparisons should yield identical implications (if care is taken to make the *denominator* in each observation identical – in either comparison, it could be the economy's position with or without international transactions). But when time is added as an element, and short-term considerations are allowed, changes in the two alternative directions may obviously differ from each other.

In this meaning, thus, the degree of openness of an economy is nothing but the size of its gains from trade: the difference made to the country's welfare by the existence of its foreign-trade transactions. Fig. 2.1 presents the effect of trade in the simplest, conventional form. Production and consumption in the economy are of two *final* consumer tradable goods. Without trade, the economy produces and consumes at A. With international trade at given prices (the "small-country" assumption), production moves to B and consumption to C; BC being the trade vector. The degree of openness of the economy is thus the change (increase) in welfare yielded by the move from *A* to *C*, either in relation to welfare at *A* or at *C*.

Any estimate of welfare effect must, of course, introduce some cardinal measure to stand for the conceptually immeasurable "welfare". We shall do it here, as it is done in all similar analyses, without specifying the obvious reservations and qualifications. In terms of fig. 2.1, the welfare effect would be described by the

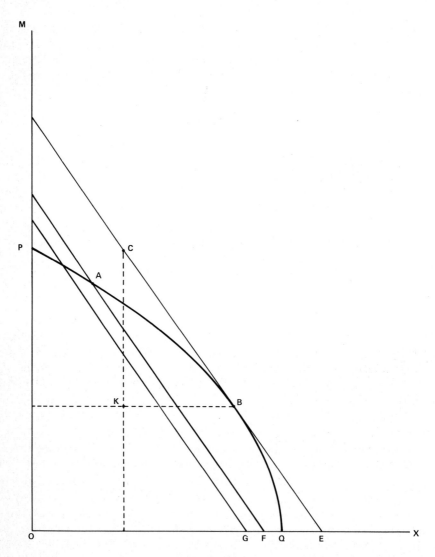

Figure 2.1

sizes of the well-known "production effect" and "consumption effect" of trade removal. With trade, the economy's income is equivalent to *OE* units of *X*, the exportable good (this could, of course, be expressed equivalently in terms of the importable good). The removal of trade (say, by the imposition of a prohibitive tariff) would lead to a "production loss" equivalent to *EF* and to a "consumption loss" equivalent to (by construction) *FG*.[1] The total loss from trade removal would thus be *EG*; and the ratio of *EG* to *OE* may thus serve as the relative measure of gains from trade, or the "ideal" measure of the economy's openness.

Had one been able to observe this ratio directly, the discussion might have largely ended here. But being denied of such an easy solution, one must resort to proxies. It is to the discussion of such proxies that this chapter will be devoted. But any such analysis must be dependent on the realization of what the ideal measure should have been.

The proxy, or yardstick, most popularly used is the size of trade (in relation to other economic activities). Much of the present analysis will indeed be devoted to this yardstick. The proportion referred to is the ratio of either exports, or imports, or their combined size, to the size of the economy's income. In fig. 2.1, expressing again all values in terms of the exportable good, at the existing price this would be the ratio of *KB* to *OE*, if exports or imports are used in the numerator; or of twice that ratio, if exports *and* imports are used in the numerator.[2]

It will be immediately apparent that there is no clear-cut relationship between either of these ratios and the measure ideally looked for. A statement such as "the ratio of *KB* to *OE* is $z\%$" would not imply that the gains from trade are $z\%$ of the economy's size; similarly, a statement that the ratio is $2z\%$ would not in any way imply that the gains from trade are twice as high, as a ratio, of what they are when the export (import) ratio is only $z\%$.

But some connection between the measure under consideration and the ideal measure does obviously exist. In a given economy (given, that is, production possibilities and demand patterns), a larger amount of trade, or a larger change from the closed to the open-economy position, *does* imply a larger increase in welfare. In a given economy the large trade would result from a larger closed-economy gap between relative prices (represented here by just a single ratio) at home and abroad. And the trade ratio may then be assumed to be an ordinal reflection of the "ideal" measure.

[1] Had a collective indifference map been introduced, *G* would be determined so that the straight line originating from it would be tangent to the indifference curve on which *A* is located.

[2] In an economy with balanced trade, as it is shown in fig. 2.1, exports are equal to imports; the use of either in the numerator of the ratio would yield identical results, and there would obviously be no sense in the use of their combined size. The rationale for distinction, and for the use of alternative indicators, lies of course in the admission of imbalanced trade. In fig. 2.1, this could easily be handled by adding to the economy, or subtracting from it, a quantity of the importable good which represents, respectively, the economy's import or export surplus.

Take, however, two economies with equal sizes of trade (in relation to income – for simplicity it may be assumed that income is equal in both), but knowing that in one economy supply and demand are more elastic than the other – that is, both the production-transformation curve and the indifference curves are flatter. An equal size of trade would then mean that the closed-economy gaps between prices at home and abroad are larger in the low-elasticities than in the high-elasticities economy. Hence, as could be easily verified, production and consumption losses from trade removal would be heavier in the former economy than in the latter. The low-elasticities economy should then be judged, with an equal size of trade, to be more "open" than the high-elasticities economy. In other words, the degree of openness is not just a function of the size of trade, but also of the difficulty of replacing imports by home-produced goods in production and consumption.

In the next chapter, the estimate of openness of the economy by the size of trade will be supplemented by measures which provide a partial expression of the difficulty or ease of such replacement. In the remaining two sections of the present chapter, on the other hand, attention will be paid to two problems of considerable significance involved in the use of the conventional measure of openness. First, in the next section, an issue will be addressed which arises from the fact that, unlike the presentation thus far, exports and imports take place in a world in which *non-tradable* activities exist. Then, in the following section, an important implication of the existence of imports of *intermediate* goods, rather than of final consumer goods, will be analyzed and evaluated.

2. Tradables, non-tradables and relative prices

Fig. 2.1 described a world of exclusively tradable goods. But a substantial fraction of an economy's transactions involves non-tradable activities. The ratio of exports (or imports, or exports plus imports) to the national product (GNP, or GDP) thus involves a ratio of an aggregate of tradable activities to another aggregate which consists of both tradable and non-tradable activities.

As long as the relative price between outputs of the tradable and the non-tradable sectors remains unchanged, this sectoral division would not introduce an added complication. Once the relative price does change, on the other hand, from one period to the next, one has to decide what set of prices to use in comparing the degree of openness of the economy at these two points. The use of different prices would not only yield different *sizes* of change over time but may also lead – as we will see – to conflicting inferences about the *direction* of change. This is equally true for cross-section, inter-country comparisons of openness of economies.

The problem is illustrated with the aid of fig. 2.2, in which the economy is divided to a tradable (T) and a non-tradable (N) activities. To reduce a 3-dimen-

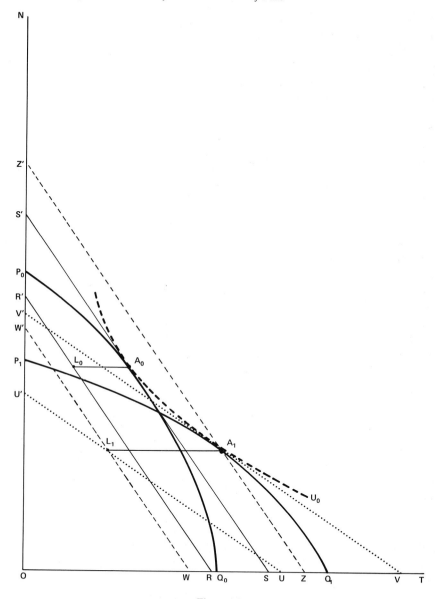

Figure 2.2

sion world (two tradable goods and a non-tradable one) to two dimensions, it is assumed for the sake of this presentation that the relative price of the two trad-able goods is fixed (through a constant world price faced by a small economy). Likewise, *within* the tradable sector all movements are equiproportional; transfor-mation curves move in a parallel way, and the preference map is homothetic. Thus, the two tradable activities are reduced into one composite good and the losses from trade removal (the gains from trade), as shown before, may be represented by a given fraction of this tradable good.

In fig. 2.2, the tradable sector is represented on the horizontal axis T, and the non-tradable sector on the vertical axis N. Initially, in period 0, the economy's transformation curve is $P_0 Q_0$. Production and consumption are at A_0, and the price ratio between the goods of the two sectors is represented by the slope SS' at this point. In terms of the tradable good, the value of the national income is OS. The size of trade (exports, or imports) is represented (by construction) as $A_0 L_0$ (this information is provided exogenously, rather than derived in the diagram). The ratio of trade to income is thus RS to OS, where RR' is a parallel to SS' through L_0.

Suppose, now, that a tradable-goods' biased technological change takes place, so that the transformation curve in period 1 becomes $P_1 Q_1$; for simplicity, this change is assumed to involve no growth, in the sense that the new transformation curve is tangent to the same community indifference curve, U_0, as the original transformation curve. The new production–consumption position is A_1 and the new price line in the economy is represented by VV'. By the earlier assumptions, the size of trade is a given fraction of the size of the tradable sector. $A_1 L_1$, the trade in period 1, is thus larger than $A_0 L_0$ by the same proportion that produc-tion of T at A_1 is larger than it was at A_0 (lines – not drawn – from L_1 through L_0 and from A_1 through A_0 would meet on the N axis).[3]

Using the *new* price line – that of period 1 – national income in period 1 is OV and the size of trade (exports, or imports) is UV (where UU' is a parallel to VV' through L_1). The trade ratio is thus UV' to OV. This could be either a higher or lower ratio than that of RS to OS, the trade ratio in period 0. This is, of course, a *current-prices* comparison; prices of period 0 are used in the estimate of the trade ratio in period 0 whereas prices of period 1 are used in the estimate for that period. The use of a *constant-prices* estimate would yield different results. Using period 0's prices for the estimate of period 1, national income at that period is OZ (ZZ'

---

[3] This equi-proportional change is guaranteed, given the assumptions, in the following way: (a) a parallel movement of the transformation curve between the export and the import goods results, with a given relative price of the two goods, in an equi-proportional change in the production of both goods. (b) A homothetic indifference map leads, at a constant relative price, to constant proportions of con-sumption. (c) Consequently, any movement of the budget constraint (the slope of which – the relative export–import price – is given) will change in the same proportion production and consumption, hence also the *excess* of one over the other, of the two goods. But this excess is, in turn, precisely the size of trade.

being a parallel to SS' through A_1) and the size of trade is WZ (equal to A_1L_1, or to UV, since the tradable good serves throughout as the numeraire). The trade ratio, WZ to OZ, must be higher than period 0's ratio RS to OS; that is, a constant-prices estimate must show, in this example, an increase of the trade ratio. And, inevitably, the constant-prices estimate would show a higher trade ratio in period 1 than the current-prices estimate.[4]

Since the trade ratio does not, in itself, provide a true representation of the "ideal" measure, estimates of the *change* in that ratio do not correspond to the inferences which would have been yielded by the use of the proper index. Hence, it is also impossible to assert whether one procedure of estimate is more appropriate than another. Suppose, for the sake of illustration, that the size A_0L_0 in period 0 just happened to be also the true size of the loss from trade removal; that is, without trade the community's welfare level would have been represented by the indifference curve on which L_0 is located. By earlier assumptions, A_1L_1 would then also happen to be the true size of the welfare loss from trade removal in period 1. Now, L_1 could be either on a lower or on a higher community indifference curve than that on which L_0 is located (or, by coincidence, on the same curve). And it is impossible to assert, in a general way, whether the constant-prices or the current-prices comparison of the trade ratios would give a better approximation to the true changes in the extent of welfare loss from trade removal.

The conclusion we may thus reach is that the alternative methods of estimating changes in trade ratios may conceivably lead to different implications, not only for the size but also for the *sign*, or direction of change; and that there is no *a priori* justification to prefer one to the other. The degree to which the issue is relevant, or important, is naturally a function of the extent to which the relative price of tradables vs. non-tradables has changed in the past, or may be expected to change in the future.

This becomes an empirical question. There is probably a widespread presumption that growth processes are generally biased towards the tradable sector in production. This may be expected if one equates the tradable sector with that of *goods*, whereas the non-tradable sector would consist of services. While such an identification is certainly highly imprecise, it is probably a close enough approximation of reality to justify some broad generalizations. It is commonly assumed that up to a certain stage of development, non-neutral growth processes express themselves primarily *within* the tradable (= goods) sector; essentially, that is, in a bias

---

[4]While conclusions concerning the *level* of the trade ratio would be different if period 1's prices rather than period 0's prices are used, the implications for the *comparison* of ratios between the two periods would be unaffected. That is, for inferences concerning the direction of change of the trade ratio, the question is not whether prices of one or of the other period are used; but whether *one period's* prices are used for both estimates (constant prices), or each period's prices are used for its own estimate (current prices).

towards manufacturing and against primary production. Beyond that stage, a bias towards goods in general vs. services – hence, towards the tradable sector – is believed to be the main non-neutral element in the growth process.[5] In consumption, on the other hand, an *opposite* bias is presumed: Beyond a certain level of (per capita) income, the income-elasticity of demand for services is assumed to be above unity whereas the income-elasticity for goods is below unity. The growth process is thus assumed to be biased in consumption towards the non-tradable sector.

An income–consumption curve – showing consumption baskets of goods of the two sectors at a given, initial price ratio – would thus be tilted towards non-tradables; whereas a production–expansion path (showing, similarly, production baskets with growth at a given price ratio) would be tilted towards the tradable sector. Obviously, hence, a given price ratio before growth cannot remain an equilibrium price after growth – at least beyond a certain level of development: The relative price of tradables must fall, and of the non-tradables rise, to lead to an equilibrium. Thus, while the effect of growth on the relative *quantities* of the two sectors is not generally predictable, the effect on the relative *price* is presumably expected; with the growth of economies, the relative price of tradables should fall.

Empirical estimates of this relative price are not generally available. Insofar, however, as the identification of the services sector with non-tradables and of the primary production and manufacturing with tradables is a good approximation, a reasonable proxy to this relative price may be feasibly derived from the ratio of two indexes the use of which is widespread: the consumer-price and the wholesale-price indexes. Wholesale prices refer to *goods* – hence, presumably, to tradables. The shift from wholesale prices to consumer, retail prices adds, by and large, the component of services, in one way or another. These may be producer services, such as those involved in the commercial activity, which are added to the goods whose prices are observed at the wholesale level; or consumer services (namely, services which are sold by themselves to the consumer, not through a combination with some good), which do not appear at all at the wholesale-price level. Thus, the change in the ratio of the consumer-price to the wholesale-price index, from one period to another, may yield a rough approximation of the change in the ratio of the combined price of tradables and non-tradables to the price of tradables alone.[6]

Table 2.1 presents the change in the ratio of the consumer-price index to that of the wholesale-price index[7] from 1950 to 1979, for all the countries for which these

[5] References to such a process are numerous – the various studies of Simon Kuznets being perhaps a prime source. And numerous hypotheses are based on this assumption – from, say, the validity or lack of it of purchasing-power-parity comparisons to the "Scandinavian model" of the source of inflation.

[6] An important component which is absent from the consumer price index (and, needless to say, at the wholesale level) is that of central-government activities, which are commonly a large fraction of services and of the non-tradable sector. The estimate of prices of government services, which are not transacted in the market, is of course conceptually a problem not subject to a satisfactory solution.

[7] In several countries, this is defined as the index of producer prices, or similar terms.

Table 2.1. Ratio of change in consumer-price index to change in wholesale-price index

	1970/1950	1979/1950
High-income countries		
Austria	1.145	1.275
Belgium	1.038	1.201
Denmark	1.446	1.540
Finland	1.012	1.006
France	1.181	1.310
Germany	1.114	1.131
Italy	1.438	1.248
Japan	1.837	2.286
Netherlands	1.385	1.613
New Zealand	1.197	1.118
Norway	1.267	1.302
Switzerland	1.260	1.479
United Kingdom	1.119	1.078
United States	1.111	1.049
Middle-income countries		
Argentina	1.078	1.170
Brazil	1.136	1.066
Colombia	0.951	0.750
Greece	0.956	0.871
Guatemala	1.008	0.993
Ireland	1.139	1.048
Korea	1.420	1.291
Mexico	1.100	1.022
Paraguay	0.873	0.590
Portugal	1.203	1.206
South Africa	1.045	0.860
Spain	1.024	1.269
Syria	1.258	1.175
Tunisia	0.965	0.861
Turkey	1.193	1.610
Venezuela	0.936	0.821
Low-income countries		
Egypt	0.870	0.888
El Salvador	1.500	1.148
India	1.124	1.022
Iran	1.127	1.262
Iraq	1.148	1.202
Pakistan	0.986	0.989
Philippines	1.126	0.727
Sudan	1.808	2.114

Source: Data from IMF *International Financial Statistics*, 1980 *Yearbook*.

data are available for this period. Since prices – absolute as well as relative sectoral prices – were particularly volatile during the 1970s, the ratio is also shown
for the more stable, or "normal", sub-period between 1950 and 1970. The 38
countries presented are classified into three categories, according to their level of
income, or the stage of economic development.[8]

As could be seen, the ratio between the two price changes — the presumed proxy
for the relative change of the price ratio of non-tradables and tradables combined
to that of tradables alone – increased in almost all countries in the high-income
category, with the exception of Finland, in which it remained practically unchanged. Among the 13 other countries in this group, the increase in the ratio
ranged from a mere 5% in the U.S. (11% in the sub-period of 1950–1970) to as
much as roughly 130% in Japan (not accidentally, perhaps, the economy which
manifested by far the highest rate of growth during the period).[9] Among middle-
income countries, increases in the ratio were still more common than decreases,
although the trend is less persistent than among the higher-income economies. In
the group of low-income countries, on the other hand, no such overall trend is
visible: increases of the ratio appear to be as likely to occur as its decreases.[10]

These revealed trends would be consistent with the expectation hypothesized
before; namely, that beyond a certain level of development (or income), growth of
economies should tend to lead to the decline of the relative price of tradables. It
also appears that this change is of a substantial quantitative significance. Thus,
the (unweighted) average change in the ratio presented in table 2.1 for the group

---

[8]"Middle-income" countries are defined as those with a 1979 per-capita income in the range of
$1000–4999. The upper limit is consistent with that used by the World Bank in its classification (in the
World Development Report). The latter uses, on the other hand, a much smaller per-capita income (less
than $400) for the lower limit. Any such boundaries are, obviously, entirely arbitrary. Those adopted
here may be somewhat more defensible than others since substantial gaps, or dichotomies, exist around
them; whereas the rest of the range is marked by a strong element of continuity. It should also be noted
that the classification of countries, in particular between the low-income and middle-income categories, would have been somewhat different had income levels of earlier periods rather than of 1979
been used. This, of course, is due to marked differences in the rate of economic development.

[9]The hypotheses specified earlier should lead to the expectation of a larger change in relative prices
the faster is the economy's growth. A formal regression analysis could not be carried out by drawing
on data from the present table, since only for 13 countries represented in this table are growth rates
available for the relevant period. Such analysis was, however, performed by correlating the price ratios
which will be presented soon in column (7) of table 2.2 with growth rates (rates of changes in per-capita
income) during the period 1960–1972, for 41 countries. The regression of price disparity on growth is
positive, as expected. The correlation is rather weak (an R^2 of 0.114); but it is significant (at the 5%
level).

[10]It should also be noticed that in this group of countries, differences between the trend, for individual countries, revealed in the sub-period of 1950–1970 and the complete period of 1950–1979 are often
very large. This may indicate that the "trends" are, in this category of countries, often the result of
short-term changes. It may also be suspected that in this category, statistical estimates are often less
reliable than among more highly-developed countries.

of the high-income countries was 33% during the period 1950–1979 (it was about 25% in the shorter period 1950–1970). This is a compounded annual change of about 1%.[11] In view of such size of change in relative prices, any implication about trends of change in the degree of openness over time must differ greatly – for a period of some duration – between estimates which use constant prices and those which employ current prices: the former must show a higher degree of openness than the latter – a more substantial increase, or a less substantial reduction, over time (or, sometimes, an increase rather than a reduction). Likewise, comparisons of change *among* countries would differ greatly. Specifically, the highly-developed economies would appear to grow more open than the less-developed economies – in comparisons of changes in countries over time – when constant-prices rather than current-prices estimates are used to calculate the trade ratio.

Let us now turn to that contrast as it is found directly in estimates of the trade ratio based on the use of the two alternative price schemes. Since constant-prices estimates require, for the purpose on hand, an unchanged base year, the length of the time period for which these alternative series could be constructed, from generally available data and without an unduly large work on country by country, is quite restricted; and so is the list of countries for which this comparison could be carried out. Table 2.2 presents the alternative series for 41 countries, during the period 1960–1978. The table shows (in columns (1) and (2), and (4) and (5), respectively) the ratio of trade (exports *plus* imports) to GDP in the beginning and end years, in both current and constant-prices estimates. It shows (in columns (3) and (6), respectively) the change in this ratio during the two periods, by the two alternatives; and, finally, (in column (7)), the ratio between changes shown by the two alternative price schemes. The countries are again divided into 3 categories, by their stage of development; note, however, that the list of individual countries only partly overlaps with that of table 2.1, particularly where lower-income countries are concerned.

The results, by and large, agree with the expectations based on the implications of the *a priori* reasoning and of table 2.1. Once more, with only two exceptions (the U.S. and Germany), the ratio of the change in the constant-prices to that of the current-prices estimate is above unity in the high-income group of countries. This is mostly true also in the middle-income group, but with more exceptions; while in the category of less-developed countries, this relationship is definitely not

---

[11] This is, we recall, the change in the price ratio of tradables and non-tradables combined to that of tradables alone. If we assume, in conformity with common patterns, that the two sectors are of roughly equal size, the average increase in the price ratio of non-tradables to tradables implied from this change would be 66%, for the period 1950–1979, for this group of countries; for Japan, it would be over 350%! But for the purpose of our discussion, which is the estimate of the trade ratio (that is, trade in relation to GNP, or GDP), the price ratio in which we are interested is indeed that of non-tradables and tradables combined, rather than non-tradables alone, to tradables.

Table 2.2. Trade ratios at current and constant prices (combined ratio of exports
and imports to GDP)

	At current prices			At constant prices			Relative price ratio
	1960 Ratio (1)	1978 Ratio (2)	(2)/(1) = (3)	1960 Ratio (4)	1978 Ratio (5)	(5)/(4) = (6)	(6)/(3) = (7)
High-income countries							
Austria	0.495	0.706	1.426	0.456	0.861	1.888	1.324
Belgium	0.688	1.028	1.539	0.640	1.126	1.864	1.211
Canada	0.362	0.511	1.412	0.330	0.471	1.427	1.011
Denmark	0.688	0.583	0.847	0.483	0.636	1.317	1.555
France	0.279	0.417	1.495	0.226	0.455	2.013	1.346
Germany	0.355	0.484	1.363	0.412	0.529	1.284	0.942
Iceland	0.923	0.801	0.868	0.785	1.122	1.429	1.646
Italy[b]	0.304	0.534	1.757	0.225	0.422	1.876	1.068
Japan	0.216	0.204	0.944	0.148	0.280	1.982	2.004
Luxembourg	1.561	1.607	1.029	1.260	1.606	1.275	1.239
Netherlands[a]	0.906	0.944	1.042	0.733	1.061	1.447	1.389
Sweden[a]	0.464	0.565	1.218	0.428	0.610	1.425	1.170
Switzerland	0.589	0.680	1.154	0.501	0.891	1.778	1.541
U.K.	0.439	0.582	1.326	0.422	0.575	1.331	1.004
U.S.	0.095	0.181	1.905	0.284	0.428	1.507	0.827
Middle-income countries							
Argentina[b]	0.214	0.173	0.808	0.214	0.228	1.065	1.318
Cyprus[b]	0.760	1.039	1.367	0.701	1.025	1.462	1.069
Greece	0.258	0.414	1.605	0.208	0.387	1.861	1.161
Guatemala	0.284	0.482	1.697	0.303	0.381	1.257	0.741
Hong Kong[a]	1.841	2.087	1.134	1.834	2.115	1.153	1.012
Ireland	0.691	1.120	1.621	0.535	0.971	1.815	1.120
Korea	0.161	0.698	4.335	0.151	0.945	6.258	1.444
Mexico	0.229	0.219	0.956	0.229	0.213	0.930	0.973
Panama	0.665	0.890	1.338	0.665	0.707	1.063	0.794
Paraguay	0.332	0.340	1.024	0.333	0.384	1.153	1.126
Peru	0.383	0.398	1.039	0.341	0.258	0.757	0.729
Philippines	0.210	0.427	2.033	0.368	0.372	1.011	0.497
Portugal[b]	0.410	0.474	1.182	0.414	0.477	1.152	0.975
Puerto Rico	1.054	1.300	1.233	1.175	1.160	0.987	0.800
South Africa	0.546	0.573	1.049	0.454	0.436	0.960	0.915
Spain[a]	0.245	0.165	0.673	0.230	0.189	0.822	1.221
Sri Lanka[a]	0.542	0.776	1.432	0.542	0.330	0.609	0.425
Syria[a]	0.496	0.543	1.095	0.496	0.402	0.810	0.740
Uruguay	0.357	0.389	1.090	0.284	0.428	1.507	1.383
Low-income countries							
Burma	0.310	0.134	0.432	0.280	0.091	0.325	0.752
Guyana[b]	1.056	1.590	1.506	1.194	0.933	0.781	0.519
Haiti	0.375	0.495	1.320	0.406	0.780	1.921	1.455
Honduras	0.449	0.802	1.786	0.423	0.686	1.622	0.908
Morocco	0.525	0.494	0.941	0.525	0.454	0.865	0.919
Nicaragua	0.475	0.657	1.383	0.485	0.623	1.285	0.929
Pakistan	0.159	0.333	2.094	0.131	0.222	1.695	0.809

[a]Starting year for Burma, Hong Kong, Sri Lanka, Sweden and Syria, is 1963; for the Netherlands and Spain, 1965.
[b]End year for Argentina is 1975; for Cyprus, 1977; for Guyana and Portugal, 1976; and for Italy, 1974.
Source: Data from U.N. *Yearbook of National Accounts Statistics.*

the rule.[12] Moreover, the contrast between the three categories of countries is even more pronounced than that found from table 2.1, despite the fact that the data of table 2.2 refer to a shorter time period. The (unweighted) average of the ratio between the two alternative changes (column (7)) is 1.307 for the high-income countries; 1.152 for the middle-income group; and 0.826 for the less-developed economies. Thus, a comparison between the high-income and the less-developed countries of the change in openness over the period, as measured by changes in the trade ratio, would show the relative openness of the first group (that is, comparing change in one group to the change in the other) higher by about 60% if constant-prices rather than current-prices estimates are used. For individual countries, the contrasts may naturally be extreme. Thus Japan shows a major increase in openness – a doubling of the trade ratio – when constant-prices estimates are used; whereas a current-prices estimate shows an unchanged degree of openness. In a country like the Philippines, on the other hand, a constant-prices estimate shows an unchanged openness; while a current-prices estimate would show a doubling of the trade ratio. The contrast between the two alternative measures in

---

[12]As could be easily verified, the ratio presented in column (7) of table 2.2 is that of the change in the relative price of GDP (tradables and non-tradables) to the price of exports and imports. Under certain conditions, this should in principle be identical with the ratio shown in table 2.1. The main sources for deviations between these two indications are as follows: (a) The price of GDP includes goods and services which are not covered by the C.P.I. – some of these are primarily tradable (investment goods), while others are non-tradable (government services); (b) Prices of exports and imports (which are a component of the ratio in table 2.2) ought, in principle, to be equal to the price of tradables. But this is a long-term proposition; in the short run, large deviations are possible. Domestic price adjustments (of exportable and import-competing goods) following a devaluation, for instance, may take years to fully materialize; (c) The estimate of exports and imports at constant prices must have required, at one stage, an estimate of changes of international prices of these goods; and these are notoriously deficient, in many countries. Likewise, the exchange rate used to express domestic prices of exports and imports is most often an inappropriate one; it is the formal exchange rate, rather than the effective rate (including tariffs, export subsidies, etc.) which should be used to arrive at the correct domestic price change. Various other deficiencies and differences in estimates of the alternative series must contribute to the existence of discrepancies in the results. It should, of course, also be noted that the periods covered in the two alternative series are not identical; one runs from 1950–1979, the other only from 1960–1978. Nevertheless, the resemblance of the two series to each other is surprisingly strong. Twenty-four countries appear jointly in both tables. For these, the correlation coefficient (r) of the ratio recorded in column (7) of table 2.2 with the ratio recorded in table 2.1 is 0.807. If the less-developed countries, whose data are in general less reliable, are excluded, this coefficient for the remaining 19 countries would become 0.879. The (Spearman) rank-correlation coefficient between the two series, for all 24 countries, is 0.771; and with the exclusion of the less-developed economies, it becomes 0.856 (all correlation coefficients being significant at any desired level). It should be noted that for the purpose of this calculation, the ratios shown in table 2.2 for the Netherlands and for Spain have been corrected, through chaining with earlier periods, to reflect the change from 1960 (rather than from 1965) to 1970. The corrected ratios are 1.708 (instead of 1.389) for the Netherlands; and 1.393 (rather than 1.211) for Spain.

comparing performances of these two countries with each other would, of course, be dramatic.[13]

3. Intermediate inputs and value-added adjustment

The recognition that imports consist not only of final but also of intermediate goods leads to several important qualifications of the use of trade ratios as the indication of openness. One implication will be discussed here whereas another aspect will appear in the analysis of the next chapter.

---

[13] In the literature, both current-prices and constant-prices estimates are used, sometimes mixed together. The latter form of estimate is often presented not directly through changes in the trade ratio, but as a comparison of rates of change of "real" trade (exports, or imports, or both) and "real" product. The amount of studies dealing with individual countries or with international comparisons is vast, and only a few of those with the widest impact will be noted here briefly. Kuznets, in his *Six Lectures on Economic Growth* (1959), used trade ratios (where the denominator was total availability of resources – adding imports to the national product) borrowed from a study by Piekarz, in which current prices were consistently used in the estimates. Later, in probably the most comprehensive study of the issue, Kuznets (1967) used estimates of varying nature. Mostly, these were again derived from current prices, but some were constant-prices estimates. In one place, Kuznets notes that: "In several countries in which the foreign trade proportion for volumes in current prices dropped significantly in the late 1950s, the proportion based on volumes in constant prices did not ... But since we should place more confidence in the proportions based on volumes in current prices, we may conclude that ... these proportions are significantly lower in the late 1950s than in the period just preceding World War I" (23–24). Presumably, the "more confidence" is due not to analytical superiority of the current-price estimates but to the deficiencies involved in price deflations. In a study destined primarily to test Sombart's celebrated "law" of the declining importance of trade, Deutsch and Eckstein (1961) use, again, mostly current-prices ratios, but constant-prices estimates are also involved, often through comparisons of rates of change of trade and product. This study's main finding is a claim that trade ratios behave, with stages of development, in an inverted *J* pattern. Kindleberger (1962), borrowing from the current-prices evidence in the studies of Kuznets and of Deutsch and Eckstein, reaches the conclusion that "while the existence of the law of declining foreign trade has been established for developed countries only very weakly, it nevertheless exists" (p. 183). The most recent comprehensive study of trade ratios, by Grassman (1980), also employs current-prices data. Lipsey (1963), in a most thorough study of prices of U.S. exports and imports, found a persistent long-term decline (concentrated heavily in the 1920s and 1930s) of the price of trade flows relative to that of the national product. He then constructed the current-prices and constant-prices estimates of the U.S. trade ratio, establishing that while the former set shows a substantial decline of the ratios over a period of more than a century, the latter set indicates either a stable ratio (in the case of imports) or fluctuations with the absence of a long-term trend (in the case of exports). Hence "... the well known decline in the value ratios has been largely a price phenomenon ... Thus, although current value export ratios have followed roughly the pattern expected by Sombart ... ratios for current dollar imports and constant dollar exports and imports for the United States appear to contradict this thesis. It is in real terms that the pessimistic outlook for the future of international trade has usually been stated and theoretically justified" (44–45).

Where the size of exports is used, either by itself or combined with the size of imports, to calculate trade ratios, the result is a hybrid of an undetermined nature. The national income, or product, which appears in the denominator of the ratio, is a *net* concept; it is the aggregate of value added in all activities in the economy, during the specified period (and not, of course, the aggregate of the values of all economic transactions, or even of the values of gross outputs in all firms). The size of exports conventionally used is, on the other hand, a *gross* concept; it is not the aggregate of value added in export activities of the economy, because it includes the value of imported intermediate goods used in the production of export goods. The ratio thus calculated is therefore meaningless. Were the import component in exports to be excluded, leaving the *value added* in the economy alone, the export ratio would regain its meaning. It would then indicate – subject to the limitations noted earlier – the fraction of the national income which is exchanged for imports, thus giving rise to gains from trade. Or, looking at it from a slightly different perspective, it would indicate the fraction of the country's economic resources employed in activities destined for sale to the outside world, and thus dependent in one way or another on the fortunes of that world. Similarly, and consistently, the import component in exports should be abstracted from in considering the size of *imports*, so that only the value of imports which are actually used in the economy, rather than shipped back abroad, will be left.

Implicitly, this principle is widely recognized by the exclusion of the so-called "transit trade" from the values of exports and imports; this is trade in which the value added in the economy is negligible. A dichotomy exists, however, in common practices: once exports have some visible component of value added, they are no longer part of "transit trade" and each export transaction is treated like another, regardless of the size of the value added in that transaction.

The identification of the import component in exports would require an inverted input–output matrix of a quite detailed nature, where in the original matrix imported inputs in each activity appear separately from home-produced inputs; or, alternatively, a thorough direct study of each export activity. Neither of these are readily available, nor do they, apparently, exist at all in the large

---

Cooper (1964), seeming implicitly to agree that constant-prices comparisons are analytically superior, notes that if Lipsey's lead is followed and price deflation is applied to Kuznets' international data, "recomputation of the ratios for real output and trade with the appropriate price deflators would certainly eliminate the decline for a number of countries; but of course the earlier rise in relative importance of trade would have been even sharper" (p. 615). In view of the inferences of the present study, this speculation seems to be amply justified. It should be noted that studies in which ratios of trade to *manufacturing* activity are examined – such as those of Lewis (1952) or Kravis (1970) – do not involve the issue under consideration, in which the change in the relative price of the tradable sector as a whole (vs. non-tradable activities) lies at the origin of potentially contradicting implications.

majority of countries.[14] What is suggested here, instead, is some rough substitute, for a limited number (and nature) of economies. The purpose of making and presenting these estimates is primarily to learn whether the issue under consideration is of quantitative significance, in particular where international comparisons are made.

The estimates presented here are based on a set of Standardized Input–Output Tables for ECE Countries, put out by the U.N. for the year 1965 (or around it).[15] The economy in these tables is classified into 24 branches, of which 14 branches define the production of goods – and the estimates here will be confined to goods (that is, the export of services and its import component will be excluded).[16] For 18 countries, the data of inter-industry input–output relationships separate between home-produced and imported inputs. This enables the construction of an import coefficient in the output of each industry. Assuming these 1965 coefficients to describe other years as well (this, of course, is a somewhat arbitrary assumption and perhaps a biased one, but unfortunately necessary), one may then apply the industry's export shares at each given year to derive the overall import component in exports of that year.[17] In table 2.3, columns (1) and (3), respectively, present the import components thus derived, for the 18 countries, for the years 1952 and 1979.[18] But this procedure yields only the *direct* import component. To derive the *overall* import component – direct and indirect – one would need not the original input–output tables but the inverse matrices. Such inversion is obviously not a feasible proposition, in the present context. Instead, resort has been made to a rough approximation; it is assumed here that *in the aggregate*, home-produced inputs purchased by the export sector are the product of the economy's original factors (its value added) and of imported inputs in the same proportion as that of the value added and import component found in the *direct* stage. In this way, the

[14] Normally, data would exist where it is felt that they are badly needed for policy – and apparently such feeling is not widespread in the present case. Probably the most notable exception was, for a while, Israel. There, for a long time, export subsidies were granted to value added, and this required a rather detailed and elaborate scheme of estimation of the import content of export activities in finely defined branches.

[15] U.N. (1977). An earlier issue (1972) presented similar input–output tables for 1959. Had the two reference years been further apart, a comparative study of the two would have been worthwhile.

[16] Moreover, the *inputs* of imported services into export industries – such as, for instance, payments to foreign capital employed in the activity – are not taken into account.

[17] This procedure assumes, implicitly, that the structure of production of *exports* in each industrial branch is identical with the average structure of that industry. Such an assumption is undoubtedly inaccurate, especially when "industries" are as broadly defined as they are in these tables; but, again, it is inevitable. It may be noted that in the aforementioned estimates for Israel, it was most often found that even when industries are finely classified, the import component in an industry's production for exports was higher than in its production for the home market.

[18] Since trade is reported by the SITC scheme, this procedure required the matching of SITC groups and the industrial branches recorded in the input–output tables. But, the SITC reporting being quite detailed (the 3-digit level), this matching has hopefully not led to any major inaccuracies.

Table 2.3. Import coefficients in exports

Country	1952		1979	
	Direct coefficient (1)	Total coefficient (2)	Direct coefficient (3)	Total coefficient (4)
Belgium	0.259	0.436	0.263	0.443
Czechoslovakia	—	—	0.081	0.184
Denmark	0.163	0.283	0.205	0.356
Finland	0.080	0.160	0.114	0.228
France	0.087	0.183	0.084	0.176
Germany	0.088	0.180	0.087	0.178
Hungary	—	—	0.114	0.211
Ireland	0.092	0.176	0.238	0.455
Italy	0.099	0.178	0.100	0.180
Japan	0.074	0.177	0.039	0.094
Netherlands	0.181	0.297	0.198	0.325
Norway	0.158	0.268	0.143	0.243
Poland	—	—	0.067	0.153
Portugal	0.105	0.169	0.148	0.238
Spain	0.048	0.104	0.095	0.205
Sweden	0.111	0.202	0.136	0.247
Turkey	0.043	0.074	0.045	0.077
U.K.	0.100	0.202	0.094	0.190

Source: Data from U.N. *Standardized Input–Output Tables, 1965* (1977) and trade data from U.N. *Yearbook of International Trade Statistics.* Method of construction explained in text.

overall import component was derived from the information about the aggregate direct import component in exports and the intermediate-input ratio in the economy's total gross output (referring, again, to goods only).[19] These coefficients, again for 1952 and 1979, are presented in columns (2) and (4), respectively, of table 2.3.

Despite the fact that the countries represented in table 2.3 belong predominantly to the high-income group, thus lying within a limited range of economies' attributes, the degree of variation of the import coefficient among countries appears to be substantial. Not accidentally, perhaps, the lowest coefficient belongs to Turkey – by far the least developed country in the group. But even among the highly-developed economies, the import coefficient varies all the way from, in 1979, less than 10% in Japan to close to 45% in Belgium. Put conversely; the share of value added in the gross value of exports varies from 90% in one country to 55% in the other. It may thus be expected that trade ratios represented in the

[19] That is, $m^t = m^d/(1-h)$, where: m^t = total (direct and indirect) import coefficient in exports; m^d = direct import coefficient in exports; and h = ratio of aggregate intermediate inputs to aggregate gross output.

Trade, income levels, and dependence

Table 2.4. Gross and adjusted trade ratios (ratio of exports and imports to GDP, in per cent)

Country	1952 Gross ratio (1)	1952 Adjusted ratio (2)	1978 Gross ratio (3)	1978 Adjusted ratio (4)
Belgium	56	32.4	103	57.8
Denmark	63	44.8	58	38.0
Finland	49	41.4	58	43.8
France	30	24.6	41	33.6
Germany	30	24.2	48	39.2
Ireland	70	59.0	112	64.6
Italy	23	19.4	56	45.6
Japan	23	18.8	20	18.0
Netherlands	93	63.4	94	63.4
Norway	84	61.4	85	64.6
Portugal	35	30.0	47	39.0
Spain	10	9.0	29	22.8
Sweden	51	40.4	57	42.6
Turkey	—	—	16	15.0
U.K.	49	39.4	58	46.6

Source: Gross trade ratios data from U.N. *Yearbook of National Accounts Statistics.* Method of adjusting the ratio explained in text.

appropriate way, abstracting from the import component of exports, would significantly qualify inferences drawn from the unadjusted trade ratio used conventionally. In table 2.4, such a comparison is made for 15 out of the 18 countries for which import coefficients in exports have been calculated.[20] This is done, again, for two years, 1952 and 1978.[21] Columns (1) and (3), respectively, show the combined unadjusted ratio of imports and exports to GDP; whereas columns (2) and (4), respectively, show this ratio when the import component of exports is deducted from both the values of exports and of imports.

It may be seen that while the proper adjustment of the trade ratio does not lead to any dramatic reversals, it does qualify significantly inferences drawn from the unadjusted estimates. The range of variation among countries, in their degree of openness, becomes substantially narrower. Extreme cases, like (in 1978) Turkey and Japan on the one hand and Ireland and Belgium on the other, become much more moderate when the adjusted ratios are observed. (The reason for this closer

[20] For the three Soviet-type economies – Czechoslovakia, Hungary and Poland – data required for the calculation of the trade ratio are not available.

[21] Each country's 1952 import coefficient in exports is used for the 1952 estimate, whereas the 1979 coefficient is used for 1978. At the time of computing these ratios, data for 1979 were not yet generally available.

Table 2.5. Import coefficients in exports by industry

Industrial branch	Mean (1)	Standard deviation (2)
1. Agriculture, forestry, fishing	0.038	0.030
2. Coal, petroleum, gas	0.025	0.026
3. Other mining and quarrying	0.034	0.026
4. Food, beverages, tobacco	0.104	0.058
5. Textiles	0.221	0.101
6. Clothing	0.145	0.097
7. Wood products, paper, printing	0.118	0.069
8. Rubber	0.242	0.078
9. Chemicals	0.221	0.091
10. Petroleum and coal products	0.488	0.187
11. Non-metallic mineral products	0.074	0.037
12. Ferrous and non-ferrous materials	0.182	0.078
13. Transport equipment	0.189	0.155
14. Machinery and other manufacturers	0.154	0.097

similarity of countries when the trade ratio is adjusted will become clear shortly.) The relative positions of countries may change substantially. Thus, for instance – again in 1978 – Norway assumes top position (along with Ireland) in the degree of openness whereas the unadjusted ratio would place her only somewhat above average – substantially below Belgium, for instance, which appears to be less open than Norway when the adjusted ratio is observed. Likewise, the change over time would appear to be significantly different. An extreme case, in this sense, is that of Ireland, in which an apparent very substantial increase in openness inferred from the unadjusted trade ratios for 1952 and 1978 turns into an only very moderate increase when the adjusted ratios are observed.[22]

Two reasons, primarily, explain the large differences among countries in their import coefficients of exports, hence the differential impacts of the adjustment of the trade ratio on the apparent degree of openness. One is the difference in *structure* of exports among countries – which is, in turn, important because there are substantial typical differences among *industries* in their intensity of using the import component. Table 2.5 presents these differences. For each of the 14 industrial branches, the (unweighted) mean of the 18 individual country coefficients is shown, along with its standard deviation. It appears that industry coefficients do indeed

[22] This is, of course, separate from the issue of the price scheme used in the estimates, which was discussed in the preceding section. The trade ratios in table 2.4 are derived from data based on *current* prices; a constant-prices comparison would have shown, for most of these countries, a substantially larger increase in openness from 1952 to 1978.

differ substantially, and often significantly, from each other.[23] In general, primary production uses significantly less imported inputs than the production of manufactures. Among the individual branches of manufactures, the differences are mostly smaller – with only petroleum and coal products being an exception, appearing to have uniformly a much higher import coefficient than any other branch of activity.

Yet differences in trade structure offer only a partial explanation of the differences among countries. The use of "standardized" import coefficients – those recorded in table 2.5 – to the export data of individual countries yields overall (weighted average) country import coefficients which only remotely resemble the coefficients actually derived (those presented in table 2.3), when each country's actual industry coefficients were used. This indicates that differences among countries in individual-industry import coefficients are of prime importance. Indeed,

---

[23] The following matrix presents the probabilities that any pair of mean coefficients of two industrial branches (represented by the intersection of a row and a column) actually belong to the same population (the heading numbers of rows and columns being the branch numbers in table 2.5):

2	3	4	5	6	7	8	9	10	11	12	13	14	Industrial branch
													Industrial branch
0.312	0.481	0.000	0.000	0.000	0.000	0.000	0.000	0.000	0.000	0.000	0.000	0.000	1
	0.375	0.000	0.000	0.000	0.000	0.000	0.000	0.000	0.000	0.002	0.000	0.000	2
		0.000	0.000	0.000	0.000	0.000	0.000	0.000	0.000	0.000	0.000	0.000	3
			0.000	0.035	0.348	0.000	0.000	0.000	0.031	0.001	0.028	0.051	4
				0.000	0.000	0.359	0.981	0.000	0.000	0.097	0.235	0.000	5
					0.159	0.000	0.001	0.000	0.001	0.010	0.137	0.591	6
						0.000	0.000	0.000	0.001	0.000	0.027	0.074	7
							0.167	0.000	0.000	0.020	0.055	0.000	8
								0.000	0.000	0.165	0.220	0.001	9
									0.000	0.000	0.000	0.000	10
										0.000	0.001	0.000	11
											0.601	0.014	12
												0.068	13

It appears that industries may be classified into six groups, where the means of industry coefficients within each group are not significantly different from each other, whereas they differ significantly from the mean coefficients of any other industrial branch. These groups are, in an increasing order of the import coefficient: (a) (2) Coal, petroleum, gas; (1) Agriculture, forestry, fishing; (3) Other mining and quarrying. (b) (11) Non-metallic mineral products. (c) (4) Food, beverage, tobacco; (7) Wood products, paper, printing. (d) (6) Clothing; (14) Machinery and other manufactures. (e) (12) Ferrous and non-ferrous metals; (13) Transport equipment; (15) Textiles; (9) Chemicals; (8) Rubber. (f) (10) Petroleum and coal products.

Interestingly, petroleum and coal appear at the very bottom; whereas the import coefficient for petroleum and coal products is by far the highest. This is, thus, the extreme case of a raw material extracted with very little use of imported inputs; and then processed, with the use of relatively little value added, in countries in which it mostly does not originate.

for most countries presented here, the *unweighted* mean of the 14 industry coefficients yield a roughly similar index to the weighted averages which describe the countries' actual overall import coefficients. This indicates, again, that for the countries presented here, differences in individual-industry import coefficients *among countries* – primarily in the branches of manufacturing – are more important than differences in trade structures.[24] And these differences, in turn, are apparently intimately related to the *overall* weight of imports in the economy: the higher the import share in the economy, the higher are the individual-industry import coefficients.

This explains the aforementioned observation of the narrowing-down of differences in openness among economies when the trade ratios are properly adjusted. The higher the overall import ratio, the higher is also the aggregate import coefficient of exports; and the more, thus, does the exclusion of this component contribute to the reduction of the trade ratio. This observation also has an important bearing upon comparisons over *time*. When the import ratio increases substantially, the import coefficient of exports is likely to do the same. Hence, the increase in openness implied from the adjusted trade ratio is likely to be smaller than the increase apparent from the unadjusted, gross ratio.[25] The aforementioned observation of the change in Ireland, from 1952 to 1978, is an example of such rule.

As has been noted before, the countries for which the necessary computations could be made belong mostly to the group of highly-developed economies, with a very poor representation of others. Implications for lower-income countries must, therefore, be inferred from the observation of the highly-developed economies. It may, thus, be quite safely assumed that the phenomenon of low-import coefficients in primary production, noted in practically all countries, will also be found in the less-developed economies. Hence, it is likely that in the latter, where primary production provides the large majority of exports, the aggregate import coefficient in exports would be found to be small. As a result, the difference between the adjusted and the gross ratio would be relatively small. When the adjusted trade ratio is used, less-developed economies would thus most probably appear to be more open, in comparison with highly-developed countries, than is apparent from

[24] But it should be recalled that the countries covered are largely similar, belonging mostly to the high-income range.

[25] This also indicates a probable bias in the method of estimation used here where – for want of a better alternative – it was assumed that in each country, the individual-industry import coefficients remained unchanged between 1952 and 1979 (both being equal to the 1965 coefficients). Since in most countries the overall import ratios increased, during this period, it is likely that individual-industry coefficients also increased. Hence, in 1979 (or 1978) in comparison with 1952, aggregate import coefficients should be higher; the adjustment factor of the trade ratio higher; and the degree of openness lower, than the changes yielded by the method followed.

the conventional, gross measure of trade ratios. Likewise, as an economy develops and its export basket contains gradually – as is typically the case – a higher share of manufactures, its overall import component in exports is likely to rise. Hence, when the adjusted trade ratio is used, in a time comparison, openness of this economy would be likely to show a smaller increase, or a larger reduction, than the use of gross ratios would seem to indicate.

CHAPTER 3

TRADE STRUCTURE AND THE HOME MARKET

We come now to the issue of the ease of replacement of trade flows by home-market transactions. As was noted in the analysis of the last chapter, this should be one of the components of an indication of the degree of openness of economies. The only *overall* indexes of the ease of replacement are, (virtually by definition) the elasticities of supply and demand for exports and imports, or, alternatively (the two measures are strictly related), the elasticities of substitution in production and consumption between exports and imports, respectively, and other activities. Estimates of aggregative elasticities of supply and demand for exports and imports are rare, and are not commonly found when the openness of economies is indicated. In the present chapter, we shall examine a few attributes of the structure of export and import flows, and their relationships to the home market, which have bearing on the present issue. This analysis could not be viewed as a good substitute for the estimate of elasticities, but it should help to illuminate factors which are presumably important components of the determinants of the ease of replacement of trade flows by home-market activities.

1. The shares of exports in industrial activities

Take, first, exports. Suppose an industrial branch sells only to the outside world: exports exhaust fully the industry's output. The (potential) disappearance of the export market would thus leave all the industry's product unsold. The replacement of exports by activities destined for the home market would then depend on the movement of factors to other industrial branches. These may be easier or more difficult, depending on the degree of specificity of factors; but in any case, it would be more difficult, and require longer time than the shift of sales of the industry's output from one market to another. To take the other extreme, suppose instead that exports occupy only a minute fraction of the industry's total sales. Here, the disappearance of the export market would be of very little consequence; a slight change in relative prices would be sufficient to insure that the output otherwise sold abroad will be sold in the home market. The ease of replacing exports by home-market activity is thus, *inter alia*, a function of the share of exports in the industry's total sales.

In any economy, it may be expected that these shares will be closely related to the aggregate export share; the larger the latter, the more can exports be expected to weigh in each individual branch. But this relationship is not unique. Two economies with the same aggregate export ratios may differ radically from each other if in one exports are concentrated in a few industries, in each of which they occupy a predominant share of the industry's sales; whereas if the other exports are evenly distributed among industries, so that the export share in each industry does not differ much from the aggregate export ratio. It is thus proposed to add to the measure of the aggregate ratio another, which will indicate this effect of varying export structures.

The measure proposed is the following index of the weighted ratio of exports to product, designated S_{jx} for country j and defined as:

$$S_{jx} = \sum_i (X_{ij}/Q_{ij})(X_{ij}/X_{\cdot j}),$$

where:

X_{ij} = exports of good i by country j;
Q_{ij} = total production of good i in country j;[1]
$X_{\cdot j}$ = aggregate exports of country j.

Given the country's size of aggregate exports, this index will be higher the more these exports are concentrated in a few branches, in each of which they occupy a larger share. The upper limit of the index is unity; this will be its value when all the country's exports are sold by industries which work solely for exports. The lower limit of the index is the aggregate ratio of exports to product; this will be the value of the index when the economy's export structure is identical with its production structure.

In any estimate of this index, the result would crucially depend on the industrial classification of activities which is adopted. Industries could always be classified finely enough so that in each activity exports will occupy an overwhelming share, and the index of weighted share of exports will approach unity. On the other hand, a very broad classification – say, for instance, into primary production vs. manufactures – would tend to yield an index of weighted share not much higher than the aggregate export ratio. There is no single classification scheme which could be defended as *the* appropriate one: there is not one level of elasticity of substitution among activities which could be offered as the appropriate level, in the

---

[1]Alternatively – with a slightly different interpretation – Q_{ij} might stand for the total *use* of the good in the economy, rather than its production – that is, adding imports to home production.

present context, to serve as the basis for classification, and, whatever the classification method adopted, elasticities of substitution among pairs of industries must in any case vary greatly from each other.[2]

Among the available scheme, the 3-digit level of the SITC would probably seem to be better, or less defective, than others.[3] In the construction of the index on hand, however, the classification scheme must be identical for trade (exports) and for production and, while trade data are usually classified by the SITC, domestic production is normally classified otherwise. In work on single economies, the matching of classifications is very often feasible (although, I suspect, usually on a broader level of classification than the 3-digit SITC); but in a multi-country comparison of the present nature, such work would not be feasible. Hence, relying on more easily accessible data, I have constructed – for the purpose of illustration – a less satisfactory index, and for only a very limited number of countries. The data are drawn again from the aforementioned U.N. (1977) set of input–output tables for 1965, where production of goods (services, once more, will be abstracted from) is classified into just 14 industrial branches. The index was constructed for 19 countries, appropriate data for which are available in the source. The element of Q_{ij} in the index consists, in this construction, not of total domestic production of the branch but of total final uses of the good in the economy. The results are presented in table 3.1.

Column (1) records, for perspective, the overall export share – the ratio of exports of goods and services to the GDP. Column (2) presents a similar ratio, but confined to goods and in which, in addition, the denominator refers not just to the national product but to the aggregate of final uses (of goods) in the economy. Column (3), on the other hand, based on the same data as those of column (2), presents the index of the weighted ratio of the export of goods. Finally, column (4) is the ratio between the weighted share in (3) and the aggregate export share in (2); it thus represents the extent to which differences between the economy's production structure and trade structure contribute to the importance of exports – in the sense just discussed – in the economy.

It appears that the latter factor is certainly of significance: despite the fact that industrial branches are classified, in this construction, in a very broad fashion, the index of weighted share of exports is usually considerably higher than the aggregate export share. Likewise, although the range of countries covered is quite nar-

---

[2] The issue of classification will be relevant and important throughout the present chapter and, indeed, most of the rest of the present part of the study. It was discussed, in a largely similar context, in Michaely (1958). In subsequent literature, Tuong and Yeats (1976) have proposed the use of a "full-information index", which incorporates indices computed at different levels of aggregation. But such an index would have no analytical content.

[3] This classifies all trade into 175 goods. The broader, 2-digit level of classification specifies 56 goods; whereas the finer classification, at the 4-digit level (for which, in any case, data are much scarcer), has 625 goods.

Table 3.1. Measures of export ratios, 1965 (in per cent)

Country	Exports of goods and services to GDP (1)	Exports of goods to final uses of goods (2)	Weighted share of exports in uses of goods (S_{jx}) (3)	(3)/(2) = (4)
Austria	25.7	23.0	40.1	1.74
Belgium	36.3	44.6	61.9	1.39
Canada	19.2	32.9	59.9	1.82
Denmark	30.7	39.8	43.5	1.09
Finland	21.3	33.9	64.1	1.89
France	13.8	20.2	30.3	1.50
Germany	18.1	26.0	41.5	1.60
Hungary	36.6	30.9	40.3	1.30
Ireland	34.8	29.4	34.9	1.19
Italy	17.2	22.9	37.1	1.62
Japan	10.7	18.2	37.5	2.06
Netherlands	45.0	42.0	51.5	1.23
Norway	40.0	32.0	54.0	1.69
Portugal	25.9	19.1	32.5	1.70
Spain	10.6	8.9	14.0	1.57
Sweden	21.8	38.4	55.7	1.45
Turkey	6.0	5.7	14.5	2.54
U.K.	19.6	34.3	46.0	1.34
U.S.	5.1	10.4	22.2	2.13

Source: Column (1) – data from U.N. *Yearbook of National Accounts Statistics*; column (2) – data from U.N. *Standardized Input – Output Tables, 1965* (1977). Method of construction of column (3) explained in text.

row – it largely coincides with the list of the world's highly-developed econo-mies – variations among individual countries are substantial. Thus, for instance, the U.S. and (once more) Japan appear, relative to other economies, to be more open than their aggregate export share would indicate, when the impact of export structure is introduced; whereas Denmark or (again, once more) Ireland appear relatively lower on the scale of openness than the exclusive use of their aggregate export ratio would indicate.

Since, this time again, data for less-developed economies are absent in this pre-sentation, one would have to speculate about the effect of introducing the consid-eration on hand on the indications of openness for these countries. It is probably not an accident that the definitely highest ratio in column (4) of table 3.1 belongs to the country, Turkey, which is significantly the least developed of those shown. Less-developed economies tend to specialize, by and large, in a very limited range of export goods, in each of which their own home market would normally be small relative to the size of exports. Thus, indexes of weighted share of exports in prod-uct would tend to exceed the aggregate export ratio, in these countries, far more than this is true for highly-developed economies.[4] Hence, the recognition of this impact of export structure would tend – it so happens, like the factor discussed in the last section of the preceding chapter – to show a relatively much higher level of openness of less-developed economies than the simple trade ratios would indicate.

2. The shares of imports in uses

Turn, now, to imports. In a similar way, the allocation of imports among various uses is relevant in the determination of the ease with which imports could be replaced in use by domestic production. The lower the share of imports in the total supply of a good, in the economy, the easier is (*ceteris paribus*) their replacement (or the higher the elasticity of demand for imports). Imports of a given aggregate size will be thus easier to dispense with the more evenly they are allocated among individual uses in the economy. Similarly to exports, the measure designed to express this factor is the weighted ratio. Designated by S_{jm}, the weighted ratio of imports to availabilities in the economy is thus:

$$S_{jm} = \sum_i \left(M_{ij}/A_{ij} \right) \left(M_{ij}/M_{\cdot j} \right),$$

where:

M_{ij} = imports of good i by country j;
A_{ij} = availability of good i in country j; and
$M_{\cdot j}$ = aggregate imports of country j.[5]

Table 3.2, largely similar to table 3.1, presents, in column (2), this measure of the weighted ratio of imports for the 21 countries for which the required data are available in the U.N. source of input–output tables. Column (1) presents the aggregate ratio of imports of goods to their availabilities;[6] whereas column (3) – the

[4]With goods classified at something like the 3-digit SITC level, indexes of weighted shares of exports in product would probably be quite close to unity in many less-developed economies.

[5]It should be noted that M_{ij} is defined as imports *of good* i – not including, that is, imports of *inputs* used in the domestic production of good i. The term A_{ij} stands for the combination of *gross* production of good i in the economy and imports of i. The economy's aggregate of A_{ij} is, hence, *not* the aggregate of final uses: it exceeds the latter – usually by much – since it includes the values of intermediate inputs.

[6]The ratios presented in this column are *not* comparable with those found in column (2) of table 3.1, where the aggregate ratio of exports to final uses is recorded. One reason is that exports of goods are not, for individual countries, necessarily equal to imports; among the countries shown, in almost all (the U.S. being the exception), the value of imports in 1965 exceeded that of exports. But this is much more than offset by the difference in the definitions of the two alternative *denominators*: in exports, it is the aggregate of final uses, whereas in imports, it is the aggregate of availabilities which, as has just been noted, far exceeds the value of final uses. Thus, the ratios recorded in column (1) of table 3.2 are universally lower – often by much – than those presented in column (2) of table 3.1.

Table 3.2. Measures of import ratios, 1965

Country	Imports of goods to aggregate availabilities of goods (1)	Weighted ratio of imports in availabilities (S_{jm}) (2)	(2)/(1) = (3)
Austria	0.204	0.268	1.31
Belgium	0.292	0.345	1.18
Canada	0.173	0.241	1.39
Czechoslovakia	0.109	0.148	1.36
Denmark	0.264	0.379	1.44
Finland	0.174	0.330	1.90
France	0.114	0.165	1.45
Germany	0.135	0.172	1.27
Hungary	0.139	0.192	1.38
Ireland	0.248	0.442	1.78
Italy	0.129	0.236	1.83
Japan	0.071	0.244	3.44
Netherlands	0.299	0.355	1.19
Norway	0.292	0.419	1.43
Poland	0.099	0.135	1.36
Portugal	0.184	0.306	1.66
Spain	0.121	0.204	1.69
Sweden	0.194	0.299	1.54
Turkey	0.102	0.316	3.10
U.K.	0.170	0.210	1.24
U.S.	0.024	0.047	1.96

Source: Data from U.N. *Standardized Input–Output Tables, 1965* (1977). Method of construction explained in text.

ratio between (2) and (1) – shows the extent by which the weighted ratio of imports to availabilities exceeds the simple, aggregate ratio between the two.

As in exports, the findings presented in table 3.2 seem to indicate that the factor under consideration may be of substantial importance. Despite, again, the fact that industries ("goods") are very broadly classified, the weighted share of imports in availabilities exceeds by much their simple, aggregated share. Likewise, despite the fact that the range of countries covered is quite narrow, substantial differences among countries appear in the relevance of the consideration on hand. It is interesting to note that by and large, whenever the ratio of the weighted share to the aggregate share is relatively high in exports, it is also high in imports (Japan's position, which almost always stands out in this study's measurements, is even more prominent when imports than when exports are concerned). Thus, as a rule (confined, at the moment, to the group of countries under consideration), whenever a country appears to be more dependent on trade than its overall trade ratio indicates due to the allocation of its exports among individual activities, it also tends to be more dependent as a result of the allocation of its imports.

3. Imports of intermediate and of final goods

Another aspect of the structure of imports which presumably has an important bearing on the ease of their replacement is the nature of the goods imported. Of particular significance is the distinction between intermediate and final goods. Imports which serve as intermediate inputs in home production are presumably more difficult to replace than imports of final goods. This may be expected on two counts. First, of the two bases for trade,[7] the exchange of intermediate goods is likely to be predominantly due to differences – very often acute differences – in factor proportions (and, to a very large extent, these factors are of a rather specific nature); whereas trade in final goods is likely to be very often based on heterogeneity of goods and product differentiation. In other words, the first category is likely to consist predominantly of "Kravis-type" goods, while the latter will include a high fraction of "Linder-type" goods. Presumably, the former category is much more difficult to replace, in both supply and demand, than the latter.

Another factor which explains the difficulty of replacement of intermediate imports is that many inputs are required, in the production process, in roughly fixed proportions in a given activity. This would be more true the shorter the time span allowed for response and adjustment and is hence a major consideration the shorter the period in which one is interested. Thus, the disappearance of certain imported inputs – which, as has just been noted, would not be easily replaced by domestic production of these inputs – would lead to unemployment of some specific home factors and to a large loss of productivity of others. On this score, the larger the number of "cycles" of production through which an imported input goes, the larger the loss from its potential disappearance: an input which serves to produce another input, which then participates in the production of still another input, and so on, would make home production dependent on it to a larger degree than an input which serves directly to produce a final good. Fuel may be the prime example of such an all-pervasive input.[8]

Thus, the distinction between imports of intermediate and of final goods would be another important measure which may be used to supplement, and qualify, the use of import or trade ratios as indicators of openness of economies: the larger the share of intermediate inputs in total imports, the more open is the economy.

---

[7] For a recent formulation of the alternative explanations of trade, see Helpman (1981).

[8] One may contemplate some overall index which would express this degree of pervasiveness of imports, reflecting the number of production cycles through which imports undergo (the minimum number being zero – for imports of final goods). I could not conceive of any formulation of this nature of an operational significance.

Multi-country estimates of this share are not readily available. To proceed, one must derive the measure by using the raw data of trade composition, classifying all goods into the two categories of intermediate inputs and final goods. Sometimes, the distinction may be easily established by the type of good; but very often this would not be possible and a large element of arbitrariness would then be inevitably involved in the classification.[9] A very fine definition and classification of all goods might have potentially minimized the distortion introduced by such arbitrariness; but available trade data are confined, when international comparisons are involved, to the 3-digit SITC level. Using this available scheme, all goods have been classified into the two categories in the way presented in an appendix table to this chapter. In view of the preceding reservation, one should bear in mind that this procedure could not yield more than tentative inferences.

An alternative method might have resorted to the use of input–output data. In the aforementioned U.N. (1977) source of input–output tables, one may readily find the distinction between imports which serve as intermediate inputs and imports destined directly for final uses. Were such data more comprehensive, they would have provided a more solid basis for the derivation of the ratios looked for. Since, however, these tables are available for only a small number of countries, and for just one point of time, they are used here instead as a partial check on the reliability of the method actually followed in this study. This is done by means of table 3.3, where the intermediate-goods ratios estimated by the two alternative methods, for the year 1965, are presented for the 15 countries for which the appropriate input–output data are available.

It appears that the trade-data estimates of the intermediate-goods ratio are universally lower than the ratios yielded by the input–output data. The method followed here may thus be judged to be leading to an underestimate of the correct ratios: some groups classified here as final goods must serve in effect, to a smaller or larger extent, as intermediate goods. Yet, the distortion is not overwhelming, and is largely of a similar proportion in most countries: the input–output estimate usually exceeds the trade-data estimate by around 20%. The rankings of countries by the two alternative schemes appear to be rather similar.[10] Thus, by this evidence, the method followed in this study probably yields a reasonably good approximation of the true measures so far as ranking of countries is concerned; and while it, apparently, generally underestimates the level of the intermediate-goods ratios, the degree of such underestimation is of moderate proportions. Yet, in trying to make inferences based on *absolute* levels of the ratios – inferences generally absent in the present, comparative study – caution would certainly be required.

[9] "Rough wood", or "fertilizers", are obviously intermediate goods; whereas "footwear", or "aircraft" are final goods. But what about "sugar", or "articles of rubber"? The latter examples characterize not an exception, but a large fraction of all goods.

[10] The (Spearman) rank-correlation coefficient of the two series is 0.711.

Table 3.3. Alternative estimates of the ratio of intermediate goods, 1965

Country	Ratio derived from input–output data (1)	Ratio derived from trade data (2)
Belgium	0.686	0.547
Denmark	0.603	0.578
Finland	0.567	0.481
France	0.711	0.565
Germany	0.735	0.582
Ireland	0.596	0.514
Italy	0.775	0.662
Japan	0.857	0.785
Netherlands	0.687	0.544
Norway	0.563	0.444
Portugal	0.651	0.547
Spain	0.620	0.566
Sweden	0.640	0.467
Turkey	0.624	0.562
U.K.	0.695	0.566
Mean, 15 countries	0.667	0.561

Source: Column 1 – data from U.N. *Standardized Input – Output Tables, 1965* (1977); column 2 – data from U.N. *Yearbook of International Trade Statistics.*

The intermediate-goods ratios are presented in table 3.4. Estimates have been derived for 1955 (practically the earliest year for which properly classified trade data are available for a reasonably large number of countries) and for the latest year for which data have been published – 1979 or another late 1970s year, as the case with each individual country may be.[11]

It seems that the spread of the intermediate-goods ratios is indeed very substantial. In 1955, the ratio ranges from 0.342 (for Liberia) to 0.761 (for Japan); whereas in the late 1970s (where the number of countries covered by the data is much larger), the range lies between 0.201 (for Qatar) and 0.770 (again, for Japan). Thus, presuming that the ratio on hand is indeed of considerable importance in determining the extent of a country's openness, it appears that it is of substantial relevance for international comparisons. A country like Japan (on this score too,

---

[11] The precise year *is* of some importance. In particular, it should be recalled that the price of oil imports – absolute and relative – has about tripled in early 1979. This by itself leads to a significant increase in the (current-prices) estimate of the intermediate-inputs ratio in 1979. Hence, the comparison of this ratio in one country's index for a year preceding 1979 with another country's estimate for 1979 tends to *under*estimate the former.

Table 3.4. The ratio of intermediate goods in total imports of goods,
1955 and 1979

	1955	1979	Excluding oil	
			1955	1979
High-income countries				
Australia	0.562	0.376	0.506	0.301
Austria	0.624	0.441	0.568	0.362
Belgium-Luxembourg	0.677	0.478	0.640	0.390
Canada	0.459	0.307	0.393	0.235
Denmark	0.722	0.565	0.655	0.457
Finland	0.592	0.568	0.535	0.412
France	0.653	0.537	0.576	0.410
Germany	0.724	0.537	0.697	0.420
Iceland	0.517	0.480	0.438	0.353
Italy	0.719	0.644	0.650	0.530
Japan	0.761	0.770	0.729	0.606
Netherlands	0.679	0.512	0.625	0.388
New Zealand	0.487	0.523	0.450	0.434
Norway	0.529	0.460	0.477	0.363
Sweden	0.584	0.512	0.497	0.374
Switzerland	—	0.425	—	0.348
U.K.	0.654	0.490	0.613	0.421
U.S.	0.634	0.512	0.596	0.305
Middle-income countries				
Algeria[a]	—	0.363	–	0.354
Argentina[a]	—	0.487	—	0.414
Brazil[c]	0.619	0.288	0.514	0.186
Chile[b]	—	0.428	—	0.292
Colombia[b]	0.432	0.467	0.406	0.428
Costa Rica[a]	0.480	0.463	0.447	0.402
Cyprus	0.476	0.527	0.429	0.459
Dominican Republic	—	0.562	—	0.403
Ecuador[b]	0.443	0.346	0.415	0.340
Fiji[a]	0.462	0.413	0.406	0.283
Greece	0.605	0.471	0.542	0.328
Guatemala[b]	—	0.482	—	0.394
Hong Kong	0.598	0.432	0.583	0.397
Ireland	0.585	0.495	0.515	0.425
Israel[a]	0.595	0.665	0.544	0.614
Ivory Coast[a]	—	0.361	—	0.293
Jamaica[a]	0.505	0.600	0.457	0.471
Jordan[a]	—	0.400	—	0.331
Korea	0.712	0.610	0.679	0.520
Macao	—	0.577	—	0.553
Malaysia	—	0.457	—	0.382
Malta[a]	0.413	0.499	0.379	0.459
Mexico[b]	0.446	0.445	0.399	0.417
Panama[a]	0.388	0.475	0.320	0.306
Paraguay[c]	—	0.468	—	0.291

Table 3.4. (*Continued*)

| | 1955 | 1979 | Excluding oil | |
			1955	1979
Portugal	0.593	0.612	0.536	0.524
Reunion	—	0.200	—	0.229
Singapore	—	0.535	—	0.375
South Africa[a]	—	0.274	—	0.271
Spain	0.628	0.657	0.549	0.508
Suriname[c]	—	0.511	—	0.379
Syria[a]	—	0.462	—	0.379
Trinidad and Tobago[a]	0.503	0.585	0.396	0.346
Tunisia[a]	—	0.463	—	0.396
Turkey	0.532	0.677	0.488	0.498
Uruguay[b]	—	0.607	—	0.472
Yugoslavia	0.594	0.525	0.557	0.434
Low-income countries				
Afghanistan[c]	—	0.460	—	0.375
Angola[c]	—	0.427	—	0.400
Bangladesh[a]	—	0.686	—	0.632
Bolivia[c]	—	0.364	—	0.358
Burma[c]	0.484	0.529	0.455	0.489
Burundi[c]	—	0.394	—	0.334
Cameroon	—	0.469	—	0.404
Central African Republic[a]	—	0.232	—	0.219
Chad[c]	—	0.461	—	0.372
Congo[b]	—	0.319	—	0.309
Egypt	0.513	0.460	0.458	0.456
El Salvador[a]	0.466	0.450	0.432	0.404
Ethiopia[c]	—	0.434	—	0.331
Gabon[b]	—	0.340	—	0.333
Ghana[b]	0.546	0.546	0.515	0.448
Haiti[b]	—	0.450	—	0.380
Honduras[a]	0.481	0.415	0.443	0.342
India[b]	0.588	0.639	0.540	0.515
Indonesia	0.659	0.485	0.637	0.420
Kenya[a]	—	0.441	—	0.318
Liberia[b]	0.342	0.351	0.305	0.236
Madagascar[a]	—	0.409	—	0.312
Malawi[a]	—	0.428	—	0.350
Mali[c]	—	0.385	—	0.282
Mauritius[c]	0.433	0.425	0.408	0.369
Morocco[a]	—	0.531	—	0.451
Nicaragua[a]	0.427	0.493	0.380	0.402
Niger[c]	—	0.383	—	0.293
Pakistan	—	0.567	—	0.479
Papua-New Guinea[c]	—	0.303	—	0.187
Peru[b]	—	0.538	—	0.431
Philippines[a]	—	0.590	—	0.464
Senegal[c]	—	0.420	—	0.342

Table 3.4. (*Continued*)

	1955	1979	Excluding oil 1955	1979
Sierra Leone[c]	0.440	0.382	0.407	0.301
Somalia[c]	0.464	0.450	0.407	0.409
Sri Lanka	0.432	0.554	0.368	0.458
Sudan[a]	—	0.330	—	0.320
Tanzania[c]	—	0.483	—	0.365
Thailand[a]	0.503	0.585	0.450	0.468
Togo[b]	—	0.399	—	0.352
Uganda[c]	—	0.515	—	0.311
Upper Volta[c]	—	0.409	—	0.351
Yemen[c]	—	0.291	—	0.265
Zaire[c]	—	0.406	—	0.341
Zambia[b]	—	0.461	—	0.363
Oil-exporting countries				
Iran[b]	—	0.386	—	0.386
Iraq[c]	—	0.340	—	0.340
Kuwait[b]	—	0.216	—	0.210
Libya[a]	0.454	0.310	0.393	0.305
Nigeria[b]	0.530	0.282	0.506	0.269
Qatar	—	0.201	—	0.189
Saudi Arabia[a]	—	0.294	—	0.289
United Arab Emirates[b]	—	0.278	—	0.230
Venezuela[a]	—	0.282	—	0.277

[a]1978 data, instead of 1979
[b]1977
[c]a year prior to 1977
Source: Data from U.N. *Yearbook of International Trade Statistics*. Classification method description in appendix.

as on others) appears to be *more* open, in relative terms, than its simple trade (or import) ratio would indicate; whereas the opposite would be true for a country like Brazil (in recent years), or Venezuela.

It will be worthwhile to inquire, again, whether countries' income levels, or levels of development, have a bearing on the measure of openness under consideration. *A priori*, the direction of such a relationship is probably not clear cut. On the one hand, low-income, less-developed economies presumably specialize in the exports of foodstuffs and raw materials, produced intensively with the aid of natural resources and low-skilled manpower found in abundance in these economies. In exchange, these countries presumably import predominantly finished goods. The opposite pattern would then follow for the trade of highly-developed with less-developed countries. On this score, thus, imports of less-developed countries would be expected to contain a small proportion of intermediate goods in comparison with the imports of highly-developed economies. On the other hand, high-income countries presumably conduct a large amount of the "Linder-type" trade; that is, exchanging among themselves finished goods, of a heterogeneous nature. This component of trade would, then, tend to *decrease* the intermediate-goods ratio in the imports of these economies, in comparison with the ratios found in less-developed countries.

In table 3.4, countries are again classified into three categories, by income level: high-income, middle-income and low-income countries.[12] In addition, oil-exporting countries (namely, those in which oil exports form a major share of total exports) are shown separately. In table 3.5, which summarizes table 3.4, (unweighted) averages for the different categories of countries are presented, for both 1955 and 1979 (or other late 1970s year). In order to be able to judge directions of *change*, averages are also shown for 1979 for only those countries, estimates of the ratios for which are also available for 1955 (a total of 51, out of a total of 109 countries covered in table 3.4). In addition, table 3.4 (and table 3.5) presents estimates of the intermediate-goods ratios, for 1955 and 1979, which exclude the imports of *oil* (from both, of course, aggregate imports and the imports of intermediate goods – the denominator and the numerator of the ratio). The threefold increase in the price of oil in 1979 (as well as a similar increase in 1974) must lead to a substantial distortion in the appearance of patterns of change. Likewise, as was noted earlier, it distorts comparisons of countries whose ratios are estimated for 1979 with countries for which estimates apply, by dictates of the availability of data, for earlier years.[13] It would have been best to overcome the effect of this distortion by adjusting the value of imports of oil, presenting it in terms of a constant price, relative to the price level of other goods. This, unfortunately, is not feasible and the alternative adopted, of abstracting from oil imports altogether, involves the obvious drawback of ignoring *real* changes over time (or differences among countries) in the significance of oil imports in the country's aggregate imports of goods.[14]

The inferences yielded by tables 3.4 and 3.5 are contradictory. Looking at the 1955 data, it appears that the intermediate-goods ratio tends to be *higher* in the high-income countries. Almost all the high-income countries have a particularly high ratio and the average ratio for this category is substantially higher than the

[12] See footnote 8 in the preceding chapter (ch. 2) for the definition of income categories.

[13] The ratios presented for *all* countries in the "high-income" category refer to 1979. In the "middle-income" category, this is true for less than half of the countries included and in the "low-income" category – for only 5 countries out of a total of 45. Thus, a cross-section comparison at the so-called "1979" point of time would tend to *over*-estimate the intermediate inputs ratio of highly-developed economies, in comparison with others, when oil imports are not abstracted from.

[14] Other relative-price changes should have also been abstracted from when patterns of change of real proportions are studied. But so far as available evidence indicates, no major relative-price changes between intermediate goods other than oil and finished goods took place during the period under consideration.

Table 3.5. Average intermediate goods ratios in categories of countries

	All imports		Excluding oil	
	1955	1979	1955	1979
High-income countries				
All countries	0.622	0.508	0.567	0.395
Countries covered in 1955	0.622	0.512	0.567	0.398
Middle-income countries				
All countries	0.530	0.486	0.478	0.393
Countries covered in 1955	0.530	0.513	0.478	0.417
Low-income countries				
All countries	0.484	0.446	0.443	0.372
Countries covered in 1955	0.484	0.483	0.443	0.408
Oil-exporting countries		0.288		0.277

Source: Table 3.4.

average for the middle-income category, which in turn is markedly higher than the average ratio for the low-income category. Thus, high-income countries should have been judged, as a group, to be more open in that period, and low-income countries to be less open, than an inter-country comparison of trade ratios alone would have indicated.

Given the relationship found in the cross-section comparison, one would expect that increased income levels over time would lead to an increase of the inter-mediate-goods ratio of imports. In fact, just the opposite has taken place. As can be seen from tables 3.4 and 3.5, the ratio has *declined* between 1955 and the late 1970s, in most individual countries and in the averages of all 3 categories of countries. This trend is strongest, and most obvious, in the category of high-income countries. Looking, in table 3.5, at the average ratios for this group, a large decline is observed from 1955 to 1979 even when oil is included; without oil, the decline is drastic. This applies also, as may be seen in table 3.4, to all individual countries in this category.[15] In the category of middle-income countries, the decline in the ratio was less dramatic and less consistent, but on average it was still substantial. In the category of least-developed countries, the decline was also in-

[15] For 11 out of the 15 countries in this group, the intermediate-goods ratio has also been calculated, and presented in table 3.3, for 1965. Excluding oil imports from the ratio, it appears that its decline was monotonic: the ratio in 1965 was lower than in 1955, and it was still lower in 1979. This pattern is true for practically all the 11 countries, with two slight exceptions: In Japan, the ratio remained unchanged between 1955 and 1965 (and then declined in 1979); whereas in Norway the rate remained at the same level between 1965 and 1979 (having declined, first, from 1955 to 1965). Hence, it may be presumed that the revealed phenomenon of a declining proportion of intermediate-goods imports represents, in this group of countries, a continuous process.

consistent, and on average still lower than among the middle-income countries.[16] Apparently, some important factors – such as the pursuance of free-trade policies, or the nature of technological progress – have led in general, and in particular among highly-developed countries, to the relative increase of trade in finished goods, and the decline of the share of intermediate goods in international trade.

As a result of the differential changes, the intermediate-goods ratio was in the late 1970s practically equal, on average, for high-income and middle-income countries and was only somewhat lower among the least-developed economies (among countries covered in 1955, it was indeed at the same level as in the higher-income economies). In this period, thus, the observation of the inter-mediate-goods ratio does not contribute much to the evaluation of comparative positions of the degree of openness of large categories of countries – distinguished by level of development – although it still appears to be very significant in the interpretation of relative positions of individual countries.

One category which still stands out is that of oil-exporting countries. In each of the 9 countries in this category the intermediate-goods ratio is distinctly low. For the category as a whole, the average ratio is only somewhat above half of what it is in other categories. Partly, this must be due to the fact that oil-exporting countries do not (almost) import oil – generally, one of the major components of intermediate-goods imports. But even when oil imports are abstracted from, the intermediate-goods ratio in this category of countries still appears to be substantially lower than in others. By and large, the typical oil-exporting country is an otherwise less-developed economy, with a manufacturing sector which is both small and unsophisticated. The revenues from oil exports – large not only as a proportion of total exports, but also in relation to the economy's aggregate income – are used, hence, primarily not to buy an assorted import of raw materials or other intermediate goods but for the import of finished goods, predominantly manufactures. In a movement over time, this is also illustrated by the two cases, Libya and Nigeria, for which data are available for both 1955 and the late 1970s. It so happens that both countries were not oil exporters in 1955 and assumed only later this status. In both countries – in Nigeria even more than in Libya – the intermediate-goods ratio fell drastically during the period. In general, it appears, the addition to wealth created by oil revenues takes predominantly the form of imports of finished goods. This leads to an exaggerated impression about the extent of dependence of such economies on trade if only the size of imports is observed: the degree of dependence would appear lower, in comparative analyses, when the structure of imports is taken into consideration.

---

[16] In both these categories, the intermediate-goods ratio (excluding oil) declined from 1955 to 1979 in about two-thirds of the countries.

Appendix: Classification of 3-digit SITC groups into intermediate and final goods

	Intermediate goods		Final goods	
Category 0				
Food and live animals	001	045	All other groups	
	041	046		
	043	047		
	044	081		
Category 1				
Beverages and tobacco	121		All other groups	
Category 2				
Crude materials, inedible	All groups			
Category 3				
Mineral fuels	All groups			
Category 4				
Animal and vegetable oil			All groups	
Category 5				
Chemicals	All other groups		541	553
			551	554
Category 6				
Manufactured goods	All other groups		612	656
			613	657
			624	665
			629	666
			642	667
			654	697
			655	698
Category 7				
Machinery and transport equipment			All groups	
Category 8				
Miscellaneous manufactured articles			All groups	

CHAPTER 4

SUSCEPTIBILITY: THE COUNTRY IN WORLD TRADE

The previous discussion, and the indications analyzed thus far of a country's dependence on international trade, were concerned with the impact of trade – and its absence, or disappearance – on the economy. That discussion was concerned with what we have termed the "mutiplicand" of the degree of dependence, ignoring the "multiplier"; it has not dealt at all with the issue of the *likelihood* of any disturbance of the country's trade patterns. That has meant, in turn, the absence thus far of the consideration of the country's position in world trade: the role of trade in the economy has been the focus of attention, while the role of the country's trade in the world has been left out.

Since, as has been stated at the start, the present study is concerned with "dependence" rather than with "power", we shall still not analyze the country's impact on others, via its trade. We shall pay attention to the country's position only because, and insofar as, attributes of this position may provide an indication of the susceptibility of the country's trade flows to disturbances of one kind or another. Given a certain measure of the "importance" of trade to the economy – in the sense discussed earlier – the country's "dependence" will be stronger the more are its trade flows expected to be subject to such disturbances. To give an extreme and obviously hypothetical example: A country with a very large size of trade – that is, a large measure of relative gains from trade – in which trade flows are entirely certain to proceed uninterrupted at a stable level, may be said to be independent of the outside world. On the other hand, a relatively small trade flow which may be judged to be highly volatile, either due to foreign economic fluctuations or to discretionary political interferences, may make a country strongly dependent.

The position of a country in world trade, and indicators of the susceptibility of a country's trade flows to disturbances, may best be analyzed by looking separately at the "world" in two different ways. First, the (outside) world will be viewed as a single unit. The country's position, and the indicators of its vulnerability, are then a function of the size of the country's trade and its *commodity* structure. Then, the fact that the world consists of many separate political units should be recognized. The measures of dependence would then have to take into account the *geographical* structure of a country's trade, and the nature of its trading partners.

The indicators analyzed in the present chapter will be based on the view of the world as a single unit (except that in one of the measures, as will be noted later, the relevant attribute of *commodities* will involve the geographical structure of trade in them). In the next chapter, the focus will turn to the geographical allocation of the country's trade, and to the nature of the country's trade partners.

1. The degree of commodity concentration

An attribute of the commodity structure of a country's trade flows which comes immediately to mind, in looking for indicators of susceptibility, is the extent of its *concentration*. The more is a country's trade (exports, or imports) concentrated in a small number of goods, the more likely is this trade as a whole to be subject to fluctuations and disturbances; from a greater dispersion in trade structure follows a greater stability.[1]

Concentration increases susceptibility and vulnerability on two counts. First, given the nature of goods in which the country trades, the more dispersed the trade structure the more are accidental fluctuations in the markets for each good likely to offset each other, thus leaving the trade flow as a whole stable.[2] With fewer goods, this tendency of movements to offset each other would become weaker, and the trade flow as a whole would become more likely to be subject to severe fluctuations (in price, or quantity, or both). The other way in which concentration contributes to vulnerability is by leading to a greater importance of the country in each of the markets in which it trades. This will be discussed specifically in the following section, in which attention will be paid to the country's share in its world markets. Anticipating that discussion, it will only be noted here that the larger a country's share in the market for a good in which it trades, the larger should be the extent to which fluctuations in that market have an impact on the trade (in

---

[1] The importance of the factor of concentration has long been recognized in the literature (as well as in policy discussions) – although the oldest references, as will be mentioned in the next chapter, are concerned with the geographic rather than the commodity concentration. Hirschman's (1945) pioneering book deals primarily with geographic concentration, but includes some mention of commodity concentration. The issue has been presented rather extensively in my book on the topic (1962a), which will be referred to on various occasions in the present and the following chapters and has since been analyzed, either as a main issue or in a subsidiary role, in a very large number of treatises and articles.

[2] "Accidental" fluctuations are understood to result from *independent* movements in individual markets. When a major, universal force – such as, say, a widespread war, or a world inflation – is the prime source of changes in world markets, movements in markets for individual goods would be in the same direction, rather than tend to offset each other; and the degree of commodity concentration would become less relevant.

that good) of the country concerned. Hence, the larger such shares, the more vulnerable is the country's trade flow.[3]

The intensity of concentration could potentially be measured by a variety of indexes – none of which, needless to say, is "ideal". The measure which has gained wide acceptance, and which will be used here, is the Gini-Hirschman coefficient of concentration.[4] For exports, the coefficient of commodity concentration, designated for any country j by C_{jx}, is defined as

$$C_{jx} = \sqrt{\sum_i (X_{ij}/X_{.j})^2},$$

where:

X_{ij} = exports of good i by country j; and
$X_{.j}$ = total exports of goods by country j.

Similarly, the coefficient of commodity concentration of imports, C_{jm}, is

$$C_{jm} = \sqrt{\sum_i (M_{ij}/M_{.j})^2}$$

where:

M_{ij} = imports of good i by country j; and
$M_{.j}$ = total imports of goods by country j.

The upper bound of the coefficient of concentration is unity; this will be its value when all the country's exports (imports) consist of a single good. The lower bound would be achieved when the country's exports (imports) are equally divided among all goods. In this case, the value of the index would be $1/\sqrt{N}$, where N is the number of goods in the scheme. With the 175 goods in the 3-digit level of the SITC, which will be used here for the construction of the indexes,[5] this value is 0.0756. For convenience of presentation, the coefficient will be multiplied by 100. Thus, its potential range is between 7.56 and 100.

---

[3] In addition, a higher degree of concentration contributes to a stronger measure of dependence by increasing the proportions of exports and imports in the home markets. This is the aspect analyzed in the preceding chapter.

[4] This measure has first been developed by Gini (1912), among various other indexes of dispersion which Gini has contributed. The index has been introduced later to the economic literature by Hirschman (1945), who provided an analysis of its attributes. As noted earlier, Hirschman was concerned with geographic concentration. The index has been applied to commodity concentration in my analysis (1958, 1962), where a discussion of some of the more important problems concerned with its use may be found.

[5] As with similar coefficients, the value of the index will crucially depend on the number of goods in the scheme of classification: the larger the number, the lower the index. Hence, also, a *uniform* scheme must be applied to all countries, in a cross-section, international comparison, or at all points of time in a study of changes over time. A discussion of the problems involved in the selection of a classification scheme for the purpose on hand may be found in my earlier study of this topic (1958, 1962).

The coefficients of commodity concentration of exports and imports in the trade flows of 1973, for most of the world's political entities, are presented in columns (1) and (2) of table 4.1.[6] The data presented reflect general tendencies which are by now well known, and will therefore be mentioned only briefly.[7]

(i) First, exports are generally more concentrated than imports. Of the 131 countries shown, in only six is the coefficient of commodity concentration higher (and even then, just barely so) in imports than in exports; in nine other countries, the export coefficient is only slightly (by, say, up to 10%) higher than the import coefficient, whereas in all the rest, the export coefficient is substantially higher, sometimes by a few multiples, than the import coefficient. On this score, thus, dependence of economies on the outside world is stronger in exports than in imports; fluctuations in foreign markets (once more, when they are "accidental" rather than dominated by universal world forces) are likely to be more important for the country where its export trade is concerned than its imports. The exceptions to the rule of the large excess of export over import commodity concentration – hence, to the rule of a larger dependence in export than in import trade – tend to be either highly-developed market economies or Soviet-type economies. Likewise, the importance of the factor on hand as a source of *differences* among countries in the degree of vulnerability is heavier in exports than in imports: the spread of the export coefficients is much larger than it is in imports. The export coefficients range between 15.73 (in the Netherlands) and 98.47 (in Libya) (out of a maximum potential range of 7.56 to 100), and only between 14.17 (in Ireland) and 72.10 (in the Netherland Antilles) in imports; and the standard errors of the series of coefficients of commodity concentration are 1.851 in exports vs. only 0.692 in imports.

(ii) By and large, when exports are highly concentrated, so do imports tend to be. The correlation coefficient (r) between the two coefficients – columns (1) and (2) of table 4.1 – is 0.288 (significant at practically any level). Thus, countries which are more vulnerable due to a high degree of commodity concentration of their ex-

---

[6]1973 was the latest year for which data were generally available when this part of the study was carried out. For a minority of the countries 1973 trade data were still missing, and 1972 data were used instead; in a few cases, data for yet earlier years have had to be resorted to. Calculation of the coefficients was also carried out for 1969, but since this yielded very similar results to those of 1973, and no new insights or different inferences would emerge from the 1969 data, these coefficients are not presented here.

Countries not covered in table 4.1 are those for which the required trade data were either absent altogether, or (in a very few cases) obviously deficient. These include several small oil-exporting countries, some Soviet-type economies and a number of newly-independent territories. Almost always, these are very small countries (of the close to 20 territories missing, the only ones of some weight are China, Taiwan and Bangladesh). In terms of the aggregate size of trade, or of the national income, the 131 countries covered in table 4.1 thus represent an overwhelming majority of the world.

[7]For a more extensive discussion of these tendencies, and their possible sources, my earlier study (1958, 1962a) may again be consulted.

Table 4.1. Commodity indicators of susceptibility, 1973

	Coefficients of commodity concentration		Commodity-weighted shares		Magnification ratios		Indexes of market position	
	Exports (C_{jx})	Imports (C_{jm})	Exports (W_{jx}^i)	Imports (W_{jm}^i)	Exports	Imports	Monopsony facing exports (PS_j)	Monopoly of imports (PO_j)
	(1)	(2)	(3)	(4)	(5)	(6)	(7)	(8)
Country								
Afghanistan	34.2	25.7	2.1	0.3	104.5	10.3	34.4	32.2
Algeria	71.0	18.3	4.5	1.0	8.3	1.3	30.0	36.5
Angola	42.0	20.8	1.8	0.2	16.1	4.9	35.4	35.3
Argentina	29.2	19.2	5.7	1.6	14.0	1.8	31.7	38.1
Australia	30.1	15.6	15.1	2.1	10.4	1.8	33.7	36.3
Austria	17.9	17.3	3.7	1.6	4.1	1.5	25.6	35.0
Bahama	67.8	60.9	1.8	0.8	90.0	7.3	29.7	34.0
Barbados	42.0	14.6	0.3	0.1	12.5	1.4	30.0	36.5
Belgium	18.1	17.6	8.2	5.7	2.3	1.6	27.1	36.5
Belize	59.2	17.0	0.2	0.1	11.5	7.0	33.0	33.2
Benin	44.0	25.0	0.8	0.3	192.7	1.7	30.9	31.9
Bermuda	62.9	17.5	0.2	0.1	23.0	2.3	22.7	33.1
Bolivia	80.5	47.2	3.8	1.2	76.2	17.1	42.3	39.7
Brazil	29.8	20.8	1.5	1.8	1.5	1.2	33.7	37.7
Brunei	94.5	27.9	0.6	0.1	4.5	4.3	28.0	35.1
Bulgaria	33.5	37.6	7.6	2.2	75.8	12.2	26.0	36.1
Burma	43.5	18.8	2.0	0.2	65.7	6.0	32.6	34.4
Cameroon	44.1	18.8	2.5	0.2	50.4	2.9	35.6	35.7
Canada	26.8	28.9	12.4	7.1	3.0	1.8	31.2	35.9
Central African Republic	50.0	18.6	0.3	0.0	29.0	3.0	38.4	36.1
Chad	70.2	24.0	0.5	0.1	52.0	8.0	29.8	31.7
Chile	69.5	18.0	9.0	0.5	45.1	2.2	31.7	36.2
Colombia	54.1	20.4	7.0	0.5	35.0	2.7	36.1	38.2
Congo (Brazaville)	47.5	20.0	0.6	0.1	20.3	2.3	43.3	35.1
Costa Rica	44.6	16.9	1.6	0.2	25.8	2.9	32.4	36.1
Cuba	79.0	24.6	19.7	2.0	140.7	9.2	33.0	38.0
Cyprus	44.2	17.3	0.8	0.2	40.5	4.0	33.1	34.5
Czechoslovakia	24.6	20.3	3.4	1.3	11.1	4.1	25.5	35.8
Denmark	17.8	16.5	6.4	2.1	6.1	1.7	30.7	34.9
Dominican Republic	51.9	23.7	2.7	0.3	24.2	3.2	31.6	31.6
Ecuador	54.0	20.3	—	—	—	—	—	—
Egypt	50.3	19.1	7.6	1.2	38.1	2.3	27.5	38.3
El Salvador	47.5	16.3	1.7	0.2	24.3	2.4	33.2	35.0
Ethiopia	53.3	20.5	1.6	0.1	51.7	3.0	36.9	35.5
Fiji	61.8	33.7	0.6	0.1	30.0	4.0	30.7	23.5
Finland	32.8	17.3	6.5	1.0	9.7	1.1	29.5	35.0
France	17.1	16.9	10.4	7.7	1.6	1.2	26.8	35.5
Gabon	54.1	19.8	1.7	0.1	13.4	—	38.4	36.2
Gambia	63.5	21.4	0.6	0.1	58.0	5.0	31.6	31.8
Germany (East)	27.3	29.4	5.8	3.2	27.5	12.6	23.5	43.3

Table 4.1. (*Continued*)

	Coefficients of commodity concentration		Commodity-weighted shares		Magnification ratios		Indexes of market position	
	Exports (C_{jx})	Imports (C_{jm})	Exports (W_{jx}^i)	Imports (W_{jm}^i)	Exports	Imports	Monopsony facing exports (PS_j)	Monopoly of imports (PO_j)
	(1)	(2)	(3)	(4)	(5)	(6)	(7)	(8)
Germany (West)	21.5	14.7	21.8	12.6	1.9	1.4	24.8	34.2
Ghana	66.7	18.8	17.6	0.3	195.4	2.5	33.8	33.8
Greece	22.6	18.8	2.3	0.9	8.3	1.4	29.7	34.7
Guadeloupe	62.3	15.7	0.2	0.1	22.0	2.5	31.3	32.8
Guatemala	38.8	16.7	1.4	0.2	18.0	2.0	32.6	35.0
Guyana	59.2	20.9	0.1	0.1	2.3	2.0	36.1	34.2
Guyana (French)	82.9	17.9	0.1	0.0	220.0	4.0	39.0	33.4
Haiti	44.0	18.3	0.3	0.1	13.0	2.7	35.3	33.3
Honduras	50.0	19.0	1.5	0.1	36.3	3.0	34.3	34.7
Hong Kong	35.1	17.0	8.2	3.1	11.2	3.9	29.2	34.7
Hungary	43.4	35.7	4.8	1.3	24.1	4.6	29.5	32.7
Iceland	60.8	20.3	3.2	0.3	79.0	5.0	34.9	34.4
India	22.8	19.8	5.0	1.8	8.6	2.5	29.7	36.3
Indonesia	51.7	19.6	4.6	1.5	7.7	2.5	34.0	35.4
Iran	80.4	19.8	9.8	1.6	4.4	1.3	29.0	36.8
Iraq	38.5	20.6	2.8	0.7	3.2	1.7	28.8	35.5
Ireland	21.7	14.2	2.5	0.6	6.5	1.5	28.7	33.7
Israel	45.7	24.3	5.0	2.5	13.5	3.6	32.1	39.3
Italy	19.0	18.7	9.0	8.3	2.1	1.9	27.1	36.9
Ivory Coast	47.3	17.0	5.6	0.3	39.9	2.4	41.0	33.8
Jamaica	69.1	16.5	5.2	0.3	52.2	2.5	39.4	35.3
Japan	23.9	23.0	18.8	18.3	2.8	2.7	26.6	32.3
Jordan	32.2	23.2	0.7	0.2	35.5	2.2	26.0	30.2
Kenya	37.9	19.1	1.0	0.3	14.1	2.4	33.6	35.5
Korea (South)	29.5	19.1	6.2	2.2	10.6	2.6	30.9	39.9
Kuwait	86.1	19.7	9.2	0.6	8.6	2.2	28.6	34.5
Lao (P.D.R.)	69.2	29.5	—	—	—	—	37.1	35.1
Lebanon	18.2	15.9	0.4	0.4	2.6	1.3	27.4	36.4
Liberia	65.1	20.8	2.1	0.1	29.4	—	42.0	34.6
Libya	98.5	20.0	10.9	0.8	15.5	1.5	28.4	34.1
Macao	73.9	27.1	0.6	0.2	56.0	12.0	32.3	30.9
Madagascar	39.0	16.8	1.8	0.1	60.1	3.0	33.3	35.7
Malawi	52.0	17.4	1.2	0.1	120.0	4.5	30.0	34.8
Malaysia	40.0	34.0	17.7	1.1	38.5	2.8	35.1	33.5
Mali	41.8	20.0	0.4	0.1	95.0	3.7	32.9	34.4
Malta	42.8	15.6	0.2	0.1	11.5	3.0	29.3	34.5
Martinique	65.8	15.8	0.6	0.1	59.0	2.8	31.3	33.8
Mauritania	66.3	21.4	2.0	0.1	68.0	5.5	43.9	35.8
Mauritius	93.7	17.5	2.7	0.2	66.3	5.8	31.0	33.9
Mexico	19.6	18.5	1.4	1.2	4.0	1.6	30.2	38.5
Morocco	34.0	19.0	11.1	0.5	58.5	1.8	29.4	38.8
Mozambique	30.1	17.6	0.9	0.2	21.3	4.8	30.5	36.2
Netherlands	15.7	18.0	8.0	5.7	1.9	1.4	27.3	35.5
Netherland Antilles	92.5	72.1	6.9	1.6	24.8	3.7	30.8	33.8
New Hebrides	76.0	18.1	0.3	0.1	32.0	1.3	40.6	34.6
New Zealand	42.5	19.4	9.8	0.7	36.3	1.8	33.8	34.9

Table 4.1. (*Continued*)

	Coefficients of commodity concentration		Commodity-weighted shares		Magnification ratios		Indexes of market position	
	Exports (C_{jx})	Imports (C_{jm})	Exports (W_{jx}^i)	Imports (W_{jm}^i)	Exports	Imports	Monopsony facing exports (PS_j)	Monopoly of imports (PO_j)
	(1)	(2)	(3)	(4)	(5)	(6)	(7)	(8)
Nicaragua	36.4	17.0	1.0	0.1	20.0	2.3	31.9	34.1
Niger	44.0	24.0	0.4	0.1	76.0	4.5	35.1	31.4
Nigeria	83.9	20.8	7.4	0.9	7.7	1.2	28.9	35.4
Norway	24.7	20.2	5.7	4.0	6.5	3.5	29.2	35.7
Pakistan	37.0	19.4	3.6	1.0	27.9	3.9	26.4	38.9
Panama	59.5	22.5	1.2	0.2	39.7	1.9	32.6	34.9
Papua-New Guinea	39.2	18.5	0.4	0.2	6.8	3.2	39.3	32.9
Paraguay	31.9	22.2	—	—	—	—	35.9	37.5
Peru	40.9	17.8	6.4	0.7	37.4	2.5	32.8	37.3
Philippines	37.9	21.1	8.2	1.0	29.2	2.3	39.8	36.9
Poland	22.0	18.6	5.0	3.2	10.6	4.1	29.1	37.2
Portugal	20.5	16.5	5.8	1.1	23.1	2.4	28.3	38.0
Reunion	82.8	16.4	1.1	0.2	109.0	2.6	30.4	34.2
Rwanda	57.9	21.6	0.2	0.1	21.0	14.0	39.4	34.2
Samoa (Western)	51.4	17.7	0.1	0.0	87.5	2.0	36.3	32.3
Saudi Arabia	91.2	23.0	17.2	—	5.0	—	25.6	30.0
Senegal	43.8	18.0	4.1	0.2	81.0	2.1	26.8	35.6
Sierra Leone	64.7	17.6	0.9	0.1	43.0	5.0	40.6	33.7
Singapore	32.4	18.7	4.8	2.1	7.3	2.2	27.6	34.4
Somalia	61.2	18.1	0.8	0.1	83.0	4.0	36.0	34.1
South Africa	24.1	22.9	3.3	1.2	5.1	1.4	30.0	36.0
Spain	17.7	18.6	3.4	2.7	3.3	1.5	29.1	39.1
Sri Lanka	63.7	22.7	19.8	1.9	330.3	24.0	30.0	33.6
Suriname	78.2	19.7	3.1	0.1	103.0	4.3	39.6	34.3
Sudan	62.6	20.6	5.4	0.5	90.2	4.5	31.1	33.9
Sweden	22.6	17.2	7.3	2.8	3.4	1.3	27.7	34.1
Switzerland	21.9	16.4	12.0	2.9	7.6	1.9	23.3	35.7
Syria	43.0	16.5	1.6	0.4	13.0	1.9	29.3	35.5
Tanzania	33.3	17.5	2.9	0.5	58.8	5.2	32.5	35.3
Thailand	29.4	18.7	3.9	0.8	10.0	2.1	27.1	33.8
Togo	55.1	18.6	2.5	0.1	124.0	4.5	29.4	33.5
Trinidad and Tobago	72.4	52.5	3.1	0.8	14.1	4.9	30.3	35.1
Tunisia	42.8	16.8	3.8	0.3	38.4	1.8	27.5	37.0
Turkey	32.2	21.2	1.6	0.7	9.1	1.3	30.0	37.1
Uganda	65.4	18.2	3.3	0.1	109.0	4.0	36.7	35.7
United Kingdom	18.0	15.7	10.6	11.0	2.0	1.8	26.5	35.8
United States	18.8	20.6	26.9	18.9	2.0	1.6	26.5	33.6
Upper Volta	50.3	17.9	0.2	0.1	24.0	3.5	34.1	34.2
Uruguay	59.5	28.3	2.0	0.1	48.8	2.2	33.1	34.8
U.S.S.R.	23.2	20.8	9.5	9.5	6.8	4.7	29.9	36.0
Venezuela	68.2	22.5	7.5	1.1	6.7	1.9	30.3	37.4
Vietnam (South)	78.8	16.9	0.2	0.5	23.0	7.8	27.6	34.0
Yugoslavia	16.1	15.6	1.6	1.2	3.3	1.3	28.9	36.2
Zaire	68.8	18.1	6.9	0.5	53.2	3.6	31.6	34.8
Zambia	92.1	19.8	14.0	0.4	139.6	3.5	30.1	34.6

ports, tend also to be more vulnerable, on this score, in their import trade. But, it should be restated, differences among countries would still be less important in their import than in their export trade.

(iii) The most important source of differences among countries in the degree of commodity concentration of their exports appears to be the level of economic development, or of income. Poor countries tend, by and large, to have an export trade which is concentrated in a very small number of dominant goods – often just one such good – whereas rich, highly-developed economies tend to have highly-diversified exports. Only very few less-developed economies – India would be the most outstanding example – will be found on the list of countries whose coefficients of commodity concentration of exports are particularly low, while no highly-developed economy would belong among countries whose trade is found to be highly concentrated. For 106 out of the 131 countries in table 4.1 for which income data are available, the coefficient of correlation (r) between the 1973 level of per-capita income and the coefficient of commodity concentration of exports is -0.471; the adjusted R^2 is 0.222, and the (Spearman) coefficient of rank correlation is -0.566 (all coefficients being significant at any desired level). Thus, given the levels of other indicators of dependence on trade, less-developed economies tend as a rule to be more dependent than highly-developed countries due to a heavier concentration of their exports in the markets for only few goods.[8] To a much smaller extent, this is also true due to a more concentrated import trade among poorer than among richer countries.

As was noted earlier, the intensity of commodity concentration of trade is relevant not only because a high concentration leads to a higher susceptibility through the absence of offsetting tendencies in the system, but also because a higher concentration contributes to a higher share of the country in the markets in which it trades. We shall now turn to the discussion of this indicator of dependence.

2. The country's shares in world markets

Suppose a country is a sole seller of its export good in the world market. Any fluctuation in that market would then be fully reflected in the position of the

---

[8] It may be noted that differences among highly-developed and less-developed economies in the degree of commodity concentration of their exports have tended to narrow down, over the years. While the level of diversification has remained without much change in the former group of countries, it has shown a definite tendency to decline in countries belonging to the latter. For the 38 countries which are covered jointly in the present and in my earlier study (1958, 1962), the standard error of the series of commodity concentration of exports was 3.543 in 1954; in 1973 it was lower, 2.897. At the same time, though, the (negative) association between income and commodity concentration has not weakened: the correlation coefficients between countries' per capita income levels and levels of commodity concentration were, for these 38 countries, -0.448 in 1954 and -0.505 in 1973.

country's export good. If, on the other hand, the country on hand is one small seller among many, the impact of the universal change in the market on its own exports must be smaller. Take, for instance, a decline of aggregate world demand for the good; for a small seller, a slight change (decline) in its relative price would be sufficient to insure that the impact on its own exports would be small. Fluctuations in world market may hence be expected to have a weaker impact on the small seller than on a monopolistic country. This is also true, for similar reasons, for the comparison of a country which is a minor buyer of its imports with a country occupying a monopsonistic position in the import markets. Hence, the smaller the shares of a country in its export and import markets the less is its trade vulnerable and the less is this country dependent, on this score, on its foreign trade.[9]

The relevant shares, for this purpose, are obviously not the country's *aggregate* proportions in world trade but its shares in the individual markets for each good. These may then be aggregated and expressed by a single index, which I have termed the "weighted share in world trade."[10] This index for exports of a country j, designated by W_{jx}^i, is defined as

$$W_{jx}^i = \sum_i (X_{ij}/X_{i.})(X_{ij}/X_{.j}),$$

where:

X_{ij} = exports of good i by country j;
$X_{i.}$ = total world exports of good i; and
$X_{.j}$ = total exports of goods by country j.

The first term in the expression is the country's share in world exports of the good, whereas the second expression is the good's weight, determined by its share in the country's aggregate exports. Similarly, for imports, the index of the country's weighted share – designated by W_{jm}^i – is

$$W_{jm}^i = \sum_i (M_{ij}/M_{i.})(M_{ij}/M_{.j}),$$

[9] This is one of the clear manifestations of the difference – here, the contrast – between "dependence" and "power". While lower shares in world markets make a country, by this reasoning, less "dependent", higher shares would grant it more "power". Hence, if one is interested not in a "gross" measurement of dependence, as we are here, but in a "net" definition (that is, netting a country's hold on others, through trade, from its dependence on them), two offsetting impacts would be attached to the factor of the country's shares in world markets. My guess would be – this is, obviously, sheer speculation – that in its "net" form, high market shares would contribute to "power", or would lower "dependence". Undoubtedly, this is the way this factor is perceived in daily practice.

[10] This index was first proposed in my earlier study (1960, 1962a). A fuller discussion of its properties – and shortcomings – may be found there. The index has since been applied in numerous studies. Estimates of its values in the trade flows of many countries have for recent years been provided annually in the UNCTAD's publication, *Handbook of International Trade Statistics*.

where:

M_{ij} = imports of good i by country j;
$M_{i.}$ = total world imports of good i; and
$M_{.j}$ = total imports of goods by country j.

The upper limit of this index is unity. This will be its value when the country is the exclusive world seller of all of its export goods, or the sole buyer of all its imports. The lower bound is the simple, aggregate share of the country in world trade (exports or imports). This would be the value of the index when a country happens to allocate its trade among goods in exactly the same proportions as world trade is allocated, so that in all of the individual markets the country has identical shares, which are equal in turn to the country's aggregate share in world trade (exports, or imports).

The indexes of weighted shares of exports and imports for 1973 (or an approximate year) are presented in columns (3) and (4) of table 4.1. They are based on the same set of data as the coefficients of concentration; that is, on the data of exports and imports of goods classified by the 3-digit level of the SITC.

As is easy to realize, the index of weighted share of a country's trade flow is determined by three factors, or components.[11] One – the most obvious – is the size of the country's aggregate trade flow; the larger it is, given a trade structure, the higher should be the country's share in each of the markets for individual goods and the larger, hence, the country's weighted share in trade. Thus, the larger the size of a country's trade, the more susceptible is this trade, on this score, to market fluctuations.

Another component is the factor discussed earlier: the degree of commodity concentration. Given the aggregate size of a country's trade flow, the more concentrated is its structure, the larger may be expected to be the country's share in each of the world markets for the goods in which it mainly trades. This, as has been mentioned earlier, is one of the channels through which a heavier commodity concentration of trade tends to lead to a larger measure of a country's dependence on trade.

The third component which participates in the determination of the index of weighted share in trade is the sizes of the world markets for the goods in which the country specializes in its export or import trade. This is purely a matter of accident. A country which happens to concentrate its exports in goods for which large world markets exist will tend to have – given the other factors – small shares in each of these markets, hence a low weighted share in world exports; whereas a country which specializes in goods with particularly small world markets may prove to be a dominant factor in these markets even though the country may be

[11]A somewhat more precise discussion of the relationships may be found in my aforementioned study (1960, 1962a).

small so far as its aggregate exports are concerned. The element of "accident" involved here will be more important (in affecting the index one way or another) the more important is the preceding component; namely, the level of commodity concentration. In a country, to cite an extreme example, which specializes exclusively in a single good, the size of the world market for this good – which is the chance component, or the element of "accident" – would be of crucial importance; whereas in a country in which exports are highly diversified, the "chance" factors of the sizes of individual markets would tend to offset each other.

To separate out partly these elements, columns (5) and (6) in table 4.1 present (respectively for exports and imports) the factor yielded by division of the indexes of weighted shares of countries' trade by the countries' aggregate proportions in world trade flows. The ratios presented in these columns, which will be termed the "magnification ratios", thus represent the combined contributions of the other two elements – the degree of commodity concentration and the sizes of individual markets – to the values of the indexes of weighted shares in trade, and through them to the level of dependence on trade.

Since the magnification ratio must be closely correlated with the degree of commodity concentration, it may be expected to reveal similar patterns to those manifested by the coefficients of concentration. Specifically, the three aforementioned general propositions concerning commodity concentration apply to the ratio on hand, namely: (i) The magnification ratio is almost uniformly higher, often substantially so, in export than in import trade flows. Since in most countries trade is roughly balanced, this must mean that the weighted shares of countries in world trade are mostly much higher in exports than in imports. Indeed, the average index of weighted share in trade for the 131 countries represented in table 4.1 is 4.61 for exports and 1.48 for imports. For the magnification ratios (columns (5) and (6)), the averages are 39.74 for exports and 3.59 for imports; the former exceeds the latter by more than tenfold![12] (ii) When the magnification ratio is high

---

[12] The discrepancy between the export to import ratios in the magnification ratios and the indexes of weighted shares in trade may seem surprising. If exports were equal to imports, these two export to import ratios should be equal to each other (with proper recording and accounting, *world* exports must equal world imports, so that a country's balanced trade would mean equal aggregate shares of the country in world exports and imports). Imbalances in individual country's trade flows could explain some discrepancy between the two ratios, but in the large majority of countries, this could not amount to much. Indeed, the two ratios are – as they must be – quite similar in most individual countries. The large discrepancy between the world *averages* of the two ratios is mostly the outcome of an implied difference in the *weighting* scheme. The index of a country's weighted share in a trade flow is affected, of course, by the size of the country's trade – the bigger the latter, the higher (*ceteris paribus*) the former. In the construction of a world average of these indexes, high individual indexes are implicitly assigned large weights; thus, large countries (in terms of trade flows) are assigned large weights. As noted, the large countries – mostly coinciding with the group of rich, highly-developed economies – are characterized by weighted shares in trade which are quite similar in exports and in imports (due to similar intensities of commodity concentration). The average world levels of the magnification ratios, on the other hand, assigns equal weights to all countries.

for exports, it tends to be also high in imports.[13] (iii) The magnification ratio tends to be higher for less-developed than for highly-developed economies, particularly in the export trade. Since less-developed economies tend to be small in economic size – including, as a rule, the size of trade – the factor under consideration tends as a rule to offset the impact of the size component on the importance of countries in world trade, and thus on its implication for the degree of dependence. The weighted shares of less-developed countries in world trade tend to be low due to the generally small sizes of the trade flows of these countries but tend, on the other hand, to be pushed upward, particularly in the export trade, by the generally high level of commodity concentration which characterizes the trade of these economies.

3. Structure of world markets of the country's trade flows

The measure just discussed, of a country's weighted share in trade, provides an indication – partial, of course – of the country's monopolistic or monopsonistic position in its world trade (exports and imports, respectively). But another element of dependence is the degree of monopoly or monopsony with which *the country is faced* in its trade.

Whatever the country's share in the world market for an export good, the intensity of its dependence on the outside world will be a function of the market structure for that good. If, to take the extreme case, the good in question is bought in the world market by a single country, the degree of susceptibility involved in this trade will be particularly high.[14] Fluctuations in this foreign economy will have a strong impact on the "world" market for this good. Likewise, the monopsonistic position of that foreign country would potentially provide it with a substantial political leverage, thus making its suppliers more vulnerable than otherwise. If, on the other hand, the market for the good consists of many buying countries,

---

[13] It would serve no purpose to examine the correlation between the series of weighted shares of countries in exports and in imports. Since each weighted share must be heavily affected by the aggregate size of the country's trade, and in most countries aggregate exports of goods are roughly equal to aggregate imports, indexes of weighted shares in exports and imports must be positively correlated on this score alone.

[14] Here, as elsewhere, the discussion disregards the question whether *within* any political entity a single firm or many firms participate (as buyers or sellers) in the market for the good: the country's composition of trade is examined, while the number of firms is overlooked. There is no doubt that the latter is a significant element in determining the intensity of dependence of countries in their foreign trade. But the incorporation of this element into quantitative indicators such as those proposed here does not seem to be feasible. Similarly, but in the opposite direction, the possibility of political-economic *alliances* will be abstracted from: each country is treated as a separate unit. Needless to say, in the concrete world the possible existence of such alliances among customers of the country's exports, or among suppliers of its imports, may be highly relevant for the determination of the degree of its dependence through trade on the outside world.

each occupying only a small share of total purchases, susceptibility of the selling country would be less severe. Fluctuations in the economies of the buying countries – whether involving their aggregate performance or just the market for the good on hand – are likely to tend to offset each other when many economies participate in the market. Similarly, the ability of manipulation of the market in one way or another as a tool of political power of the foreign country would be very limited when each country is only a minor component in the market for the good.

In a similar way, a country will be more susceptible, thus more dependent on the outside world, the more is the market for a good which it imports dominated by a single foreign country; and less susceptible when the world supply of the good is shared by a large number of countries of origin, each providing only a minor fraction of the total.

The issue under consideration, and the measure which will be proposed shortly to handle it, is in a sense a transition (or a cross) between the approach followed in the discussion of the present chapter thus far and that which will form a basis for the analysis in the next chapter. Until now, the country's commodity structure of trade has been observed while the nature of the outside world has been ignored. In the next chapter, on the contrary, the underlying factor under consideration will be the geographical structure of the country's trade, and its implications, disregarding in the process the commodity structure. In the present section, analysis is still focused on the *commodity* structure of trade of the country, but the relevant *attribute* of commodities will be the geographic structure of their world markets, thus abandoning the implicit view of the outside world as a single unit.

The proposed indicator of this element of dependence will be an index of *monopsonistic* position faced by the country's *exports*, and a similar index of *monopolistic* position faced by the country's *imports*. Like other measures, this will be a weighted average. Its presentation must be preceded by the introduction of another measure, on which it is based. Our object is, first, to determine the extent of monopsony (in the market for an export good) or monopoly (for an import good) in world trade. Needless to say, no perfect indicator of the degree of monopolistic or monopsonistic position may be offered. The measure I shall employ here is the index of *geographic concentration* in the world trade of a *good*: the heavier the concentration of trade in the good in a small number of countries, the higher the degree of monopolistic or monopsonistic position in that market. The index of concentration will again be the Gini-Hirschman coefficient. Thus, in the world market for good i, the coefficient of country concentration in the *selling* of the good, designated by C_{ix}, will be[15]

$$C_{ix} = \sqrt{\sum_j (X_{ij}/X_{i.})^2} ,$$

[15]A more detailed discussion of this index may, again, be found in my earlier study (1960, 1962a).

where:

X_{ij} = exports of good i by country j; and
$X_{i.}$ = total world exports of good i.

The higher this coefficient, the stronger is the monopolistic element in the structure of the world market for the good. Similarly to the coefficient of commodity concentration discussed earlier, the upper bound of the value of the coefficient is unity, a value which would be reached in the case in which the good is provided exclusively by a single country. The lower bound will be, again, $1/\sqrt{N}$, where N this time is the number of *countries* participating in world trade. In the recorded statistics of the last decade, this number has been roughly 150, so that the lower bound is about 0.08. For convenience of presentation, again, the coefficient will be multiplied by 100; its potential range will be, thus, between 8 and 100.[16]

In a similar way C_{im}, the coefficient of country concentration of imports of good i, is defined as

$$C_{im} = \sqrt{\sum_{j} \left(M_{ij}/M_{i.} \right)^2},$$

where:

M_{ij} = imports of good i by country j; and
$M_{i.}$ = total world imports of good i.

The potential range of the imports' coefficient is identical with that of the exports' coefficient. The higher it is, the heavier is the domination of world imports of the good by a small number of countries, and the stronger is the monopsonistic attribute of the structure of world imports of the goods.

Given this description of the world-market structure of each *good*, the index of the position faced by trade of each *country* then follows: It is simply the weighted average of the indicators of monopolistic or monopsonistic positions – the country coefficients of concentration – in the markets for individual goods in which the country trades. Thus, the index of *monopsonistic* position faced by country j's *exports*, designated by PS_j, is defined as

$$PS_j = \sum_{i} C_{im} \left(X_{ij}/X_{.j} \right)$$

where, we recall:

C_{im} = coefficient of country concentration in world imports of good i;
X_{ij} = exports of good i by country j; and
$X_{.j}$ = total exports of goods by country j.

---

[16]At the present level of number of countries, the precise value of N is largely immaterial: the sensitivity of the lower boundary of the index to changes in N is quite low. Thus, for instance, with $N = 120$, the lower bound will be 9.13; with $N = 180$, it will be 7.45.

Similarly, the index of *monopolistic* position faced by country j's *imports*, PO_j, is defined as

$$PO_j = \sum_i C_{ix}(M_{ij}/M_{i.}),$$

where:

C_{ix} = coefficient of country concentration in world exports of good i;
M_{ij} = imports of good i by country j; and
$M_{.j}$ = total imports of goods by country j.

The higher the index of monopsonistic position facing the country's exports, the more are its export markets characterized by a monopsonistic structure, and the more vulnerable is the country in its export trade. Similarly, a higher index of monopolistic position facing the country's imports would indicate a stronger susceptibility of the country's flow of imports from abroad. The potential range of each of the indexes is, given a *carte blanche*, the potential range of the coefficients of country concentration of exports and imports of goods (that is, with the present number of countries, from about 8 to 100). Given, however, the *actual* values of the country coefficients of concentration of exports and imports of goods, the potential range of the index of monopsonistic position would lie between the lowest and the highest coefficients for imports; and, similarly, the potential range for the indexes of monopolistic position with which countries' imports are faced would be determined by the lowest and highest coefficients of country concentration of exports of goods.

The coefficients of country concentration of trade in goods are presented in column (1) (for exports) and column (2) (for imports) of table 4.2; and the indexes of the positions of countries which are derived from these coefficients are presented in columns (7) and (8) of table 4.1 for, respectively, the monopsonistic position faced by the country's exports and the monopolistic position faced by its imports. A number of general observations about these indicators may be made.

First, both the coefficients of country concentration of exports and imports spread over most of their potential ranges: from 21.14 (for good 291, "crude animal materials") to 73.11 (for good 261, "silk") in the case of exports and from 17.09 (for 541, "medical and pharmaceutical products") to 78.17 (for 012, "meat – dried, salted, smoked") in the import trade. But in fact, most of the coefficients, in both exports and imports, are not wide apart; the standard errors of the series of coefficients are 0.722 in exports and 0.703 in imports.

While, thus, the distributions were not very uneven *within* the export and import sets of coefficients, there seems to be a substantial difference among the *averages* of the two sets: the mean coefficient is 37.1 for exports and only 28.6 for imports. Exports of each good, it thus appears, tend to be more heavily concentrated among a few countries than imports. As a result, countries should tend to have, as a rule, a higher index of monopolistic position facing their purchases

Table 4.2. Coefficients of country concentration of goods, 1973

Commodity (SITC No.)	Exports (C_{ix}) (1)	Imports (C_{im}) (2)	Commodity (SITC No.)	Exports (C_{ix}) (1)	Imports (C_{im}) (2)
001	28.7	37.8	251	44.5	30.7
011	30.1	32.7	261	73.1	76.1
012	58.7	78.2	262	48.9	36.9
013	48.7	45.4	263	34.7	29.8
022	34.9	22.4	264	66.1	25.5
023	37.4	41.5	265	33.3	28.0
024	36.9	35.5	266	35.6	22.6
025	44.4	44.7	267	45.1	27.5
031	22.6	40.5	271	51.2	24.0
032	31.9	27.7	273	28.5	28.5
041	60.9	22.5	274	40.4	24.9
042	44.8	19.2	275	36.6	32.9
043	48.4	32.9	276	31.7	25.9
044	68.6	32.6	281	36.0	46.8
045	60.0	46.9	282	51.4	39.4
046	38.3	20.6	283	32.0	43.5
047	42.2	33.1	284	33.5	33.1
048	30.4	20.7	285	47.2	59.3
051	24.1	31.3	291	21.1	29.6
052	37.0	29.8	292	35.1	31.5
053	23.7	34.0	321	50.6	38.7
054	31.9	31.7	331	34.4	28.2
055	27.9	36.0	332	25.1	31.2
061	29.7	31.0	341	47.7	40.2
062	32.3	25.8			
071	33.9	40.9	411	52.5	25.8
072	36.3	32.6	421	30.2	25.4
073	33.0	29.3	422	28.6	28.6
074	44.2	30.6	431	37.1	24.4
075	29.1	26.6			
081	33.5	27.8	512	34.9	22.8
091	33.5	36.2	513	29.8	23.7
099	29.3	19.1	514	32.5	18.2
			515	60.8	39.8
111	38.7	31.3	521	39.1	30.2
112	40.1	33.7	531	49.9	19.3
121	46.6	29.6	532	37.3	18.2
122	36.9	22.3	533	36.1	19.6
			541	31.6	17.1
211	30.6	31.6	551	33.4	25.1
212	36.1	40.0	553	42.2	20.1
221	64.0	35.8	554	34.7	19.5
231	37.3	27.1	561	30.7	20.8
241	27.8	30.9	571	30.3	19.5
242	36.7	60.8	581	36.0	22.0
243	40.4	34.0	599	34.9	19.5
244	63.8	25.6			

Table 4.2. (*Continued*)

Commodity (SITC No.)	Exports (C_{ix}) (1)	Imports (C_{im}) (2)	Commodity (SITC No.)	Exports (C_{ix}) (1)	Imports (C_{im}) (2)
611	27.2	28.7	693	34.9	30.0
612	30.1	27.0	694	35.7	33.0
613	34.4	34.0	695	35.1	20.7
621	34.8	21.1	696	37.5	28.1
629	31.9	26.1	697	29.0	24.0
631	25.0	34.2	698	32.5	22.1
632	25.1	33.1	711	38.2	26.3
633	64.0	28.8	712	36.6	23.4
641	33.5	28.6	714	39.1	27.1
642	28.9	20.9	715	43.7	21.5
651	28.2	21.4	717	41.6	20.9
652	23.8	22.0	718	39.6	17.3
653	31.2	22.3	719	37.2	19.1
654	32.1	22.8	722	35.4	18.8
655	31.1	21.9	723	30.8	18.4
656	25.4	19.4	724	37.1	29.2
657	32.2	34.3	725	35.4	23.3
661	29.2	25.0	726	40.8	24.7
662	35.8	27.4	729	35.1	23.9
663	34.4	24.6	731	35.4	18.8
664	35.6	24.1	732	36.6	32.7
665	33.0	22.8	733	33.6	31.1
666	43.3	34.6	734	66.7	22.9
667	41.0	41.0	735	42.9	31.5
671	27.6	30.4			
672	41.1	26.5	812	31.8	23.7
673	36.1	25.2	821	32.9	29.6
674	39.0	24.7	831	31.5	35.5
675	39.1	24.9	841	27.2	32.9
676	30.9	20.7	842	26.5	46.8
677	36.1	26.8	851	41.1	41.5
678	39.5	21.6	861	37.8	23.7
679	39.7	27.1	862	39.3	22.9
681	40.6	39.1	863	35.4	20.2
682	28.8	29.7	864	53.5	26.1
683	45.7	40.1	891	42.5	33.3
684	28.2	25.7	892	30.7	23.9
685	33.6	32.3	893	31.4	26.5
686	32.8	34.9	894	30.5	32.6
687	53.6	37.8	895	36.7	19.1
689	31.9	34.2	896	43.3	43.0
691	30.7	21.4	897	35.7	28.6
692	28.9	18.8	899	29.1	27.3

of imports than an index of monopsonistic position with which they are faced as sellers of their exports.

Turning to the latter indexes, we see that the average index of monopsonistic position faced by exports, 31.3, is indeed somewhat lower than the average level, 34.4, of the index of monopolistic position facing imports. But it is the former index which accounts for most of the differences that exist among countries in this indication of dependence on trade. The spreads of the two indexes happen to be very similar; between 22.7 (for Bermuda) and 43.9 (for Mauritania) for the index of monopsonistic position (out of a potential range of 21.1 to 73.1) and from 23.5 (for Fiji) to 43.3 (for East Germany) for the index of monopolistic position (with a potential range spreading from 17.1 to 78.2). But, in fact, the dispersion of the former index is substantially larger than that of the latter; the standard error of the distribution is 0.379 for the index of monopsonistic position and only 0.194 for the index of monopolistic position. In the series of the latter, very few countries deviate by any substantial margin from the average for all countries. Thus, while *conceptually* the degree of monopolistic position faced by a country's imports is a potential source of differences among countries in the intensity of their dependence on foreign trade, not much importance could be assigned to this factor in the concrete world.[17] The reason for this should be obvious. Most countries, we have seen, have a highly diversified commodity structure of imports. Hence, since countries import a large variety of goods, differences *among commodities* in their market structure would lead to only small differences among countries. In the export trade, on the other hand, the situation is different. There, many countries have a highly concentrated trade. Hence, a country which happens to specialize in goods whose market structure is highly monopsonistic, may be expected to manifest a relatively high overall index of monopsonistic position faced by exports; whereas in a country which exports goods the geographic market for which is widespread, the overall index of monopsonistic position would be low.

No clear-cut association appears to exist between the nature of goods – their physical attributes – and the degree of country concentration of their trade flows; specifically, no general distinction may be made, on this score, between primary goods and manufactures. It is interesting to note, on the other hand, that a relationship does exist between the income levels of the participants in the trade flow of a good and the degree of country concentration of that flow. In the second part of this study an index will be developed for the measurement of income levels of participating countries. At this juncture, it is enough to note that the higher this index in the exports of a good, the higher is the average income of the countries which export it; and similarly for imports. In the export trade, the rank-

---

[17] This statement – like others referring to the indicator under consideration – is obviously predicated on the presumption that countries buy and sell in a "world" market and are not precluded *beforehand* from parts of this market. If a country is restrained, by one form or another and for one reason or another, from dealing in part of the world market, its dependence on trade (in the sense of its vulnerability) is to that extent *enhanced*.

correlation coefficient of the index of income level of a good and its coefficient of country concentration is 0.373; in the import trade it is substantially higher, 0.655. As we have just seen, in the concrete world it is in any case differences in the country concentration of imports which are primarily relevant for implications about the extent of vulnerability and dependence. It thus appears that countries who happen to specialize in the export of goods which tend to be imported primarily by high-income countries, are likely to be selling their exports in markets which tend to have a relatively high degree of monopsonistic structure. Thus, on this account, such exporting countries are vulnerable. Countries which specialize, on the other hand, in goods which are sold mostly to low-income, less-developed economies, would tend to be less vulnerable and dependent.

4. Price fluctuations in world markets

Still another potential indicator of susceptibility will now be presented briefly. The discussion will be limited to the conceptual level since, as will be noted shortly, the practical application of the measure under consideration must be highly restricted.

The more stable the levels of export earnings and of expenditures on imports, the less vulnerable is the economy which conducts these trade flows. The levels involved are products of prices and quantities, and the two may conceivably fluctuate in offsetting directions. Thus, fluctuations of the monetary levels of trade are not identical with those of price levels: as a rule, the former are likely to be higher than the latter (this would be highly probable if price movements are due to supply rather than demand changes). Yet, a positive relationship of fluctuations of prices and of earning levels certainly exists. Specifically, when a country specializes in goods which tend to fluctuate severely (whether due to changes in supply or in demand in the world markets for these goods), its export earnings are liable to be highly volatile. Similarly, this would be true for levels of expenditures on imports when the prices of import goods are likely to be unstable.

The concern for this aspect, of price fluctuations, is implied in some other measures, either those which have already been discussed or others that will still be dealt with later. But, this concern may also be expressed by a direct measure of this aspect of susceptibility. Each good may be assigned an index of the degree of fluctuations of its international price – assuming that past performance is a good yardstick for future expectations. Based on these individual indexes, an overall index of price fluctuations of a country's trade flow may be constructed; as usual, this will be a weighted average of the individual measures. Thus the index of price fluctuations of country j's exports, designated by F_{jx}, will be

$$F_{jx} = \sum_i \tilde{F}_i (X_{ij}/X_{.j}),$$

where:

$\tilde{F}_i$ = index of fluctuations of the international price of good i;
X_{ij} = exports of good i by country j; and
$X_{\cdot j}$ = total exports of goods by country j.

Similarly, the index of price fluctuations of country j's imports, F_{jm}, will be

$$F_{jm} = \sum_i \tilde{F}_i \left(M_{ij} / M_{\cdot j} \right),$$

where:

M_{ij} = imports of good i by country j; and
$M_{\cdot j}$ = total imports of goods by country j.

This measure is proposed here since, had its construction been feasible, it would have been a useful component in the array of tools designed for the evaluation of vulnerability and dependence of countries. Unfortunately, however, the data of $\tilde{F}_i$ – the indexes of fluctuations of international prices of individual goods – are neither generally available nor could be feasibly constructed. Each such index would require a sufficiently large number of *reliable* observations, over time, of the prices of individual goods.[18] As will be appreciated from the discussion of international price data towards the end of this study, no such body of observations may be obtained for international trade in manufactures, which constitutes over a half of total trade. The existence of roughly adequate data for most primary goods would be insufficient for the construction of multi-country overall indexes of export and import price fluctuations – although a comparative study of just the *export* trade of a small number of countries which specialize almost exclusively in exporting primary goods may be carried out by use of such data. It is not entirely unrealistic, however, to speculate – or, at least, hope – that future availability of international price data of manufactures may still make feasible, *inter alia*, a study of a measure such as the one suggested here.[19]

---

[18] Changes over time of *inaccurate* observations are more likely to reflect deviations due to errors in the estimates than actual price fluctuations. Thus, while inaccuracies may not be fatal for the study of a *long-term* price trend, they would invalidate the study of *fluctuations*.

[19] Had such a measurement actually been carried out, a detailed and specific discussion of the nature of $\tilde{F}_i$ – the index of price fluctuations of any good – as well as of similar problems, should have been in order. This, obviously, would be superfluous at the present state of knowledge.

CHAPTER 5

SUSCEPTIBILITY: THE COUNTRY'S TRADE PARTNERS

As noted earlier, the country's foreign trade has been viewed thus far as if it is undertaken within a framework of one uniform "world market" (for each good). In the present chapter, on the other hand, the subdivision of the outside world, and the world "market", into many separate political units will be admitted. The degree of susceptibility of a country's trade flow must depend on the number of foreign partners to this exchange, on their nature and on the significance of the country in question in trade with each of these partners – beyond its significance in the "world" as a whole. These will be the elements examined in the present chapter. On the other hand, the commodity structure of trade, so heavily emphasized thus far, will in the present context be ignored altogether: just as before all geographical units were viewed as one aggregate of a "market", in the present discussion all commodity markets in the trade with each geographic-political unit will be considered as a uniform, aggregate entity.

1. The degree of geographic concentration

The most obvious implication of the recognition of many partner countries to trade, rather than a single outside world, is that the *number* of such partners is an important element in the determination of the extent of vulnerability of a country's trade flow, hence dependence on it. A country which conducts its trade exclusively with a single foreign country is highly vulnerable: fluctuations in the relevant parts of the foreign economy would not be compensated by fluctuations in other markets.[1] In addition, the home country is clearly subject to a discretionary policy of its trade partner, aimed to exert pressure on it in one way or another, when that foreign county is the exclusive trader with the home country. An econ-

---

[1]As before, such statement is predicated on the assumption that fluctuations in foreign markets (this time, in individual political units rather than in individual commodity markets) are accidental and not synchronized. Fluctuations which are due to some general, universal cause – such as world war, or world inflation or recession – will be shared by all, or most, countries and the offsetting element will then be missing.

omy, on the other hand, which trades with many (and presumably varied) foreign countries, must on this score be considered less susceptible to either foreign economic fluctuations or discretionary foreign policies.[2]

The index adopted for the indication of the strength of this element of vulnerability will again be the Gini-Hirschman coefficient of concentration. This time, it is concentration among *countries*, rather than among goods; and to distinguish it from the earlier measure, of commodity concentration, the present index will be referred to as the *geographic* concentration of trade flows. Thus, the coefficient of geographic concentration of country j's exports, designated by G_{jx}, will be

$$G_{jx} = \sqrt{\sum_k (X_{kj}/X_{.j})^2},$$

where:

X_{kj} = exports to country k by country j; and
$X_{.j}$ = total exports of goods by country j.

And similarly, the coefficient of geographic concentration of imports, G_{jm}, will be

$$G_{jm} = \sqrt{\sum_k (M_{kj}/M_{.j})^2},$$

where

M_{kj} = imports of country j from country k; and
$M_{.j}$ = total imports of goods by country j.

Once more, the coefficients are multiplied by 100, for convenience of presentation. The coefficients of geographic concentration of exports and imports in 1973 (or an approximate year), for 151 countries (which are practically the whole world), are presented in columns (1) and (2) of table 5.1. Here, too, a few general observations may be made and they serve, again, to reconfirm inferences which are already well established, hence will be noted only briefly.

First, unlike the case of commodity concentration, geographic concentration appears by and large to be similar in countries' export and import flows. The

[2] This element of vulnerability is perhaps one of the most popular in practical policy considerations, and one which has been recognized early in the literature and whose acknowledgement has been widespread. Hirschman's (1945) treatise is largely concerned with it. Hirschman cites (pp. 73–74) a colorful discussion of Adam Smith, in which trade with only a few countries is compared with a body containing several major blood arteries, a stoppage in each of which would be fatal, whereas trade with many partners is comparable to a body with many minor blood vessels, a stoppage in each of which is easily overcome. Somewhat later, during the celebrated debates on the Corn Laws, Macaulay has stated the principle in what may be its strongest fashion: "Next to independence, and indeed, amounting to practically the same thing, is a very wide dependence, a dependence on the whole world, on every state and climate." (Quoted in Hirschman, 1945, p. 7)

Table 5.1 Geographic indicators of susceptibility, 1973

Country	Coefficients of geographic concentration		Geographically-weighted shares		Magnification ratios		Indexes of size of partners	
	Exports (G_{jx}) (1)	Imports (G_{jm}) (2)	Exports (W_{jx}^k) (3)	Imports (W_{jm}^k) (4)	Exports (5)	Imports (6)	Exports (7)	Imports (8)
Afghanistan	33.6	36.6	0.2	0.2	12.1	6.6	0.70	0.98
Algeria	41.6	38.4	1.1	2.2	2.0	2.9	2.80	1.82
Angola	48.9	28.3	0.7	1.0	5.8	18.7	1.20	0.51
Argentina	22.0	55.1	1.9	3.7	4.7	4.3	0.87	1.73
Australia	32.9	32.7	5.2	2.4	3.6	2.1	1.37	2.34
Austria	27.7	42.6	2.5	3.0	2.7	2.7	1.59	2.11
Bahama	72.3	40.1	0.9	2.2	4.6	8.6	1.64	0.94
Bahrain	32.1	54.3	0.7	1.2	5.4	8.9	1.02	1.13
Bangladesh	23.2	35.6	0.4	0.5	8.9	2.8	0.64	1.77
Barbados	48.0	34.6	0.8	0.3	6.7	11.2	1.10	0.75
Belgium	35.3	34.6	7.2	7.7	2.1	2.2	2.49	2.34
Belize	58.6	49.2	0.1	0.1	6.2	7.0	1.25	1.20
Benin	33.9	35.4	0.1	0.1	7.1	4.9	0.89	1.15
Bermuda	38.0	37.5	0.0	0.1	7.0	2.9	0.98	1.81
Bolivia	33.8	36.3	0.4	0.5	7.7	7.2	0.86	0.95
Brazil	25.3	32.6	1.9	3.0	1.8	2.0	2.46	2.45
Brunei	85.0	55.3	1.5	1.4	11.4	45.7	1.09	0.66
Bulgaria	23.3	31.6	0.6	0.6	6.2	3.4	0.77	1.37
Burma	29.3	33.6	1.4	0.2	53.2	5.8	0.41	1.00
Burundi	50.7	30.8	0.2	0.2	34.2	43.9	1.74	0.43
Cameroon	37.8	49.2	0.5	0.5	8.8	6.9	0.86	1.21
Canada	63.8	66.5	13.7	15.4	3.4	3.8	1.96	2.09
Central African Republic	43.4	48.2	0.4	0.4	57.8	42.0	1.14	0.62
Chad	30.9	41.3	0.1	0.2	12.5	16.4	0.66	0.74
Chile	27.2	38.2	0.5	2.4	2.7	11.1	1.57	0.81
China	34.3	41.2	6.0	3.0	8.6	4.0	0.82	1.48
Colombia	40.1	45.9	0.5	0.5	2.5	2.6	2.11	2.30
Congo (Brazaville)	38.5	58.8	0.7	0.3	24.5	8.6	0.59	1.21
Costa Rica	43.0	39.5	1.4	1.4	22.8	17.6	0.64	0.70
Cuba	39.5	34.2	0.9	0.9	6.7	4.1	1.00	1.27
Cyprus	38.8	28.5	0.1	0.3	6.3	7.7	1.03	0.74
Czechoslovakia	25.3	30.7	1.3	1.8	4.3	5.7	1.01	0.93
Denmark	29.9	29.4	4.4	3.1	4.1	2.6	1.16	1.63
Dominican Republic	66.7	60.1	0.5	0.4	4.5	4.8	1.59	1.68
Ecuador	49.0	45.4	1.8	0.3	14.6	2.5	0.79	2.38
Egypt	34.7	28.1	1.5	1.2	7.6	2.3	0.87	1.77
El Salvador	38.6	40.8	1.6	2.3	23.3	32.4	0.60	0.59
Ethiopia	29.8	28.9	0.1	0.1	4.8	2.0	1.03	2.25
Faeroe Islands	32.8	70.2	0.1	0.7	9.1	49.5	0.78	0.74
Fiji	55.8	39.0	0.3	0.5	15.4	16.1	0.82	0.71
Finland	33.0	30.3	2.9	3.8	4.3	4.3	1.19	1.09

Table 5.1 (*Continued*)

	Coefficients of geographic concentration		Geographically-weighted shares		Magnification ratios		Indexes of size of partners	
	Exports (G_{jx}) (1)	Imports (G_{jm}) (2)	Exports (W_{jx}^k) (3)	Imports (W_{jm}^k) (4)	Exports (5)	Imports (6)	Exports (7)	Imports (8)
France	24.7	26.9	12.6	11.6	2.0	1.8	2.18	2.33
Gabon	35.2	64.2	1.1	0.6	8.5	9.5	0.84	1.22
Gambia	53.1	33.7	0.0	0.1	6.9	10.9	1.14	0.74
Germany (East)	26.1	26.1	1.6	2.4	7.4	9.7	0.75	0.60
Germany (West)	22.1	24.4	18.0	16.3	1.6	1.8	2.82	2.16
Ghana	30.2	26.1	0.2	0.3	1.8	2.9	2.86	1.28
Greece	27.3	25.3	0.8	1.8	3.0	2.9	1.42	1.25
Greenland	45.7	87.6	0.2	1.2	15.8	75.2	0.74	0.74
Guadeloupe	74.9	75.6	0.3	1.0	31.5	29.3	0.73	0.88
Guatemala	31.6	39.7	2.3	1.4	27.6	15.3	0.51	0.74
Guinea-Bissau	52.1	41.7	0.1	0.3	41.7	62.5	0.58	0.50
Guinea Republic	32.2	37.1	0.1	0.1	5.7	7.3	0.98	0.96
Guyana	38.3	41.7	0.3	0.8	7.5	19.2	0.93	0.71
Guyana (French)	70.2	72.1	0.0	0.1	10.8	9.1	1.03	1.32
Haiti	80.7	65.8	0.1	0.1	5.3	4.1	1.56	1.98
Honduras	49.2	48.3	0.3	0.6	7.3	13.0	1.06	0.90
Hong Kong	31.9	33.6	1.8	7.2	2.5	9.1	1.89	0.80
Hungary	28.8	32.6	0.7	1.1	3.4	3.9	1.31	1.26
Iceland	36.5	27.9	0.2	0.3	5.4	4.7	1.09	0.95
India	24.7	28.7	2.5	1.8	4.4	2.5	0.98	1.64
Indonesia	51.5	39.3	3.6	2.0	4.2	3.4	1.50	1.63
Iran	31.4	33.2	5.8	2.1	2.6	1.8	1.76	3.08
Iraq	30.0	27.7	3.2	1.1	3.7	2.6	1.26	1.55
Ireland	56.0	50.4	1.9	2.3	4.9	5.2	1.42	1.45
Israel	40.9	39.8	1.1	–	2.9	–	1.81	–
Italy	26.3	26.4	6.6	7.9	1.6	1.8	3.40	2.42
Ivory Coast	33.8	41.8	2.2	0.6	15.2	4.2	0.65	1.46
Jamaica	46.1	43.2	0.4	0.9	4.4	6.9	1.38	1.11
Japan	24.2	27.6	15.9	21.2	2.3	3.2	1.69	1.27
Jordan	27.9	26.3	0.2	0.3	8.9	3.6	0.72	1.09
Kenya	23.9	30.3	0.6	0.5	7.8	4.4	0.33	1.09
Korea (North)	38.2	39.5	0.1	0.3	3.8	4.2	1.39	1.39
Korea (South)	42.7	44.8	1.2	2.8	2.2	3.4	2.58	1.80
Kuwait	33.1	30.0	2.3	0.7	2.1	2.6	2.33	1.68
Lao (P.D.R.)	48.9	44.0	0.1	0.3	52.6	43.5	0.53	0.57
Lebanon	27.9	26.8	2.0	0.7	14.1	2.7	0.59	1.43
Liberia	34.9	31.7	0.2	1.1	2.4	5.5	2.08	0.98
Libya	37.0	31.9	2.0	2.1	2.9	4.1	1.74	1.20
Macao	34.1	61.5	0.1	0.7	5.9	54.1	0.99	0.67
Madagascar	38.8	57.8	1.1	0.2	33.3	6.9	0.54	1.33
Malawi	43.3	37.1	0.2	0.2	12.5	12.2	0.79	0.76
Malaysia	32.3	29.4	2.6	1.8	5.5	4.4	1.00	1.05
Mali	37.2	43.7	0.1	1.4	16.9	55.0	0.65	0.54
Malta	35.4	36.1	0.1	0.1	3.0	2.7	1.62	1.28

Table 5.1 (*Continued*)

	Coefficients of geographic concentration		Geographically-weighted shares		Magnification ratios		Indexes of size of partners	
	Exports (G_{jx}) (1)	Imports (G_{jm}) (2)	Exports (W_{jx}^k) (3)	Imports (W_{jm}^k) (4)	Exports (5)	Imports (6)	Exports (7)	Imports (8)
Martinique	73.3	69.2	1.9	0.3	147.1	8.0	0.50	1.37
Mauritania	35.1	58.2	0.1	0.3	3.9	11.0	1.32	1.08
Mauritius	69.2	28.2	0.4	0.2	8.9	6.1	1.11	0.83
Mexico	62.5	63.4	1.3	2.8	3.8	3.7	1.76	2.07
Morocco	28.1	35.0	0.6	1.0	2.9	3.5	1.51	1.46
Mozambique	27.1	30.2	0.4	0.7	11.6	15.5	0.63	0.58
Nepal	62.8	60.6	0.2	0.8	53.5	65.8	0.59	0.63
Netherlands	36.9	33.0	8.7	7.8	2.0	1.9	2.60	2.72
Netherland Antilles	69.3	64.1	1.3	16.7	4.7	38.2	1.58	0.75
New Caledonia	63.7	47.2	0.3	0.4	6.0	9.5	1.32	1.01
New Hebrides	61.1	41.6	0.0	0.4	13.8	28.8	0.88	0.62
New Zealand	31.0	34.5	1.0	1.7	3.8	4.5	1.24	1.20
Nicaragua	33.8	38.7	0.9	1.7	16.5	28.7	0.63	0.59
Niger	69.8	46.9	0.1	0.2	9.2	10.4	1.10	9.70
Nigeria	38.1	33.3	2.8	1.4	2.9	2.0	1.77	2.46
Norway	32.6	30.1	3.1	3.6	3.5	3.2	1.37	1.37
Oman	43.2	34.5	0.8	1.7	4.7	17.0	1.29	0.63
Pakistan	20.5	25.4	0.9	0.9	7.2	3.7	0.65	1.01
Panama	61.3	34.5	0.1	1.6	3.8	14.0	1.73	0.68
Papua-New Guinea	45.3	53.0	0.2	1.1	3.5	19.8	1.61	0.82
Paraguay	37.1	35.8	0.2	0.3	10.1	15.0	0.80	0.68
Peru	30.9	38.3	0.7	0.9	4.2	3.0	1.16	1.81
Philippines	48.7	27.8	0.9	1.1	3.1	2.6	1.86	2.06
Poland	23.5	27.5	1.0	1.7	2.1	2.1	1.88	1.96
Portugal	27.4	24.3	1.4	1.8	5.6	4.0	0.90	0.92
Qatar	35.4	36.2	3.6	0.3	19.8	4.1	0.60	1.34
Reunion	94.5	64.4	0.2	1.7	13.6	25.5	1.05	0.85
Romania	25.9	26.5	3.3	3.9	6.3	7.3	0.81	0.70
Rwanda	54.1	31.0	0.0	0.5	3.7	55.6	1.68	0.41
Samoa (Western)	44.8	41.4	0.0	0.2	13.8	36.8	0.77	0.58
Saudi Arabia	28.3	34.6	7.4	5.8	2.1	6.9	2.08	0.93
Senegal	53.0	44.9	1.0	0.5	18.8	7.2	0.74	1.11
Sierra Leone	56.0	32.3	0.1	0.1	6.4	5.4	1.21	1.01
Singapore	26.9	29.4	7.2	4.6	11.0	4.9	0.64	0.98
Somalia	41.6	29.4	0.5	0.3	49.8	13.0	0.50	0.61
South Africa	33.5	35.4	1.0	1.5	1.6	1.7	3.94	3.31
Spain	24.4	25.7	1.8	3.8	1.7	2.0	2.63	1.98
Sri Lanka	22.8	24.5	0.4	1.2	6.6	16.0	0.73	0.46
Suriname	46.1	43.3	0.1	0.4	3.2	15.2	1.75	0.79
Sudan	29.6	28.3	0.4	0.6	6.5	5.0	0.87	0.93
Sweden	24.2	27.5	6.4	5.6	3.0	2.6	1.31	1.50
Switzerland	23.0	35.1	2.2	3.0	1.4	1.9	4.20	2.78
Syria	29.4	23.3	0.5	0.9	4.0	4.5	1.17	0.80
Taiwan	39.1	42.8	1.6	2.1	2.5	3.0	2.07	1.93

Table 5.1 (*Continued*)

	Coefficients of geographic concentration		Geographically-weighted shares		Magnification ratios		Indexes of size of partners	
	Exports (G_{jx}) (1)	Imports (G_{jm}) (2)	Exports (W_{jx}^k) (3)	Imports (W_{jm}^k) (4)	Exports (5)	Imports (6)	Exports (7)	Imports (8)
Tanzania	22.9	26.6	0.4	0.9	9.5	8.9	0.61	0.64
Thailand	35.8	37.0	1.6	1.4	4.2	3.7	0.48	1.45
Togo	49.1	39.0	0.1	0.1	5.4	4.0	1.25	1.43
Trinidad and Tobago	68.6	40.1	1.9	1.2	8.8	7.1	1.12	1.04
Tunisia	33.0	38.6	0.6	0.5	5.6	3.2	1.00	1.69
Turkey	28.7	30.5	0.5	1.6	2.8	2.9	15.80	1.54
Uganda	33.5	40.1	0.1	0.4	10.0	63.3	1.74	0.40
United Arab Emirates	56.1	27.3	1.6	0.9	2.2	2.9	2.36	1.63
United Kingdom	18.6	20.4	9.9	11.5	1.8	1.9	1.96	1.63
United States	25.3	27.7	28.6	35.5	2.2	3.0	1.91	1.36
Upper Volta	45.5	48.2	0.5	0.6	137.0	32.5	0.44	0.65
Uruguay	25.7	27.6	0.2	0.5	3.5	7.5	1.18	0.72
U.S.S.R.	24.4	26.2	4.8	7.1	3.5	3.5	1.15	1.11
Venezuela	47.0	48.7	14.9	1.3	13.2	2.4	0.80	2.69
Vietnam (North)	57.8	42.1	0.0	0.1	8.0	7.5	1.09	1.04
Vietnam (South)	35.9	54.8	0.5	0.5	7.7	7.3	0.89	1.25
Virgin Islands	54.4	46.8	0.1	6.2	26.3	27.5	0.68	0.68
Yemen (Arab Republic)	56.1	27.3	0.1	0.5	90.1	15.7	0.50	0.53
Yemen (P.D.R.)	65.7	28.0	0.9	0.6	21.2	25.7	0.78	0.46
Yugoslavia	30.6	27.4	3.3	3.4	6.5	3.8	0.88	1.09
Zaire	42.9	31.7	0.7	0.4	5.1	2.7	1.22	1.69
Zambia	34.8	29.6	0.3	0.5	2.9	5.2	1.70	0.96

averages of the coefficients for the 151 countries are practically equal, 39.3 for exports and 38.9 for imports. In 73 countries the export coefficient exceeds the import's, while in 77 others the opposite is true (in one country, the two coefficients happen to be identical). The spread of the coefficients, too, is roughly the same. They range from 18.6 (for the U.K.) to 94.5 (for Reunion) for exports and from 20.4 (again, for the U.K.) to 87.6 (for Greenland) for imports, and the standard errors of the series are not too far apart, 1.203 for exports and 1.005 for imports. Thus, by the description of these coefficients, geographic concentration of trade contributes to its vulnerability roughly as much in export flows as in import flows.[3]

---

[3] Hirschman's study (1945), conducted for the inter-war period, revealed a clear tendency of exports to have a higher degree of geographic concentration than imports. In my earlier study of the issue (1958, 1962), this tendency was just barely confirmed for an early post-war year (1954); at that time, the two coefficients were already almost equal, on average. Twenty years later, it seems now, any such difference disappeared altogether.

Moreover, this is by and large true not just as an attribute of the series as a whole but also for individual countries. In most countries, the coefficients of geographic concentration of exports and imports do not deviate much from each other. This implies, obviously, a positive association of the two coefficients; indeed, the correlation coefficient (r) of the two series is 0.569. It thus appears that whenever a country's trade is particularly vulnerable due to a high degree of geographic concentration of exports, it tends to be so also due to a highly-concentrated import trade.

Another inference of a general nature is that in export flows of countries, geographic concentration and commodity concentration are positively associated with each other: the correlation coefficient (r) between the series of the two indexes of concentration is 0.477 (significant at any level). Thus, accentuated susceptibility of a country due to a high measure of commodity concentration of exports tends, as a rule, to be reinforced by a high level of geographic concentration. In imports, on the other hand, no similar association between the two types of concentration exists (the correlation coefficient between the two indexes is 0.025, and is insignificant).

In both export and import flows, a high measure of geographic concentration of trade tends to be associated with a low level of development, or of income, although the association is not very strong: the correlation coefficients (r) between countries' per-capita income level and the index of geographic concentration are -0.258 in exports (significant at better than the 1% level) and -0.204 in imports (significant at better than 2%). Thus, it appears, low-income, less-developed economies tend to have a more vulnerable trade due, in addition to other causes, also to a high level of its geographic concentration.[4]

2. The country's share in its partners' trade

Similarly to its relevance when commodity markets were analyzed, the weight of a country in its *geographic* markets is significant in evaluating the vulnerability of its trade flows. If the home country, to cite one extreme, is the sole provider of another country's imports, fluctuations in the foreign country would be fully borne out by exports of the home country; whereas if a country is only one of many participants in the foreign market, accounting for only a minor share of its im-

---

[4] The associations of geographic concentration with commodity concentration and with low levels of income and development are, of course, interrelated. The findings of both types of associations conform with observations of the attributes of trade flows in the early post-war period. An attempt at an explanation of these relationships may be found in my aforementioned study (1958, 1962a).

ports, fluctuations in it would presumably be easily overcome by minor adjustments in prices of the home-country's export flow to the foreign market.[5]

The indication of the size of this element will be again through an index of the weighted share of the country in foreign markets – where "markets" are now distinguished by separate foreign countries rather than by separate commodities. Thus, the index of country j's geographically-weighted share of exports, designated by W_{jk}^x, will be

$$W_{jx}^k = \sum_k (X_{kj}/M_{.k})(X_{kj}/X_{.j}),$$

where

X_{kj} = exports of country j to country k;
$M_{.k}$ = country k's total *imports* of goods; and
$X_{.j}$ = total exports of goods by country j.

Similarly, the index of geographically-weighted share of the country in imports, W_{jm}^k, is

$$W_{jm}^k = \sum_k (M_{kj}/X_{.k})(M_{kj}/M_{.j}),$$

where

M_{kj} = country j's imports from country k;
$X_{.k}$ = total *exports* of goods by country k; and
$M_{.j}$ = country j's total imports of goods.

The indexes of geographically-weighted shares of countries in exports and imports, for 1973 (or thereabouts), are presented in columns (3) and (4), respectively, of table 5.1. A few comments on some general attributes may be suggested.[6]

Similarly to the index of commodity-weighted share of trade flows, the present index is a function of three elements. First, the size of the country; that is, the aggregate size of its export and import trade. Second, the degree of geographic concentration of trade: the heavier the concentration, given an aggregate size of a trade flow, the larger the shares of the home country's trade in the markets of its main trade partners. Third is the element of size of the *partner* countries: the

[5] It is perhaps worthwhile recalling again, on this occasion, that it is (gross) *dependence* rather than *power* which is the issue of concern to the present analysis. If it were the latter, a higher share of the home country in foreign markets would, of course, carry quite different implications. As before, it may be presumed that the indicator on hand is more important for the determination of the degree of power than it is for the intensity of vulnerability and dependence. This is probably the context in which this phenomenon is mostly discussed in practical political considerations. The thrust of Hirschman's (1945) analysis is, indeed, the evaluation of acquisition of power through domination of foreign markets.

[6] This index, too, has been developed in my earlier study (1960, 1962a); and a more thorough discussion of its properties, as well as of some inferences drawn from its observation, may be found there.

smaller (in terms of trade flows) the foreign countries with which the home country trades, the larger the role of the home country's trade in these foreign markets, and the *higher* its indexes of geographically-weighted trade shares.

Since in most countries the aggregate sizes of exports and imports are roughly equal, and since the element of size of partners is "accidental", and could not be expected to lead to a systematic bias, any general discrepancy between the indexes of exports and those of imports could be due only to differences in the degrees of geographic concentration of exports and imports. In fact, however, it has just been noted that no such general difference emerges from the data; hence, no systematic discrepancy between the export and import indexes of geographically-weighted shares should be expected. Indeed, none is found. The average levels for the 151 countries represented in table 5.1 are practically equal: they are 2.10 for the export index and 2.22 for imports. This is also true for what have been termed before the "magnification ratios" – the product of the division of the index of weighted share by the country's aggregate share of trade flows in world trade. These ratios are presented, respectively for exports and imports, in columns (5) and (6) of table 5.1. The averages of these ratios for all countries are almost identical: 11.30 for exports and 11.39 for imports. Thus, due to generally similar intensities of geographic concentration in export and import trade flows, this indicator of vulnerability shows no systematic differences in dependence on export vs. import trade flows.

The geographic "magnification ratio" is a function of two elements: the degree of geographic concentration of a country's trade flow, and the size of the geographic markets (i.e. countries) with which the trade is conducted, namely, the sizes of trade of the country's main trading partners. It should be interesting to try to separate out these two elements. This will be done in the following way: The magnification ratios (columns (5) and (6) of table 5.1) are regressed on, respectively, the coefficients of geographic concentration (a logarithmic regression form has been found to fit better than a regression of original values). From these regressions, predicted values of the magnification ratios are then derived. The division of predicted values by observed values yields still another ratio, which represents the other element in the function and which may be viewed as an index of the "size of the partners" to a country's trade flow. If the size of customers of the country's exports is "average", the ratio on hand would be unity; if it is above average, the ratio would be above unity (the "magnification ratio" would be, in this case, *lower* than the value predicted from the intensity of the country's geographic concentration of exports); and if the size of the customers of the country's exports is smaller than average, the ratio would be *below* unity. In general, the higher the ratio on hand, the *larger* the size of the country's customers. Similarly, an above-unity ratio of predicted to observed values of the magnification ratio for imports indicates an above-average size of the country's suppliers; and the higher the ratio, the larger is the size of the countries from which the home country's imports originate.[7] These ratios of predicted to observed values of the magnification ratios, the indicators of the sizes of partners to the country's exports and imports, are presented in columns (7) and (8) of table 5.1.

It is immediately evident that by and large, the major, highly-industrialized, high-income countries tend to manifest *high* indexes of size of partners, in both their export and import trade flows; that is, these countries are inclined, as a rule, to trade more than on average with other large countries (in terms of trade volumes), rather than with small foreign countries. This impression is confirmed by regressing the indexes of the size of partners (columns (7) and (8), respectively, for exports and imports) on the level of per-capita income of countries. The correlation coefficients (r's) yielded are 0.388 for exports and 0.343 for imports; and the adjusted-R^2's are, respectively, 0.151 and 0.118 (significant at any desired level). It appears, thus, that the trade of high-income countries tends to be less vulnerable than that of low-income countries due to the tendency of the former to be directed to large markets, whereas the latter, on average, flows to and from relatively small foreign markets.[8]

Before turning to other indicators, it may be worthwhile to mention briefly that the relevant size of foreign countries, for the purpose of the evaluation of trade vulnerability, may be not just the volume of their foreign *trade* (imports, when the home country's exports are concerned, and vice versa), but the size of their *incomes*. For similar reasons to those proposed before, the vulnerability of the home country's flow of exports would be weaker if it forms a minor proportion of *income* of the foreign country to which it is directed and would be stronger when

---

[7] This is, needless to say, just one possible measure of the element under consideration, namely, of the size of countries (in terms of trade flows) with which the home country trades. At least two other indexes of this attribute of trade may be found in the literature. In Hirschman's forementioned study (1945), the size of partner countries constituted a major element in the discussion of the manipulation and re-direction of trade as an instrument of political power. To estimate it, Hirschman proposed (pp. 87–91) a measure designated by R and termed "the index of preference for trade with small countries." Replacing partly Hirschman's notation by the one used here, this index will be, for country j's exports, $R = U.A./W.A.$ [$U.A.$ (unweighted average) $= (1/N)\Sigma_k(X_{kj}/M_{.k})$; and $W.A.$ (weighted average) $= (1/M..)\Sigma_k(X_{kj}/M_{.k})M_{.k} = (X_{.j}/M..)$], where: N = number of foreign countries; X_{kj} = country j's exports to country k; $M_{.k}$ = country k's total imports; $X_{.j}$ = country j's total exports; and $M..$ = total foreign imports (i.e. world minus home country's).

In my earlier study (1962, p. 45), I have used an index of the "size of the partner countries", designated by Z_{jx}, which is (again, for country j's exports and with some change in notation) defined as,

$$Z_{jx} = \sum_k (X_{kj}/X_{.j})^2 / \sum_k (1/M_{.k})(X_{kj}/X_{.j})^2$$

[8] Once more, the implication for *power* acquired by trade would be the opposite: the direction of trade of the large, high-income countries to relatively large markets *lowers* their potential domination of foreign countries through trade relations. Hirschman (1945, ch. 6), studying the geographic trade patterns of six major trading nations during the inter-war period, concluded that large countries manifested a preference to trade with small countries. Evidently, recent trade patterns are characterized by an opposite tendency.

the proportion is high, so that any fluctuation in the foreign country is liable to be borne heavily by the home country's exports. The indicator of the extent of this factor would be, again, an index of geographically-weighted share, where the *shares* are now proportions of foreign *income* rather than of foreign trade. Thus for country j's exports W_{jx}^y, the index of geographically-weighted share of exports in incomes, will be

$$W_{jx}^y = \sum_k (X_{kj}/Y_k)(X_{kj}/X_{.j}),$$

where

X_{kj} = exports of country j to country k;
$X_{.j}$ = total exports of goods by country j; and
Y_k = aggregate income of country k.

The index would be similar, with the appropriate changes, for the country's geographically-weighted share of *imports* in incomes.

Actual statistical work on this measure has not been carried out, in the present study so that it will not be dwelt upon at any length. It may only be noted that this index is again a function of three elements. Two of these are shared with those of the indexes of weighted shares in foreign *trade*, namely, the size of the home country (in terms of trade flows) and the intensity of geographic concentration of its trade. The third element, the size of the foreign markets to which the home country's trade is mainly directed, is different: it is now concerned with the size of foreign income, rather than with foreign trade. But the two must give roughly similar indications. Even though trade proportions are not equal in different countries, the size of trade is undoubtedly highly correlated with the size of income. Thus, "magnification ratios" calculated from the indexes of shares in income would most likely largely resemble those derived from the indexes of weighted shares in trade. Hence, it also appears likely that comparative inferences about the vulnerability of trade flows would be similar, where trade shares in foreign incomes are examined, to those drawn from the observation of the indexes of geographically-weighted shares in foreign trade.

3. Attributes of trade partners

In this last section, several measures of attributes of partner countries to trade flows will be surveyed. The concepts will be discussed without empirical illustrations, either because the empirical work has not been carried out or because the empirical findings do not offer significant insights.

A country's trade flow would be more susceptible the less "stable", in one way or another, are its trading partners and trade relations with them. Absence of stability may have various representations and manifestations. Some are political in nature. One country is more prone than another to use its trade relations as an instrument of foreign policy. Trade with such a foreign country would be more susceptible, *ceteris paribus*, than trade with other countries. Similarly, political regimes are more stable in some countries than in others; and since a change in political regime would often lead to changes in trade relations and trade policies, trade flows with countries which are unstable in this sense are more vulnerable than other components of trade. These considerations are rather obvious and must very often be extremely important in the practical examination of the degree of dependence of individual countries on their foreign trade. Yet, they do not feasibly lend themselves to quantitative definition, hence also to an international comparison. Thus, beyond mentioning such factors, little could probably be done by way of estimating their significance or drawing some rules and inferring patterns of dependence.

Other elements of instability are "economic" rather than "political" and these may, conceptually at least, be subject to quantitative evaluation. Several indicators of this nature will be mentioned here briefly.

Trade flows with partner countries in which *real income* is highly fluctuating are relatively unstable and vulnerable: supply and demand volatility in the foreign country would make the home country's exports and imports too highly volatile. The relevant intensity of fluctuations is, of course, the one expected in the future – a measure which is not observable. As on other occasions, it probably could be approximated reasonably well by the observation of past performance. In this way, an index of the strength of the fluctuations of real incomes among partners to the home country's trade may be devised. As usual, this will be a weighted average of the indicators for individual partner countries. Thus, the index of real-income fluctuations of the customers of country j's export flow, designated by F_{jx}, will be

$$F_{jx} = \sum_k \tilde{Y}_k \left(X_{kj} / X_{.j} \right),$$

where

$\tilde{Y}_k$ = index fluctuations of real income of country k;
X_{kj} = exports of country j to country k; and
$X_{.j}$ = total exports of goods by country j.

F_{jm}, the index of fluctuations of real incomes in the foreign countries which provide country j's imports, is similarly defined, replacing X_{kj} and $X_{.j}$ by, respectively, M_{kj} and $M_{.j}$.

The index of fluctuations of real incomes *in* each country, $\tilde{Y}_k$, has been determined by the standard deviation around the trend of the series of annual changes in per-capita G.D.P. in the post-war years. From these, the indexes F_{jx}

and F_{jm} have then been constructed. The results are not presented here since they do not seem to be instructive. Specifically, a very large degree of uniformity among countries seems to be indicated, and the few exceptions – particularly high or particularly low indexes – do not seem to suggest a definite pattern. To some extent, this uniformity is due to the fact that the $\tilde{Y}_k$s – the indicators of fluctuation of own country's real incomes – do not deviate dramatically from each other; but the series of F_{jx} and F_{jm} are still far more uniform than the series of $\tilde{Y}_k$. It appears that geographic diversification of trade is, by and large, sufficiently high to lead to a high degree of uniformity of the measure under consideration. More generally, in view of this uniformity, it appears that differences among countries in the intensity of geographic concentration of trade – the factor analyzed earlier – are more important than differences in the measure of fluctuations (F_{jx} or F_{jm}). Two countries with the same measure (say, same F_{jx}) would face quite different intensities of vulnerability of their export flows if one sells its exports to many countries, real-income fluctuations in which may be expected to offset each other (unless due to some worldwide forces); whereas the other markets its exports exclusively in one country, or in very few, so that offsetting tendencies are absent or are relatively weak.

Fluctuations in other foreign variables constitute other elements of susceptibility of the home country's trade flows. These fluctuations, it may be noted, might be closely related to each other – as well as to changes in real income – being the result, partly at least, of common factors. Variables of this nature which would look, *a priori*, to be important are fluctuations, in foreign countries, in the levels of real exports and imports; in the levels of *prices* of exports and imports[9] as well as in general price levels in the foreign countries. For all such elements, indexes similar to F_{jx} or F_{jm}, replacing each time $\tilde{Y}_k$ by the measure of fluctuations of the variable under consideration, might be adopted; but actual estimates of such indexes have not been carried out in the present study.

Finally, an element should be mentioned which is concerned not with the nature of economic performance in foreign countries, nor indeed with the geographic structure of the country's export and import trade flows taken separately, but with the degree of *reciprocity* in trade; namely, the degree to which a country's trade relations with foreign countries tend to be *bilateral*, rather than be settled in a multilateral fashion.

The intensity of bilateralism in a country's trade relations may definitely be presumed to have a bearing on the extent of susceptibility of the country's trade flows, hence on the degree of its dependence on foreign trade. But the impact of

---

[9]An index of fluctuations of foreign prices related to this element should be distinguished from the one discussed towards the end of the previous chapter. There, it was a weighted average of price fluctuations of the *commodities* which constitute the country's trade flows; whereas here, it will be an average of the degree of fluctuations in price levels of foreign *countries* with which the home country trades.

this factor is not clear-cut: several elements are involved, operating in conflicting directions.

Suppose a country's trade relations are purely bilateral (whether with a single foreign country or with many – a factor, of course, of great importance but of a separate nature). Fluctuations in a foreign country would then affect jointly, in each case, the home country's exports and imports. Such effects may be either offsetting, in a way relevant to the present issue, or reinforcing. In the first case, bilateralism would lower vulnerability; whereas in the latter instance, it would increase vulnerability and dependence. Thus, for instance, a fall in foreign demand would tend to diminish the real size of the home country's exports and increase its imports (through the increase in the foreign supply of these imports), with both tendencies reinforcing each other in their impact on the home country's real trade balance, or its employment; but foreign *prices* of both the home country's exports and imports would tend to fall – a factor which would tend to diminish, for instance, the effect of the foreign fluctuation on the *value* of the home country's imbalance of trade.

Similarly, the impact of bilateralism on the degree of susceptibility due to *political* manipulations by foreign governments is ambivalent. On the one hand, such action by a foreign government would be doubly damaging, since it would involve both the exports and the imports of the home country. On the other hand, such foreign action may be less likely than in the case in which trade relations are unilateral, where no reciprocal response by the home country would be threatened when the foreign country's activity is contemplated.

Thus, although it would seem that the degree of bilateralism in a country's trade is an element which participates in determining the extent of trade susceptibility and dependence on trade, an index of the intensity of bilateralism would not provide a general indication of the direction, or strength, of the impact of this element. No quantitative evaluation has therefore been attempted in the present study, which is international and comparative in nature. But in studies of individual countries, where the knowledge of specific circumstances provides additional information, such an evaluation might probably often be fruitful.[10]

---

[10]An index of bilateral vs. multilateral balancing of trade has been proposed in my study of this subject (1962b).

PART II

INCOME LEVELS AND TRADE PATTERNS

CHAPTER 6

INCOME LEVELS OF TRADE: CONCEPT AND MEASUREMENT

Certain goods are exported by rich nations and other goods by poor; likewise, some goods are imported primarily by rich countries and others by poor. Does a good exported by rich countries tend to be also imported by their likes, or by their poor partners? Have the patterns of income level of the structure of trade been stable, or have they changed much or fluctuated over time? What are the possible explanations of the income levels of exports and imports? How do these explanations square with a priori theories of the determinants of the pattern of international trade? And how have the terms of exchange of rich countries' for poor countries' goods behaved?

These, and a few associated questions, are the subject matter of the second part of the study. In the present chapter an index for the measurement of the income level of trade flows will be proposed, and be estimated by the use of trade data for 1973. This index will serve as the basic tool for the rest of the present part of the study. In chapter 7, trade theories will be tested through the application of the concept of the income level of trade. This will be followed, in chapter 8, by a study of the time-profile behavior of the income levels of trade. The last two chapters apply the tools developed in this study to issues of concern for economic development and economic policy. In chapter 9, this is done for the analysis of the terms of trade between poor and rich countries; whereas in chapter 10 the concept of income level of trade is utilized for the investigation of possible discrimination in trade policies.

1. An index of income level of traded goods

The income level of world exports of good i is defined by the following index, y_{ix}.

$$y_{ix} = \sum_j y_j \left(X_{ij} / X_{i.} \right),$$

where:

X_{ij} = exports of good i by country j,
$X_{i.}$ = world exports of good i, and
y_j = index of income of country j.

The latter term is, in turn, defined as follows

$$y_j = 100\left(Y_j / Y_n\right),$$

where:

Y_j = per capita GNP of country j; and
Y_u = US per capita GNP.

The index is defined, thus, as an average (weighted by the share of each country in world exports of the good) of the income levels of the countries exporting the good. A good's index of income level of exports will be higher the richer are the countries which export it, the degree of richness being determined by two elements – the proportions of high-income countries in total exports of the good and the income levels of individual countries. A country's "richness" or "poorness" is defined by its per capita GNP – still the best possible single measure, despite its various well-known shortcomings (especially in international comparisons). The income level is presented as an index, by showing it as a ratio of the US per capita income – the world's highest during the period covered in the present study.[1]

In this way the highest possible level of the index is 1, or 100, as it is put here for convenience: this would be the income level of.exports of a good exported exclusively by the United States. The lowest boundary of the index is, of course, the index of the income level of the poorest country which conducts any trade. In this study this lowest index is 1.0 (for Laos).

The income level of world *imports* of good i, designated by y_{im}, is defined in an exactly parallel way; that is, it is defined by the formulation given above, where X_{ij} and $X_{i.}$ are replaced by, respectively, M_{ij} and $M_{i.}$ – country j's imports and world imports of the good.

The indexes of income levels of exports and imports, classified by the three-digit SITC into 174 goods,[2] have been calculated for the year 1973.[3] The results are

---

[1] The division of each country's income level by that of the USA is entirely immaterial in the present context: each country's income could instead be represented by its absolute level (dollars per year), or divided by any other *common* number. But the principle of dividing each country's income level by that of the richest country does become significant in a *time-series* study, such as the one presented in the next chapter.

[2] The SITC contains 175 goods. But for commodity no. 688 – uranium and thorium – the required data are not available. The omission of a single good is immaterial for the following analysis.

[3] To shift from the index as it is presented here to an expression of the income level in absolute terms (in US dollars), the index shown (taken as a fraction of 100) should be multiplied by 6200 which is the level of US per capita GNP in 1973.

Table 6.1. Indexes of incomes levels of exports and imports, by commodity, 1973

SITC code	Income level of exports (y_{ix})	Income level of imports (y_{im})	SITC code	Income level of exports (y_{ix})	Income level of imports (y_{im})
			221	73.92	60.52
0			231	29.89	52.99
001	60.85	49.84	241	55.73	56.75
011	58.56	63.64	242	37.43	53.35
012	74.86	49.53	243	69.56	65.63
013	58.29	70.88	244	22.14	53.02
022	70.05	34.91	251	80.83	61.90
023	69.11	51.39	261	19.10	57.45
024	71.69	64.75	262	58.31	55.61
025	69.43	60.98	263	33.64	43.88
031	46.80	67.73	264	9.67	42.84
032	52.04	62.17	265	31.83	55.31
041	88.30	29.95	266	68.02	46.43
042	53.20	16.80	267	79.70	38.63
043	78.37	56.37	271	32.08	51.65
044	81.70	51.32	273	63.63	64.61
045	76.04	54.90	274	64.36	49.47
046	72.24	12.12	275	56.60	69.46
047	70.50	38.74	276	60.18	58.71
048	71.08	49.33	281	51.46	67.64
051	30.79	66.65	282	84.14	45.62
052	40.13	54.41	283	39.55	64.76
053	43.92	67.74	284	75.33	64.77
054	47.50	63.26	285	59.46	71.94
055	44.52	68.10	291	50.57	65.49
061	24.74	52.16	292	53.42	64.66
062	61.23	62.10			
071	11.39	76.82	3		
072	16.80	69.25	321	83.12	60.39
073	66.69	67.27	331	23.45	55.48
074	10.12	40.31	332	38.49	67.71
075	13.45	45.60	341	65.66	72.98
081	58.51	59.22			
091	68.14	44.51	4		
099	67.28	47.20	411	80.46	44.56
			421	50.53	41.06
1			422	24.91	57.92
111	65.98	55.86	431	69.41	53.62
112	54.30	68.21			
121	54.85	59.73	5		
122	71.69	43.19	512	75.00	53.49
			513	69.20	56.18
2			514	71.81	47.81
211	60.74	52.07	515	86.44	76.90
212	69.28	70.88	521	56.24	57.47

Table 6.1. (*Continued*)

SITC code	Income level of exports (y_{ix})	Income level of imports (y_{im})	SITC code	Income level of exports (y_{ix})	Income level of imports (y_{im})
531	81.06	45.20	679	75.24	48.89
532	49.51	32.54	681	62.29	72.03
533	71.04	48.22	682	42.96	63.26
541	71.34	41.90	683	74.22	80.08
551	61.97	54.13	684	69.93	60.51
553	66.36	49.97	685	57.62	55.64
554	70.94	48.20	686	64.47	62.86
561	68.26	37.41	687	19.07	66.89
571	63.86	46.18	689	62.79	71.71
581	73.50	54.58	691	68.79	47.52
599	72.78	46.31	692	64.40	45.38
			693	65.49	60.81
6			694	71.06	67.75
611	44.72	62.20	695	74.81	54.01
612	55.53	65.66	696	61.71	62.28
613	64.30	65.78	697	58.27	57.25
621	71.81	52.54	698	69.82	58.60
629	65.61	62.14			
631	50.91	67.40	7		
632	64.23	72.76	711	76.86	59.32
633	30.70	65.67	712	75.94	50.87
641	76.57	60.40	714	75.53	64.25
642	68.92	53.78	715	77.35	49.71
651	56.54	49.46	717	74.53	41.07
652	47.08	53.48	718	77.71	42.14
653	56.91	55.22	719	75.99	49.50
654	65.33	53.07	722	74.64	50.00
655	68.49	57.23	723	66.38	46.72
656	40.45	50.04	724	67.54	60.72
657	56.16	72.04	725	67.26	61.56
661	46.50	51.40	726	80.13	58.89
662	62.20	59.88	729	72.54	57.71
663	71.41	59.99	731	69.76	29.60
664	70.74	61.78	732	76.21	67.81
665	66.12	55.66	733	66.81	68.86
666	61.51	68.48	734	87.17	55.47
667	50.52	62.62	735	66.84	57.38
671	56.53	68.06			
672	66.74	40.39	8		
673	71.23	58.01	812	67.83	58.25
674	68.05	55.32	821	67.94	72.64
675	75.18	55.66	831	46.24	73.96
676	65.12	28.63	841	45.33	73.15
677	71.80	55.61	842	57.41	79.05
678	70.18	56.08	851	41.12	78.84

Table 6.1. (*Continued*)

SITC code	Income level of exports (y_{ix})	Income level of imports (y_{im})	SITC code	Income level of exports (y_{ix})	Income level of imports (y_{im})
861	75.12	60.03	893	68.72	67.50
862	76.79	57.73	894	58.40	71.16
863	55.67	43.67	895	72.63	49.43
864	79.68	54.69	896	73.21	71.49
891	66.76	68.18	897	60.71	67.36
892	67.62	61.26	899	56.46	62.06

presented in table 6.1 and a few simple characteristics of the findings shown in this table are pointed out below.

First, the dispersion of the indexes of income levels is much more substantial in exports than in imports. The range of the index in exports is from 9.7 (in good (264) – jute) to 88.3 (in good (041) – wheat) – the maximum possible range being, we recall, from 1.0 to 100. In imports, the range is from 12.1 (good (046) – wheatmeal or flour), to 80.1 (good (683) – nickel).[4] The weighted averages of the indexes are 61.8 for exports, and 58.3 for imports. The coefficient of variation – the ratio of the standard deviation to the mean – is 0.29 in exports and 0.20 in imports.

It might be expected that the extreme cases, both high and low, of income levels of exports would be associated with a high degree of country concentration of these exports, with very few rich countries exporting the high-income good, and similarly very few poor countries exporting the low-income good. This, of course, is immediately evident for the two most extreme cases – wheat being exported primarily by the USA, one of the world's richest countries, and jute being exported predominantly by Bangladesh, one of the world's poorest. But it is also true as a general rule. Thus, if we take the ten goods with the highest income level in exports,[5] the (unweighted) average coefficient of country concentration of these exports[6] is found in 1973 to be 54.7 – in comparison with an average of 37.3 for all exports. The average for the ten goods with the lowest income levels[7] is 46.4; in

---

[4] Interestingly enough, practically the same good (wheat, or wheat flour) which is exported by the richest countries, is imported by the poorest – and that is a purely agricultural product. As we shall see later, this polarization of income levels in exports and imports is not clearly evident in general.

[5] These are, in a descending order of income level: (041) Wheat; (734) aircraft; (515) radioactive materials; (321) coal; (282) iron and steel scrap; (044) maize; (531) synthetic dyes; (251) pulp and waste paper; (411) animal oils and fats; and (726) electrical-medical equipment.

[6] See chapter 4 for the concept.

[7] These are, in an ascending order of income level: (264) Jute; (074) tea; (071) coffee; (075) spices; (072) cocoa; (687) tin; (261) silk; (244) cork; (331) crude petroleum; and (061) sugar.

Table 6.2. Levels, dispersion and association of exports and imports, by major categories

	Category	y_{ix} Mean (1)	y_{ix} Coefficient of variation (2)	y_{im} Mean (3)	y_{im} Coefficient of variation (4)	Spearman rank-correlation coefficient of y_{ix} and y_{im} (5)
0	Food and live animals	55.4	0.39	53.7	0.28	−0.418
1	Beverages and tobacco	61.7	0.09	56.8	0.18	
2	Crude materials, inedible	53.2	0.38	57.4	0.17	0.151
3	Mineral fuels, lubricants	53.2	0.52	64.1	0.12	
4	Animal and vegetable oils	56.3	0.43	49.3	0.16	
5	Chemicals	64.4	0.29	49.8	0.20	0.159
6	Manufactured goods, by material	61.4	0.19	58.6	0.15	−0.238
7	Machinery and transport equipment	73.8	0.08	54.0	0.19	−0.098
8	Miscellaneous manufactured articles	63.2	0.18	65.0	0.15	−0.534
	All goods	59.0	0.29	56.7	0.20	−0.232

this group, it is not as high as in the former because some of the goods with the lowest income levels, such as sugar, coffee, or cocoa, are exported by several low-income countries.

It is interesting to note that, as a general rule, a positive association exists between the income level of exports of a good and the degree of country concentration of these exports. The Spearman rank-correlation coefficient between the two series is 0.38; this should be considered quite high, particularly in view of the fact, noted above, that the extremely low-income goods have a *higher* than average level of country concentration. In imports, the association is even stronger: the rank-correlation coefficient of the income level and the country concentration of imports is 0.66. We can thus see that the higher the income level of exports and imports of a good, the more these exports and imports tend to be concentrated in a small number of countries.

When goods are aggregated into large categories, the dispersion among the aggregates should naturally be substantially smaller than among individual goods. When the major categories of the SITC are used (nine categories, 0 to 8), the dispersion becomes surprisingly small. This may be seen from columns (1) and (3) of table 6.2. It appears that the (unweighted) average income levels for these categories only range from 53.2 (for category 3 – mineral fuels) to 73.8 (for category 7 – machinery and transport equipment), whereas the range for imports is between 49.3 (category 4 – animal and vegetable oils and fats) and 65.0 (category 8 – miscellaneous manufactured articles). This low dispersion *among* categories must imply a high degree of dispersion within each category; this may in fact be seen from columns (2) and (4) for exports and imports, respectively. It appears, indeed, that in the case of exports the degree of dispersion within each group is in the majority of categories *higher* than for the total of individual goods: only two categories – 1 and 7 – appear to be relatively homogeneous. This indicates, there-fore, that the category to which a good belongs is not one of the characteristics which determine the income level of the good's exports or imports – an indication which is not inconsistent with the findings which will be presented later on in the investigation. The only clear-cut exception to this rule, for the export trade, is cat-egory 7 (machinery and transport equipment). In this category both the average income level is substantially above all the rest and the dispersion within the cate-gory is particularly low. This is, then, the only major category of goods which may be clearly designated as a high-income category of exports.

2. Means and dispersion

The index of the income level of a trade flow which has been used in this study all along is, of course, a weighted mean of the income levels of the (geographic) com-ponents of such flow – where, for instance in exports, the X_{ij}/X_i is the weight assigned to the exports of each country j. It may be asked, however, what the *dispersion* of this series (of X_{ij}/X_i) is around its mean. The lower this dispersion, the more can the mean be said to be an indication of the income level of the "typical" country which exports that good.

The levels of dispersion of the export and import series of each individual good are presented in table 6.3. It will be noticed that most measures of dispersion are quite close to each other – particularly in imports, but by and large also in ex-ports. Thus, the degree of "representativeness" of the index of income level used here is rather similar for most goods.

3. An alternative measure of income levels

The analysis of this study will be conducted all along through the use of the specific index of the income level of exports and imports which has been proposed, namely a weighted average of the income levels of the trading countries – with some re-gard being paid to the dispersion around this average. Alternative indexes of the income level are, however, conceivable, and one such alternative will be presented and discussed in this section.[8]

[8] This measure has been suggested to me by Alexander Yeats.

Table 6.3. Measure of dispersion (σ) of income levels of exports and imports

SITC	Exports	Imports	SITC	Exports	Imports
001	26.47	24.37	264	18.67	27.45
011	24.24	23.05	265	33.23	22.29
012	20.12	15.01	266	20.07	27.98
013	26.43	25.97	267	22.31	26.89
022	14.80	27.89	271	41.84	22.76
023	13.37	22.14	273	23.34	20.39
024	15.50	23.39	274	35.43	27.25
025	16.51	25.77	275	36.61	23.97
031	32.27	25.66	276	30.21	23.60
032	29.35	24.07	281	36.61	18.98
041	18.96	26.15	282	18.62	23.39
042	42.34	22.05	283	37.87	21.93
043	18.08	27.34	284	21.56	23.30
044	30.49	20.92	285	36.78	24.08
045	31.97	18.73	291	28.87	22.15
046	22.98	21.83	292	27.08	22.54
047	33.97	29.21	321	14.86	17.95
048	18.66	27.58	331	22.64	26.28
051	29.77	22.04	332	29.47	24.36
052	35.14	24.30	341	26.86	24.73
053	29.99	19.96	411	24.76	27.66
054	31.31	23.24	421	35.62	27.73
055	26.53	22.65	422	31.01	27.20
061	27.63	31.51	431	21.93	23.58
062	20.82	25.08	512	20.19	26.95
071	18.27	22.32	513	21.10	26.19
072	24.74	22.67	514	21.25	27.14
073	20.09	19.08	515	20.30	19.81
074	19.69	28.37	521	38.59	24.56
075	22.50	33.61	531	19.66	27.75
081	34.73	22.09	532	31.94	28.40
091	23.85	22.30	533	19.16	26.84
099	22.97	26.23	541	23.14	27.07
111	16.69	27.28	551	29.55	26.12
112	23.60	23.32	553	20.96	27.02
121	42.20	24.78	554	23.07	24.79
122	25.95	26.12	561	25.05	33.63
211	27.92	23.14	571	26.59	29.07
212	25.27	21.06	581	18.25	23.29
221	37.33	19.10	599	20.58	26.67
231	31.31	28.03	611	31.60	24.55
241	36.54	23.06	612	24.36	23.48
242	43.32	18.07	613	25.57	23.28
243	28.91	23.44	621	21.04	24.00
244	11.96	29.64	629	20.92	24.94
251	20.82	25.45	631	32.26	21.35
261	25.16	13.03	632	27.48	21.06
262	20.49	19.74	633	20.11	22.35
263	41.09	26.60	641	18.23	24.85

Table 6.3. (*Continued*)

SITC	Exports	Imports	SITC	Exports	Imports
642	20.67	24.63	697	24.54	25.54
651	27.09	27.35	698	21.52	24.15
652	33.32	24.24	711	21.53	25.97
653	25.27	25.55	712	21.61	29.49
654	25.08	25.53	714	23.21	23.06
655	21.71	24.63	715	20.03	28.79
656	34.96	27.09	717	20.72	31.99
657	27.62	18.15	718	20.09	28.50
661	27.18	30.03	719	20.57	27.04
662	22.32	23.83	722	20.89	26.95
663	20.27	22.57	723	23.30	28.76
664	19.62	24.00	724	22.27	27.18
665	22.09	26.15	725	22.25	22.53
666	18.37	25.46	726	16.56	26.93
667	26.64	23.40	729	24.39	26.46
671	29.83	22.57	731	24.96	29.89
672	16.02	28.22	732	18.81	23.58
673	19.64	26.05	733	21.61	23.59
674	17.80	29.37	734	20.34	26.66
675	15.58	26.95	735	17.74	22.58
676	27.43	31.62	812	23.24	23.06
677	16.94	29.43	821	22.76	17.78
678	20.23	26.63	831	26.91	21.91
679	25.65	31.28	841	27.15	19.71
681	27.61	23.37	842	29.90	18.41
682	35.56	22.90	851	22.11	18.42
683	20.74	25.21	861	20.35	24.62
684	23.94	22.61	862	19.83	25.07
685	29.54	24.65	863	32.07	31.27
686	27.59	30.28	864	24.39	30.07
687	24.38	25.21	891	20.14	24.89
689	30.81	21.44	892	23.47	22.36
691	21.18	28.86	893	22.80	20.47
692	20.38	26.82	894	27.42	22.37
693	18.78	27.10	895	69.74	25.39
694	21.00	24.22	896	26.59	22.31
695	22.02	25.99	897	27.94	25.79
696	22.98	25.37	899	27.19	25.07

The index used in this study, we recall, is (say, for exports)

$$y_{ix} = \sum_j y_j (X_{ij}/X_{i.}),$$

where

X_{ij} = exports of good i by country j;

$X_{i.}$ = world exports of good i; and

y_j = country j's per capita income (as proportion of US income).

However, instead of *multiplying* X_{ij}/X_i (country j's share in world exports of good i) by y_j (country j's income level), one could draw a *regression* of the two, showing their relationship to each other. In such a regression, where y_j is the independent and X_{ij}/X_i the dependent variable, the slope will indicate the tendency of the country's share in exports to change with the country's income level. This could be, then, another measure of the income level of exports; and similarly for imports.

Such linear regressions have been run for all 174 goods. They have the general form

$$X_{ij}/X_i = a + by_j,$$

where the b's yield the measure under consideration (and similarly for imports). The results are presented in table 6.4.

A glance at this table will show immediately that the slope measures for practically all goods are positive. In the few cases where they are negative, they are mostly not significantly different from zero.[9] This should come, of course, as no surprise: as a rule, the higher the country's per capita income, the higher its total income and, in an even stronger way, its share in world exports and imports, and this should be reflected, generally, in each of the goods in which the country trades. The measures of slope presented in table 6.4 do not therefore tell us, by themselves, whether the exports (imports) of a good tend to be concentrated in high-income countries. They could be made, however, to give such indication when compared with an "average" tendency. This average is yielded by a regression of the shares of countries in *all* goods on the countries' income levels, similar to the regressions for each individual good. The outcome of this procedure is as follows

$$X_{\cdot j}/X_{\cdot\cdot} = -0.135 + 0.049y_j \quad (R^2 = 0.396, \text{ and significant at practically any level}), \text{ and}$$

$$M_{\cdot j}/M_{\cdot\cdot} = -0.0138 + 0.045y_j \quad (R^2 = 0.391, \text{ and significant at practically any level},$$

where:

$X_{\cdot j}, M_{\cdot j}$ are country j's total exports and imports of goods; and
$X_{\cdot\cdot}, M_{\cdot\cdot}$ are total world exports and imports of goods.

Whether a given slope for an individual good indicates that the good tends to be exported by high-income countries may thus be inferred by comparing this slope with the magnitude 0.049; in imports, it would be compared with 0.046.

One would be inclined to repeat, with this measure, the various experiments, comparisons and tests which will be conducted in this study by the use of the weighted average as the index of income levels of exports and imports. Such re-experimentation seems, however, to be redundant. The rank-correlation coeffi-

[9] The significance levels of the negative-sign slopes are as follows. In exports: Good 071-0.534; 072-0.892; 074-0.453; 075-0.851; 264-0.582; 895-0.116. In imports: 046-0.880.

Table 6.4. An alternative measure of income levels

SITC	Exports	Imports	SITC	Exports	Imports
001	0.056	0.042	264	−0.012	0.034
011	0.053	0.060	265	0.017	0.049
012	0.074	0.041	266	0.065	0.040
013	0.052	0.070	267	0.080	0.031
022	0.067	0.027	271	0.018	0.046
023	0.066	0.045	273	0.060	0.062
024	0.069	0.062	274	0.061	0.043
025	0.067	0.058	275	0.050	0.067
031	0.042	0.065	276	0.056	0.056
032	0.046	0.060	281	0.043	0.064
041	0.091	0.019	282	0.086	0.036
042	0.046	0.004	283	0.032	0.060
043	0.078	0.051	284	0.075	0.061
044	0.082	0.044	285	0.054	0.069
045	0.075	0.048	291	0.047	0.063
046	0.070	−0.001	292	0.048	0.063
047	0.068	0.032	321	0.087	0.055
048	0.069	0.046	331	0.009	0.051
051	0.021	0.064	332	0.032	0.068
052	0.028	0.050	341	0.062	0.071
053	0.036	0.066	411	0.082	0.037
054	0.040	0.061	421	0.043	0.034
055	0.035	0.067	422	0.010	0.054
061	0.012	0.048	431	0.067	0.050
062	0.057	0.061	512	0.074	0.049
071	−0.068	0.077	513	0.068	0.054
072	−0.002	0.067	514	0.070	0.045
073	0.063	0.065	515	0.089	0.076
074	−0.010	0.032	521	0.055	0.054
075	−0.002	0.040	531	0.081	0.040
081	0.055	0.055	532	0.041	0.025
091	0.065	0.038	533	0.069	0.045
099	0.065	0.043	541	0.070	0.038
111	0.060	0.054	551	0.059	0.051
112	0.048	0.067	553	0.064	0.047
121	0.049	0.056	554	0.069	0.045
122	0.071	0.037	561	0.066	0.030
211	0.059	0.045	571	0.060	0.044
212	0.066	0.068	581	0.072	0.052
221	0.073	0.056	599	0.072	0.042
231	0.015	0.047	611	0.036	0.058
241	0.048	0.052	612	0.050	0.064
242	0.027	0.046	613	0.061	0.062
243	0.067	0.063	621	0.070	0.050
244	0.005	0.047	629	0.062	0.061
251	0.083	0.058	631	0.045	0.065
261		0.050	632	0.061	0.073
262	0.052	0.049	633	0.015	0.064
263	0.021	0.035	641	0.076	0.059

Table 6.4. (*Continued*)

SITC	Exports	Imports	SITC	Exports	Imports
642	0.067	0.052	697	0.054	0.055
651	0.051	0.045	698	0.068	0.058
652	0.040	0.050	711	0.076	0.057
653	0.051	0.052	712	0.075	0.048
654	0.061	0.049	714	0.075	0.062
655	0.066	0.055	715	0.077	0.044
656	0.035	0.047	717	0.073	0.035
657	0.043	0.071	718	0.078	0.038
661	0.040	0.048	719	0.075	0.046
662	0.057	0.058	722	0.074	0.047
663	0.069	0.058	723	0.063	0.044
664	0.068	0.060	724	0.064	0.059
665	0.063	0.053	725	0.064	0.060
666	0.056	0.068	726	0.080	0.056
667	0.042	0.057	729	0.071	0.055
671	0.051	0.066	731	0.067	0.022
672	0.063	0.032	732	0.075	0.068
673	0.057	0.056	733	0.063	0.069
674	0.065	0.053	734	0.090	0.052
675	0.074	0.052	735	0.063	0.053
676	0.061	0.018	812	0.065	0.056
677	0.070	0.054	821	0.065	0.072
678	0.068	0.054	831	0.038	0.074
679	0.074	0.044	841	0.039	0.073
681	0.058	0.070	842	0.052	0.079
682	0.033	0.060	851	0.032	0.080
683	0.072	0.080	861	0.074	0.058
684	0.069	0.058	862	0.076	0.055
685	0.051	0.050	863	0.049	0.039
686	0.060	0.060	864	0.080	0.051
687		0.064	891	0.063	0.067
689	0.059	0.070	892	0.065	0.059
691	0.066	0.044	893	0.066	0.067
692	0.062	0.042	894	0.053	0.071
693	0.062	0.060	895	−0.054	0.046
694	0.069	0.068	896	0.071	0.069
695	0.074	0.052	897	0.056	0.067
696	0.057	0.061	899	0.050	0.060

cient of the slope measure and the weighted-average measure is, in exports, 0.952; and the simple (Pearson) correlation coefficient is 0.829. In imports, the rank-correlation coefficient is 0.972 and the simple correlation coefficient is 0.939. It thus appears that tests conducted by the use of the slope measure of income level would have yielded roughly the same results and inferences as those that will be presented in the following chapters of the study.

CHAPTER 7

INCOME LEVELS, NATURE OF GOODS AND TRADE THEORIES

In the present chapter, the determination of income levels of trade will be analyzed in relationship to the fundamental theories which are designed to explain patterns of trade. The 1973 estimates, shown in the last chapter, will serve for this purpose. This use will be justified later, in the time-profile study of the next chapter.

1. Income levels in exports and imports

Conventional, factor-proportions theory of the determinants of trade patterns would lead us to the following expectation: A country with an abundance of certain factors will *export* goods intensive in these factors, and *import* goods intensive in the other factors. In a world of two factors, labor and capital, the result is obvious. A country with an abundance of capital (relative to labor) is a rich country, and this country will export to its poor partner capital-intensive goods. A country, on the other hand, abundant in labor is a poor country and it, in turn, will export (to its rich partner) other labor-intensive goods. Hence, the income level of the *exports* of a certain good, and the income level of its *imports*, should be radically different. Even if the factor-proportions theory is viewed less crudely – with more factors admitted, or when factors such as technological innovations, for instance, are introduced – the expected result remains basically unchanged; namely that, in general, the higher the income level of the exports of a good, the lower should be the income level of its imports, and vice versa.

A product-differentiation, demand-determined theory, on the other hand, such as that suggested by Linder (1961),[1] would lead to the opposite expectation. By this theory, countries of a similar income level trade mainly among themselves, in a range of goods which are inherently quite similar, although somewhat differenti-

---

[1] For recent formalization and further development of the theory, see Lancaster (1980) and Helpman (1981).

ated. Thus, rich countries export and import (by trade among themselves) one class
of goods. Hence, a good whose income level is high in exports may be expected
also to have a high level of income in imports; whereas a low-income level in exports would be associated with a low level in imports.

We thus have clearly conflicting expectations from the two sets of theories and
we may test the expectations against the actual findings, by the use of rank-correlation coefficients. The factor-proportions pattern would lead to a high *negative*
rank correlation of the series of income levels of exports and imports; whereas the
Linder theory would lead to a high *positive* rank correlation. The rank-correlation
coefficients are presented in column (3) of table 7.1, which partly reproduces table
6.2.

It appears that when all commodities are included, the rank-correlation coefficient, -0.232, is *negative*, but quite small. The sign would indicate a vindication
of the conventional factor-proportions expectation. But the fact that the correlation is weak suggests that *both* forces – the forces indicated by both sets of theories – are working, with varying strength or weight in the case of each good.

Table 7.1. Association of income levels of exports and imports,
by major categories

	Category	y_{ix} (1)	y_{im} (2)	Spearman rank-correlation coefficient of y_{ix} and y_{im} (3)
0	Food and live animals	55.4	53.7	-0.418
1	Beverages and tobacco	61.7	56.8	
2	Crude materials, inedible	53.2	57.4	0.151
3	Mineral fuels, lubricants	53.2	64.1	
4	Animal and vegetable oils	56.3	49.3	
5	Chemicals	64.4	49.8	0.159
6	Manufactured goods, by material	61.4	58.6	-0.238
7	Machinery and transport equipment	73.8	54.0	-0.098
8	Miscellaneous manufactured articles	63.2	65.0	-0.534
	All goods	59.0	56.7	-0.232

It may be worthwhile, therefore, to see whether the rank-correlation coefficients would be different when ranking is done within each *class* of goods separately. This is shown, in column (3), for the major categories (the one-digit) in the SITC classification (categories 1, 3 and 4 are omitted because there are only four goods in each). In a very rough way this classification system orders and ranks classes by the level of fabrication – the value added in manufacturing, and the level of sophistication. It appears that the signs of the rank-correlation coefficients do indeed vary among major classes, but the coefficients themselves are again mostly rather small. In two categories – the first (0) and the last (8) – they are quite substantial (-0.418 and -0.534, respectively); and here, they are again *negative* in both cases. That is, within each of these categories it may be stated more strongly that the higher the income level of a good in exports, the lower it tends to be in imports – the result expected by conventional theory.[2]

Since the argument for similarity of exports and imports of a country is intimately associated with the hypothesis that high-income countries tend to both export and import goods of a highly heterogeneous nature, one further test has been conducted. A measure of the degree of product differentiation – which will be mentioned later – is available for 120 out of the total of 174 goods. These have been divided into three groups of 40 goods each, according to the degree of product differentiation – group 1 including the goods with the highest measure of differentiation, and group 3 those with the lowest differentiation. According to the hypothesis tested – Linder's – it is mainly in group 1 that a positive association of the income level of exports and imports should be expected. In fact, the rank-correlation coefficients within each of these three groups are as follows: -0.222 in group 1; -0.392 in group 2; and -0.317 in group 3 (for the 120 goods as a whole, it is -0.234). Thus, although the negative association of the income levels of exports and imports is somewhat weaker for goods in group 1 than for the rest, it is *negative* – in contrast to the hypothesis postulated, and in accordance with the predictions of "conventional" theory.

It has been noted in chapter 6 that the *average* income levels do not differ radically among the major categories. In addition, it should be pointed out now that inasmuch as such differences do exist, they do not reveal any clear-cut order. It might have been expected, intuitively, that the higher the level of fabrication, the higher will be the share of high-income countries in exports of the good and of low-income countries in its imports. That is, that the income level of exports should increase as one moves from category 0 to category 8, and the income level of imports should fall. In fact, if such an order appears at all, it would seem to be a very weak one. A simple explanation of the determination of the income levels of degree of fabrication would thus seem to be rejected outright. But we can now

---

[2] This is also true for categories 7 and 8 together – these two sharing among them most highly fabricated goods. The export–import rank correlation for this combined group is -0.490.

proceed to attempt to explain the determination of income levels of trade in goods by other elements.

2. Income levels and attributes of goods

A high-income export good is, by definition, exported by high-income countries. What would a highly-developed, high-income country be expected to export?

One such expectation – the most obvious – has already been noted. A high-income country is, almost invariably, a country with an abundance of physical capital; hence, it may be expected to export capital-intensive goods. A rich country is – again, almost invariably – abundant in human capital as well; hence, it may be expected that such countries will export goods intensive in human capital. These two factors, physical and human capital, may be considered as two components of one aggregate – the total size of an economy's capital – with attention given only to the total. Recent evidence suggests, however, that the two are not close substitutes, and should therefore be better treated as separate factors.[3]

A closely related attribute is the abundance of human skills, which may be expected in highly-developed countries. The correlation of an "average" level of skills in a country and the size of its human capital will undoubtedly be very high. Yet, the two are not entirely identical by definition: separate hypotheses are found in the literature with regard to the effect of a "skill ratio".[4] Hence, if data are available, the "skill" factor may be better treated separately from human capital.

Another explanation of the nature of the exports of a highly developed country, popular in various versions in recent years, lies in technological aspects – the "technology gap" or "product cycle" explanations of trade patterns. The rich country is expected, by these hypotheses, to export primarily goods in which the embodied technology is the result of new, recent innovations. A corollary – in the "product cycle" version – is that each such "good" would be highly heterogeneous, whereas standardized goods would be exported by lower-income countries. The heterogeneity (or diversification) attribute is stressed by the Linder theory: this expects both exports and imports of a rich country to be of highly heterogeneous goods, as a result of the greater variations in demand introduced by high income.

The testing of such hypotheses has become readily feasible due to the well-known work of Hufbauer (1970), where the attributes of each good are quantified. Beside estimates relating to the possible determinants of trade mentioned above (excluding human capital, which is not incorporated in Hufbauer's study), Hufbauer also provides estimates of the wage level in the production of each good. This might be regarded as a proxy estimate of human capital, or of the level of skills; but it is designed to test directly Kravis' hypothesis (1956), that the export

---

[3] See Branson and Monoyios (1977).

[4] The main reference here is, of course, the series of studies by Keesing – such as (1965) or (1971).

industries of rich countries are high wage-level industries. In addition, Hufbauer introduces a measure of scale economies; since a rich country tends, due to its very richness, to also be a *large* economy in the relevant sense (that is, in terms of total income, or total demand), it may be expected to have an advantage in industries where scale economies are positive and large (in the relevant range of production). This assumes, of course, less than perfect mobility of goods (in the full sense – including, for instance, perfect information) in world trade. Still another characteristic estimated by Hufbauer is the degree to which a good is sold to final consumers, rather than being an intermediary in the production of other goods. This is intended to test the contention that less-developed economies tend to export intermediate goods, whereas highly-developed economies tend to produce and export goods which are required mainly by final consumers, the production of which presumably tends to be more sophisticated.

We shall, therefore, test the following attributes of goods as possible explanatory variables of the income level of exports of the good; unless otherwise specified, the estimates of the variables are taken from the Hufbauer study.[5]

X_1 = physical-capital/labor ratio
X_2 = human-capital/labor ratio[6]
X_3 = a measure of skill ratio
X_4 = wage level
X_5 = a measure of economies of scale
X_6 = ratio of sales to final consumers
X_7 = a "first-trade date", as a measure of recentness of technological innovation (in this study, the *later* the date, the higher the index)
X_8 = degree of dispersion of unit prices of the good, as a measure of product differentiation.[7]

[5] The data appear in Hufbauer (1970) (table A2, pp. 212–20) and their construction is explained in the following notes to the tables (pp. 221–3), as well as in a few places in Hufbauer's text. Despite the great amount of work and great ingenuity invested in the construction of these data, they are obviously imperfect; and occasionally based, inevitably, on assumptions of an arbitrary nature. Yet I believe that it is, by and large, a body of data sufficiently accurate for a purpose such as the present one – the test of general hypotheses – especially when the number of observations (that is, goods) is as large as in the present case. One specific argument that has been levelled against Hufbauer's series is that they are based on data of the US alone (except in one instance, in which they draw on Japanese data). This, of course, might be a serious problem for some purposes. But, again, for a purpose such as the present one reliance on US data would not be damaging, as Hufbauer himself pointed out, unless factor-intensity reversals are common; and most available studies suggest that they are not.

[6] Estimate of the human-capital/labor ratio have been provided by William Branson, from the worksheets to Branson and Monoyios, op. cit. These estimates refer to 1967; Hufbauer's estimates are based on data for various years in the 1960s.

[7] Although explanations and details are provided in the source, and will not be repeated here, one point concerning this measure should probably be indicated: Hufbauer's estimates, like those of the present study, are provided for "goods" classified by the three-digit SITC, but the measures of price dispersion for each such "good" are *averages* of measures of dispersion of "goods" classified by the *seven-digit* SITC. This, of course, lends these measures greater credibility.

The discussion thus far has referred to exports. For imports we have, again, two alternative hypotheses. "Conventional" theories would lead to the expectation that a variable which contributes to a high-income level of the exports of the good should make the opposite contribution – to a low-income level – in imports. The Linder hypothesis, on the other hand, of exchange of basically similar goods, should lead to the expectation that a contribution of a variable to a high-income level of exports should do the same for the income level of imports.

Of the total of 174 goods altogether, Hufbauer's study provides data for 120: a sample of nineteen goods[8] (out of a total of 73) which belong to the SITC major (one digit) categories 0–4 (where most of the value added is derived from natural resources or from non-manufacturing activity); and all (101) goods which belong to categories 5–8 – roughly, the semi-manufactured and manufactured goods. Human-capital data (from the Branson-Monoyios study) are available only for the latter group (of 101 goods). I have therefore run three multiple regressions: (1) A regression for all (120) goods for which Hufbauer's data are available, where the explanatory variables exclude X_2 (human capital); (2) the same regression, with same data, but only for the (101) goods in categories 5–8; and (3) a regression covering again only the latter group (of 101 goods), but in which human capital is added to the explanatory variables.[9] Regressions (4) to (6) perform, similarly, the respective tests for imports. The results are summarized in table 7.2.

The performed tests seem, from table 7.2, to yield the following findings:

(1) When all (120) goods are tested, all variables together provide a modest part of the explanation of the determination of the income level of exports and none at all for imports. The adjusted R^2 is 0.382 for exports; and nil (and, of course, insignificant) for imports.

(2) As might be expected, the performance improves substantially when only the (101) goods in the categories 5–8 are included: the adjusted R^2 rises then to 0.462 in exports and to 0.178 in imports (the latter being this time significant at the 5% level). The fact that the exclusion of only nineteen goods improves the explanation to this extent suggests that if these goods are an approximately representative sample of all goods in the categories 0–4, inclusion of these (had the data been available) would probably have reduced the explanation to nil, for exports as well as for imports. It also suggests, on the other hand, that had the removal of the effect of natural resources been done more thoroughly than by just excluding goods in the categories 0–4 (that is, primarily, if a finer classification and selection of goods for coverage had been made), the variables under consider-

[8] These goods are: (013) canned, prepared meat; (032) canned, prepared fish; (046) wheatmeal or flour; (047) non-wheatmeal or flour; (048) cereal preparations; (053) preserved fruits; (055) preserved vegetables; (061) sugar; (062) sugar preparations; (091) margarine, shortening; (111) non-alcoholic beverages; (112) alcoholic beverages; (122) tobacco manufactures; (231) crude synthetic rubber; (242) rough wood; (251) pulp and waste paper; (266) regenerated synthetic fibers; (332) petroleum products; and (421) fixed vegetable oils, soft.

[9] In this regression, the data for physical-capital/labor ratio were also taken from the Branson-Monoyios study.

Table 7.2. Explanatory variables of income levels: Correlation coefficients

Equation number	Adjusted R^2	Partial correlation coefficient (r) of							
		X_1	X_2	X_3	X_4	X_5	X_6	X_7	X_8
Exports									
(1)	0.382	−0.096		0.084	0.349	−0.108	0.128	0.328	0.169
(2)	0.462	−0.093		0.311	0.204	0.363	−0.313	0.199	0.374
(3)	0.392	−0.061	0.093	0.236	0.289	0.024	0.085	0.217	0.306
Imports									
(4)	0.048	−0.001		−0.130	0.079	−0.151	0.036	0.014	0.012
(5)	0.178	0.063		−0.318	0.036	−0.193	0.201	−0.024	0.060
(6)	0.193	−0.175	0.065	−0.320	−0.051	−0.168	0.219	−0.064	−0.001

Underlined figures are significant at the 5% level.

ation would have yielded together a substantially better explanation of the income level of trade.

(3) Partial correlation coefficients show that, in general, each variable separately performs better in explaining exports than in explaining imports, as has been seen before to be true for all explanatory variables together. This applies (again as it was for the aggregate) particularly when all 120 goods – including, that is, those of the 0–4 group – are tested.

(4) The most surprising finding, from the partial correlation coefficients, is the poor showing of X_1 – the physical-capital/labor ratio. Intuitively, again, this variable might have been expected to provide the most obvious explanation: rich countries might first and foremost be expected to export capital-intensive goods. In fact this characteristic of the good – its capital intensity – contributes practically nothing to the determination of the income level of trade.[10]

(5) The human-capital variable (X_2) also appears – again, quite surprisingly – to contribute little: its partial correlation coefficient in exports is significant, and is of the "right" sign, but it is rather low. In imports it is not significant (at the 5% level). Its addition to the list of explanatory variables *lowers* somewhat the R^2 of the regression as a whole (from 0.462 to 0.392) in exports and leaves it practically unchanged for imports.[11]

[10] Moreover, most of the coefficients for X_1 appear with the "wrong" sign. But this should probably be disregarded in view of the fact that the coefficients are not significant at the 5% level.

[11] The relevance of these comparisons may be somewhat impaired, though, by the fact that in regressions 3 and 6 the physical-capital/labor ratio is estimated by a different set of data than in 2 and 5. It might be thought that the poor showing of the human-capital variable may be due to it (probably) being highly correlated with other explanatory variables, which "get the credit"; this might be true particularly in relation to the variable of skills. To test this possibility, I have eliminated the latter variable X_3 (this is not shown in Table 7.2). This leaves the multiple correlation coefficient for exports practically unchanged, and lowers somewhat this coefficient for imports. More important, however, the partial correlation coefficients of the human-capital variable are still very low – for exports, the coefficient is even *lower* (0.041) than when the skill variable is included!

(6) Six variables, out of those tested, seem to contribute to the determination of the income level of exports (and – less clearly, as is implied by our former observations – of imports): The level of skill (X_3); the wage level (X_4); the ratio of sales to final consumers (X_6); the "newness" of the good, as measured by "first-trade date" (X_7); the degree of heterogeneity of the good (X_8); and, somewhat less clearly, the degree of economies of scale (X_5). Of these, all but one (X_6) influence the income level of exports in the hypothesized direction; in other words, they contribute to its increase. The degree to which the good is destined to final consumers (X_6) operates, on the other hand, in the opposite direction: the higher this degree, the *lower* the income level of exports and the higher the income level of imports.

(7) Whenever the significant (at the 5% level) pairs of coefficients for exports and imports are matched (that is, the partial-correlation coefficients of X_i in regression 1 and 4, 2 and 5, and 3 and 6 – seven such pairs altogether), their signs are in *opposite* directions. That is, when a variable contributes to a high-income level of exports, it also contributes to a low-income level of imports. This agrees with the expectations of "conventional" theory, in contrast to those of Linder's theory. It also agrees with the results of the rank correlations that have been observed in table 7.1. There, it may be noticed that among the categories 5–8, in three (6, 7, 8) the rank correlation coefficients of the income levels of exports and imports are negative, within each category; and only in one category, 5 (containing 16 goods, out of the total 101 in categories 5–8) is the rank correlation positive.

In this connection, the degree of heterogeneity of a good – variable X_8 – deserves special attention, since the rationale of the Linder theory is intimately connected with this measure. It is contended that high-income countries will trade with each other in the same range of goods, each "good" being more heterogeneous than in trade of lower-income countries. Hence, a positive correlation of the income levels of exports and imports should be expected particularly when goods are highly heterogeneous.

Table 7.2 shows positive signs (and relatively substantial levels) of the partial correlation coefficients for this variable, X_8, in the export regressions 2 and 3 (which are the relevant ones for the present purpose); and insignificant results in imports. No conclusion can thus be drawn from the matching of the export and import coefficients for this variable (except, perhaps, that the absence of significant correlation coefficients in imports with opposite signs to exports, whereas such opposite coefficients are found for some other variables, may give some slight support to the Linder contention). This finding is in agreement, thus, with the conclusions indicated earlier by the rank-correlation analysis of the income levels of exports and imports.

If we consider that indexes of income levels are more meaningful, in some way, when the dispersion around the average is small, it may be worthwhile to try and

Table 7.3. Explanatory variables of income levels: Correlation coefficients for a subgroup

Dependent variable: Index of income level of	Adjusted R^2	Partial correlation coefficients (r) of						
		X_1	X_3	X_4	X_5	X_6	X_7	X_8
Exports (y_{ix})	0.455	−0.057	0.180	0.661	0.134	0.444	0.277	0.151
Imports (y_{im})	0.074	0.129	−0.028	−0.196	−0.266	0.035	0.199	0.116

Underlined figures are significant at the 5% level.

see whether just the "more meaningful" indexes give the same indications and yield the same inferences as the rest. In attempting to test this, commodities have been ranked according to their levels of dispersion in exports and imports separately (starting with the *lowest* dispersion measure), and the top half (60 out of 120 goods for which the relevant data are available) have been selected to consist of a new population of observations. For this group, the effect on income levels of exports and imports of the various attributes with which these levels are presumed to be connected has been tested by a multiple regression, in the same way which has been done before for all (120) goods. The results, which should be compared with those of table 7.2, are presented in table 7.3. The test has been carried out only through the regressions equivalent to those which are represented in lines (1) and (4) of table 7.2.

On the whole, table 7.3 would lead to roughly the same conclusions as table 7.2. The R^2s are somewhat higher, but not by any substantial margin. The showing of variable X_4 (the wage level) in exports and of X_5 (the measure of scale economies) in imports are of the same sign as in table 7.2 but more impressive. In particular, one of the major inferences made earlier is supported again: the physical-capital variable fails to assert itself as influencing the pattern of specialization and trade. It appears again with the "wrong" signs, but its correlation coefficients are not significant.

3. Total-income levels of trade

So far this study has dealt with the *per capita* income level of the structure of trade. But, by way of some digression, the *total* income of exporters and importers can be observed. Similarly to the per capita index, the index of total income of exports of a good, $\hat{y}_{ix}$, is defined as

$$\hat{y}_{ix} = \sum_j \hat{y}_j \left(X_{ij} / X_{i.} \right)$$

where $\hat{y}_j$ stands for country j's total GNP (relative to the US GNP), and X_{ij} and X_i, as before, are country j's and the world's exports of good i. Similarly, $\hat{y}_{im}$ will be a measure of the total income level of imports of good i. The values of these indexes are presented in table 7.4. Averages for the major categories are shown in columns (1) and (2) of table 7.5.

By and large, the indexes of total -income level reveal the same pattern as those of per capita income levels – as witnessed, for instance, by comparisons of the appropriate columns in table 7.5 and table 7.1. Some of the results seem to be indicated even more strongly by the total-income indexes; in particular, the high-income level of exports of commodities in category 7 (machinery and transport equipment). Column (3) of table 7.5 presents the correlation coefficients of export and import income levels, within each category and for all goods. These coefficients appear to be negative, by and large – again, an indication which comes out stronger than that which follows from column (3) of table 7.1. In other words, goods tend to be traded more between large (by total-income yardstick) and small countries than among similar countries.

The similarity of indications yielded by total-income and per capita income measures is of course not surprising. A country's level of total income is the result, by definition, of its level of per capita income and its size, in terms of population. The measures of total income of the trade structure may thus be expected to reflect, first, the effect of the level of per capita income. But they should also reflect, in comparison with the measures of per capita income level, the added impact of the size of the economy. A small-sized economy may be expected to manifest a different production pattern and to specialize, partly at least, in a different range of goods than would a large country with a similar level of per capita income. In particular, it is usually expected that large economies have the advantage, and will tend to specialize, in industries in which economies of scale are strongly pronounced – the aircraft industry, or railroad equipment, are obvious examples.[12]

The particularly high total-income level of the exports of machinery and transport equipment may be an indication, indeed, of the added impact of scale economies on the pattern of specialization. A simple regression of the index of total-income level of exports on Hufbauer's measure of scale economies which has been used in the earlier analysis, for the commodities for which this measure is available, yields a correlation coefficient (r) of 0.257; in imports, the correlation coefficient is -0.300. Both coefficients are significant and of the expected sign. This might conceivably be, however, due to the positive correlation which exists between scale economies and the per capita income level of exports and the negative correlation in imports. A multiple regression of the total-income measure on

---

[12]Analyses of this issue may be found in various contributions in Robinson (1960), particularly that of Kuznets. See also Chenery and Taylor (1968).

Table 7.4. Indexes of total income level of trade ($\hat{y}_j$)

SITC code	Exports	Imports	SITC code	Exports	Imports
001	17.2	16.6	261	6.8	27.3
011	10.4	27.1	262	7.9	19.6
012	9.5	13.2	263	28.6	13.4
013	6.0	44.3	264	2.2	12.1
022	12.0	11.4	265	6.1	15.4
023	7.8	13.8	266	26.3	11.3
024	9.7	24.0	267	47.8	9.4
025	11.5	16.5	271	26.7	10.6
031	12.5	42.2	273	15.2	16.3
032	17.7	24.2	274	27.3	14.2
041	61.6	9.0	275	24.3	30.6
042	43.5	2.6	276	19.0	22.9
043	27.7	14.6	281	6.4	32.1
044	69.7	13.4	282	54.5	15.0
045	59.0	17.4	283	7.6	28.1
046	30.6	1.3	284	31.8	20.2
047	37.9	3.0	285	12.5	45.8
048	23.6	15.9	291	13.4	24.5
051	14.3	21.5	291	13.2	21.4
052	22.0	14.0	321	44.8	17.4
053	18.7	21.6	331	1.1	31.0
054	14.9	19.8	332	8.9	31.0
055	11.6	26.5	341	11.7	41.5
061	5.0	32.2			
062	14.4	21.5	411	54.7	13.6
071	4.9	44.3	421	25.5	10.4
072	3.3	31.9	422	9.3	26.4
073	11.5	19.4	431	18.9	11.6
074	3.5	16.0			
075	4.9	23.0	512	31.2	17.0
081	33.2	13.0	513	24.2	23.7
091	24.1	9.5	514	28.5	13.4
099	23.9	12.1	515	64.11	41.8
			521	33.6	15.0
111	15.4	10.7	531	20.5	14.4
112	12.9	33.9	532	14.9	12.7
121	45.6	21.3	533	22.6	9.4
122	32.4	9.9	541	23.9	11.0
			551	21.9	22.6
211	27.0	17.6	553	21.4	12.6
212	21.5	23.6	554	26.0	9.6
221	64.3	18.1	561	26.4	16.9
231	10.3	23.4	571	24.5	17.1
241	16.6	12.7	581	26.6	11.8
242	28.3	21.6	599	29.5	12.5
243	14.9	33.5	611	15.9	21.0
244	2.5	21.1	612	15.9	24.7
251	19.2	29.4	613	21.0	16.2

Table 7.4. (*Continued*)

SITC code	Exports	Imports	SITC code	Exports	Imports
621	28.1	8.1	695	28.5	16.8
629	22.3	25.6	696	21.1	29.8
631	16.8	31.1	697	19.1	21.6
632	17.1	33.9	698	25.4	19.8
633	5.9	19.4			
641	18.2	27.1	711	38.3	24.5
642	22.4	12.2	712	36.6	18.9
651	16.7	12.7	714	41.6	23.6
652	17.6	18.2	715	28.9	14.2
653	18.4	17.8	717	24.2	19.9
654	16.9	15.9	718	36.3	11.6
655	21.9	16.6	719	32.1	13.8
656	16.7	14.7	722	31.1	14.2
657	14.4	19.4	723	23.9	15.9
661	11.0	19.6	724	27.3	29.9
662	20.9	15.9	725	22.1	17.9
663	23.0	15.5	726	31.0	23.3
664	24.4	20.7	729	35.1	22.1
665	20.9	18.5	731	32.7	7.5
666	20.8	36.6	732	30.7	32.1
667	15.6	24.7	733	23.4	30.1
671	11.9	28.5	734	69.7	19.4
672	20.2	9.4	735	19.9	7.8
673	14.3	21.9			
674	21.4	23.3	812	19.7	15.6
675	22.4	14.9	821	15.3	23.9
676	22.0	6.8	831	14.7	38.2
677	17.2	27.0	841	11.0	29.8
678	26.0	18.2	842	13.1	21.4
679	38.1	13.8	851	10.0	43.5
681	20.5	40.5	861	35.0	20.3
682	11.11	22.1	862	38.1	18.0
683	14.3	47.9	863	30.9	16.3
684	19.7	20.2	864	13.6	24.7
685	12.6	21.7	891	29.3	35.1
686	10.8	36.5	892	25.6	16.2
687	5.2	39.1	893	23.0	23.6
689	22.9	28.6	894	24.8	35.3
691	25.0	9.2	895	31.2	13.6
692	19.6	9.2	896	40.3	39.0
693	17.5	31.0	897	22.4	26.0
694	25.9	34.3	899	18.3	28.9

Table 7.5. Total-income levels and association of exports and imports, by major categories

	Category	$\hat{y}_{ix}$ Average for category (1)	$\hat{y}_{im}$ Average for category (2)	Spearman rank-correlation coefficient of $\hat{y}_{ix}$ and $\hat{y}_{im}$ (3)
0	Food and live animals	20.2	19.3	−0.658
1	Beverages and tobacco	24.1	19.0	
2	Crude materials, inedible	20.8	20.9	−0.353
3	Mineral fuels, lubricants	16.6	28.5	
4	Animal and vegetable oils	27.1	15.5	
5	Chemicals	27.5	16.2	0.241
6	Manufactured goods, by material	19.1	22.0	−0.402
7	Machinery and transport equipment	31.9	19.3	−0.310
8	Miscellaneous manufactured articles	23.1	25.5	−0.426
	All goods			−0.361

the per capita measure of the income level and on the measure of economies of scale yields the following partial-correlation coefficients: In exports, the coefficient of the two income measures is 0.650, and the coefficient of correlation with economies of scale is 0.146 (not significant at the 5% level; $R^2 = 0.425$); in imports the two coefficients are, respectively, 0.787 and -0.210 ($R^2 = 0.797$). The expected relationship of the total-income level of trade flows to economies of scale is thus still borne out, particularly in the pattern of imports.

In the rest of the analysis, the measures of income level of trade will once more refer exclusively to *per capita* income. But, in view of the similarity of inferences indicated in the present section, it may be speculated that quite similar findings would have been yielded by the application of the *total*-income indexes.

4. The income levels of trade of countries

Having at our disposal the index of (per capita) income level of trade of each *good*, we may now move back to the trade of a *country* and inquire about the income level of the goods traded by the country: Does the country trade in high income-level goods, or in low-level goods? We shall confine this inquiry to the export side and conduct it by using an index of the income level of the country's exports.[13] This index, y_{jx}, is defined as

$$y_{jx} = \sum_{i} (X_{ij} / X_{.j}) y_{ix}.$$

The income level of exports of a country must by definition be, *on average* for all countries, simply the country's level of per capita income. For individual countries, however, there is no need for this equality to hold: some countries may be expected to export "above" their income level, that is, to have an index of the income level of exports higher than their per capita income levels, whereas other countries may be expected to export "below" their income levels.

Column (1) of table 7.6 presents the per capita income level of each country. A comparison of these levels with those presented in column (2) shows immediately that almost all countries export "above" their income levels. The exceptions are partly a few oddities such as oil-exporting and Soviet bloc countries, to which further reference is made below. Mainly, however, the group of countries which export "below" their income levels consists of the top high-income countries (whose shares in total exports, it should be recalled, are very high). These are (in alphabetical order); Australia, Belgium-Luxembourg, Canada, Denmark, France, Germany, Netherlands, Norway, Sweden, Switzerland and the United States. The income level at which a country turns from exporting "above" to exporting "below" appears to be around 60 (as a percentage of US per capita income).

Upon reflection, however, it would appear that this finding of "above" and "below" exporting countries represents merely a technical attribute, rather than any phenomenon of substance in world exports. A rich country shares its exports with other countries, which on average may be expected to be poorer than the country involved. The index of income level of the goods which the country exports may therefore be expected to be lower than the country's own income level; and the opposite must hold for a relatively poor country. This may easily be visualized by considering the two extreme cases. Take, on one hand, the US – the highest-income country. Assuming that each of the goods exported by the US is also exported, to some extent at least, by other countries (which are, by definition of the case, poorer than the US), each of the goods exported by the US will have an index of income level of exports lower than 100 and so inevitably will be the index of income level of the US exports, which is the weighted average of the indexes of individual goods. And the opposite must be true, in the same way, for countries such as Laos, Cambodia, Mali, Rwanda, or Upper Volta – which appear to have the lowest per capita income levels (just 1% of the US level).

---

[13]An attempt to analyze similarly the imports of countries has proved to be rather fruitless, due to the fact that the indexes of income level of imports are remarkably similar among countries.

Table 7.6. The income level of exports of countries

Country	Per capita GNP (in percentage of US) (y_j) (1)	Index of income level of exports	
		Actual (y_{jx}) (2)	Expected ($\bar{y}_{jk}$) (3)
Afghanistan	1.5	49.6	38.5
Algeria	9.2	32.2	40.7
Angola	7.9	31.5	40.4
Argentina	26.5	60.0	45.7
Australia	70.2	54.9	58.2
Austria	56.6	68.9	54.4
Belgium-Luxembourg	73.5	58.9	59.2
Bolivia	3.7	36.8	39.2
Brazil	12.3	37.7	41.6
Bulgaria	25.6	32.3	45.5
Burma	1.3	47.6	38.5
Cambodia	1.1	41.3	38.4
Cameroon	4.0	27.7	39.3
Canada	87.9	60.3	63.3
Central African Republic	2.6	37.0	38.8
Chad	1.3	39.0	38.5
Chile	11.6	45.2	41.4
Colombia	7.1	26.0	40.1
Congo	5.5	42.8	39.7
Costa Rica	11.5	32.6	41.4
Cuba	8.7	28.8	40.6
Czechoslovakia	46.3	63.0	51.4
Denmark	84.0	60.9	62.2
Dominican Republic	8.4	29.4	40.5
Ecuador	6.1	31.6	39.9
Egypt	4.0	39.0	39.3
El Salvador	5.6	30.0	39.7
Ethiopia	1.5	34.6	38.5
Finland	58.1	64.5	54.8
France	73.2	60.3	59.1
French Guiana	1.8	48.9	38.6
German Democratic Republic	48.4	39.1	52.0
German Federal Republic	85.8	63.9	62.7
Ghana	4.8	29.1	39.5
Greece	30.2	48.2	46.8
Guatemala	8.1	34.7	40.4
Haiti	2.1	32.5	38.7
Honduras	5.2	38.4	39.6
Hong Kong	23.1	50.7	44.7
Hungary	29.8	10.5	46.7
India	1.9	42.7	38.7
Indonesia	2.1	29.2	38.7
Iran	14.0	27.3	42.1
Iraq	13.7	50.7	42.0

Table 7.6. (*Continued*)

Country	Per capita GNP (in percentage of US) (y_j)	Index of income level of exports	
		Actual (y_{jx})	Expected ($\bar{y}_{jk}$)
	(1)	(2)	(3)
Ireland	34.7	53.6	48.1
Israel	48.5	47.1	52.0
Italy	39.5	58.0	49.4
Ivory Coast	6.1	24.5	39.9
Jamaica	16.0	35.8	42.7
Japan	58.5	63.3	54.9
Jordan	5.5	48.9	39.7
Kenya	2.7	32.3	38.9
Laos	1.0	58.6	38.4
Lebanon	15.2	57.5	42.5
Liberia	5.0	46.8	39.5
Libya	56.9	24.2	54.4
Malawi	1.8	44.5	38.6
Malaysia	9.2	30.7	40.7
Mali	1.1	51.9	38.4
Mauritania	3.2	49.1	39.0
Mexico	14.4	47.9	42.2
Morocco	5.2	39.6	39.6
Mozambique	6.1	41.1	39.9
Netherlands	69.8	56.9	58.1
New Zealand	59.4	57.8	55.1
Nicaragua	8.7	40.4	40.6
Niger	1.6	56.4	38.6
Nigeria	3.4	32.2	39.1
Norway	75.2	60.7	59.7
Pakistan	1.9	48.6	38.7
Panama	14.8	34.6	42.3
Papua-New Guinea	6.6	24.2	40.0
Paraguay	6.6	51.2	40.0
Peru	10.0	47.0	41.0
Philippines	4.5	38.2	39.4
Poland	33.7	54.1	47.8
Portugal	22.7	51.5	44.6
Rwanda	1.1	20.9	38.4
Saudi Arabia	26.0	21.2	45.6
Senegal	4.5	49.6	39.4
Sierra Leone	3.6	45.5	33.8
Singapore	29.5	45.8	46.6
Somalia	1.3	51.5	38.5
South Africa	16.9	45.9	43.0
South Korea	6.5	51.6	40.0
Spain	27.6	51.6	46.0
Sri Lanka	1.9	18.1	38.7
Sudan	2.1	46.4	38.7

Table 7.6. (*Continued*)

Country	Per capita GNP (in percentage of US) (y_j)	Index of income level of exports	
		Actual (y_{jx})	Expected ($\bar{y}_{jk}$)
	(1)	(2)	(3)
Sweden	95.3	65.0	65.5
Switzerland	98.4	65.7	66.3
Syria	6.5	38.8	40.0
Thailand	4.4	41.9	39.4
Tanzania	2.1	30.8	38.7
Togo	2.9	28.5	38.9
Trinidad and Tobago	21.1	36.6	44.2
Tunisia	7.4	42.1	40.2
Turkey	9.7	42.4	40.9
Uganda	2.4	18.9	38.8
United Kingdom	49.4	59.6	52.3
United States	100	63.9	66.8
Upper Volta	1.1	54.6	38.4
Uruquay	15.3	52.8	42.5
Venezuela	26.3	29.6	45.7
Yemen Arab Republic	1.6	38.6	38.6
Yemen Democratic Republic	1.8	34.3	38.6
Yugoslavia	16.3	53.8	42.8
Zaire	2.3	41.8	38.8
Zambia	6.9	43.7	40.1

To overcome this technical difficulty, and arrive at comparisons which may reveal any substance, a (linear) regression of the index of income level of exports of countries on the countries' level of per capita income was run. The inference of this procedure is that a country may be said to export at its income level if the index of income level of its exports is similar to what would be expected from this regression. Likewise, a country would be judged to be exporting "above" or "below" its income if its index of income level of exports is, respectively, higher or lower than the expected value. The regression fitted is

$$\bar{y}_{jx} = 38.11 + 0.287 \, y_j,$$

where:

$\bar{y}_{jx}$ = expected income level of country j's exports; and
y_j = per capita income level of country j (in percentage of US income)

R^2 is 0.368, and the result is significant at practically any desired level. The values of the income level of exports expected from this regression are presented in column (3) of table 7.6.

Table 7.7 Countries with deviating indexes of income level of exports

Country	Per capita income (in percentage of US)	$(y_{jx} - \bar{y}_{jx})/$Standard deviation
Exporting "above" income		
Afghanistan	1.5	1.11
Argentina	26.5	1.44
Austria	56.6	1.46
Czechoslovakia	46.3	1.18
French Guiana	1.8	1.03
Korea	6.5	1.18
Laos	1.0	2.04
Lebanon	15.2	1.52
Mali	1.1	1.36
Mauritania	3.2	1.02
Niger	1.6	1.80
Pakistan	1.9	1.00
Paraguay	6.6	1.13
Senegal	4.5	1.03
Somalia	1.3	1.32
Upper Volta	1.1	1.63
Uruguay	15.3	1.04
Yugoslavia	16.3	1.11
Exporting "below" income		
Bulgaria	25.6	−1.33
Cameroon	4.0	−1.17
Colombia	7.1	−1.43
Cuba	8.7	−1.19
Dominican Republic	8.4	−1.13
German Democratic Republic	48.4	−1.30
Ghana	4.8	−1.05
Hungary	29.8	−3.65
Iran	14.0	−1.50
Ivory Coast	6.1	−1.55
Libya	56.9	−3.05
Malaysia	9.2	−1.01
Papua-New Guinea	6.6	−1.59
Rwanda	1.1	−1.77
Saudi Arabia	26.0	−2.46
Sri Lanka	1.9	−2.08
Togo	2.9	−1.05
Uganda	2.4	−2.01
Venezuela	26.3	−1.62

A comparison of columns (2) and (3) of this table would show, naturally, that the actual and expected indexes of income level are never precisely equal; and the decision as to what is a "large" or a "small" deviation of the two from each other is a rather arbitrary matter. I have selected one standard deviation of the distribution as a dividing line, and termed a country as one which trades "above" if its actual income level of exports is higher than its expected value by more than one standard deviation, or as trading "below" if its actual income index is lower than its expected value by more than the standard deviation. These countries are listed in table 7.7.

It appears that the large majority of the countries listed in table 7.7 share one common attribute: whether they trade "above" or "below," they are mostly relatively poor countries. Such countries tend, by and large, to be relatively specialized in their exports – to have, that is, a high measure of commodity concentration of their exports. In such instances chance plays a heavier role. If the few goods in which the country specializes happen to be high-income goods, the country will have a relatively high index of income level of its exports and will hence appear to be trading "above"; and the opposite would be true if the very limited list of the country's exports happens to consist of goods exported largely by relatively low-income countries.

Two groups of countries seem, from table 7.7, to share other specific attributes. One consists of the oil-exporting countries: all oil countries covered in the data – Iran, Libya, Saudi Arabia and Venezuela – appear on the list of countries which export "below." This phenomenon is explained rather simply. Oil appears to be a good exported primarily by low-income countries. At the same time, *some* of the oil-exporting countries are made relatively rich, in per capita income terms, by the very export of oil; Libya and Saudi Arabia are most obvious examples, beside other countries and territories which are not included in the study. This leads to the appearance of such countries as exporting "below" their income level.[14] Also, the exporting of oil is done primarily by rather similar countries, having roughly the same (low) range of per capita income (with the exception of the small-population exporters of oil). Since in each of these countries oil is the major export good, total exports of such countries tend to have a low-income index and thus to deviate from the values expected from a regression whose results were determined by the fact that low-income countries mostly share their exports with higher-income countries.

The other group which may be distinguished is that of Soviet bloc countries. Of the six countries in the bloc covered in this study, five appear in the list in table

---

[14] It should be recalled that the study's data refer to the year 1973, only at the end of which has the oil price risen dramatically. At present-day prices, oil-exporting countries would appear, as a whole, to be relatively richer; and the income level of exports of oil would not be nearly as low as the level recorded in 1973.

7.7 (the sixth, Poland, has an index of income level exceeding its expected value by 0.64 standard deviations). Of these five, Czechoslovakia appears to be trading "above"; whereas the four others – Bulgaria, Cuba, East Germany and Hungary, the latter by a very wide margin – seem to be trading "below". The number of observations here is small and the appearance they give may be a result of accident. Yet, the assertion often made that the trade structure in the Soviet bloc leads its peripheral countries to specialize in goods normally exported by low-income countries may find some support in these observations.

Is there a consistent difference between exporters "above" and "below" their income levels in the success of their export performance? This question seems to be of some significance. Assertions are often made that a high rate of increase of exports of a country, particularly a less-developed one, requires, *inter alia*, specialization in "advanced" goods; and this would imply an export structure which yields a relatively high index of income level.

A casual look at table 7.7 does not seem to disclose any systematic difference in export performance between the countries exporting "above" and those exporting "below" their income level. On the other hand, some positive indication is yielded by observation of the group of countries whose average export growth in the last two decades has been most rapid. This group would include Greece, Hong Kong, Israel, Japan, Jordan, South Korea, Portugal and Yugoslavia (data for Taiwan, a country with another remarkable export performance, are not available in this study). It appears, from table 7.6, that countries in this group predominantly export "above" – Israel being the only exception and Greece being a borderline case. Thus, some support may be claimed for the above-mentioned assertion, of the benefit in export performance derived from specialization in relatively high-income goods, but the evidence is too sporadic to yield, on this issue, more than a suggestive indication.

CHAPTER 8

A TIME-SERIES PROFILE: POSITIONS
IN THE INCOME LADDER

Until now, the study of the income level of trade has been based on a single point of observation: the data of trade flows referred to the year 1973. The present chapter will go beyond the cross-section study and examine the time-series profile of the indexes of income levels of exports and imports. The purpose of this extension is two-fold.

First, it may be questioned whether any single year may provide a sound enough basis for generalizations. If trade patterns fluctuate wildly from one year to the next, or even undergo a regular, consistent change over time but at a very rapid pace, data for a single year would provide an insufficient basis and may lead to unreliable, and conceivably misleading, inferences. It is thus important to see whether trade patterns, as they are represented by the indexes of income levels, have been quite regular and consistent, each point of observation not differing widely from another; or whether, to mention an extreme possibility, fluctuations and trend changes have been so strong as to make not just a single point of observation, but even an average of several such points an inadequate basis for tests and inferences.

Second, a time-series study might make possible the examination of the nature of changes in trade patterns over time, inasmuch as any longer-term trends are revealed. Have exports of certain goods tended to move from the richer to the poorer countries, or vice versa, and have import patterns changed – a good earlier imported by rich countries shifting to the poorer, or vice versa? And insofar as such trends of change are found, do they reveal any regularities, that is, can any common attributes be found which are shared by goods which move " upward" or "downward" on the ladders of income levels of exports and imports? In other words, can any meaningful "product cycle" be traced?

In the first section of this chapter, the nature of the data and the construction of time series will be described. The second section will discuss the first of the aforementioned issues, namely, the degree of consistency of the time-series; whereas the third, last section will analyze the second issue – the existence and the nature of trends over time.

1. Time series of the indexes of income levels

It will be recalled that the index of income level of trade is concerned not with measures of *absolute* incomes but with *relative* income levels. For a time-series study, this is an essential element. If, for instance, all income levels (as measured by per capita GNP) have doubled between two points of observation, and a weighted average of the income levels of countries from which exports of a certain good flow has also doubled, this good would still be described as being exported by countries as rich, or as poor, in one observation point as in the other. "Richness" or "poorness" are, that is, measures of *relative* income. As the denominator for all the ratios of relative income levels of countries the U.S. (per-capita) income level has been selected, because it has been the world's highest throughout the period of observation covered in this study.

A time-series study requires, for obvious reasons, the availability and use of data classified in a uniform fashion throughout the period of observation. World-wide recording of trade data by the 3-digit SITC started only in the early 1950s. This restricts the period of the present study to the post-war era, starting with the observation of 1952.[1] The last year of observation is 1973, the latest for which universal data were available when this study started (which is, we recall, the year that served for the earlier, cross-section analysis). The study thus covers a period extending over 21 years. As a historical perspective for trends of change, this is probably a rather short stretch. Future studies, hopefully, will be able to extend over a more impressive length of time – provided, of course, that the classification scheme used for recording trade flows does not suffer from drastic changes and revisions. Yet, a period of over 20 years is already long enough, presumably, to detect trend changes in trade patterns, if these trends are of a substantial order of magnitude. And it should certainly be long enough to infer from its data the degree of regularity and consistency vs. randomness in the nature of trade patterns.

To construct a time-series, a study of each single year is both too effort consuming and non-essential for the purposes of the present study. Hence, a sample of a few years, spaced about equally, has been selected. In addition to the beginning and end years, 1952 and 1973, data for four other years have been compiled: 1955, 1960, 1965 and 1970. Altogether, thus, the series of the study contain six points of observation.

The "revised" SITC contains, in its 3-digit specification, 175 goods. This scheme has been used in the U.N. recording, on which this study draws, since 1960. Earlier, the "original" SITC scheme had been used, with a specification of only 150 goods. On occasion, a concordance of the original and the revised classification schemes – where changes have been made – could be easily handled so as to make

---

[1]An attempt to match the classification employed in records of trade in a pre-war year, 1936, with the 3-digit SITC, has proved futile.

an unbroken series possible. On other occasions, however, such concordance was not feasible and no long-term series, including both pre- and post-1960 years, could hence be yielded for the goods involved. As a result, the number of goods for which the time series data have been constructed, in this study, is only 108. Their proportion in total world exports in 1970 was 75.5%.[2] In this sense, thus, although the study is not fully comprehensive, it is certainly adequately representative, covering the large majority of world trade. The major category mostly affected by changes in the classification scheme was "machinery and transport equipment". Among the 9 major categories of the SITC, this might be thus the only one whose representation in this part of the study is deficient.

The time series of the indexes of income levels of exports and imports are presented in an appendix, in tables 8.A.1 and 8.A.2. The following analyses are based on these findings.

2. The degree of consistency of relative positions

To test whether the positions of various goods, in their income levels of exports and imports, have been similar or widely dissimilar in different points of observation, Spearman's rank-correlation coefficients of the various time series have been calculated; the more similar the series, the higher the coefficient should be, with a coefficient of unity for series with identical positions.[3]

Table 8.1 presents the rank-correlation coefficients of the series of each of the six years with each other, separately for exports (part A) and imports (part B). Several conclusions emerge from the observation of these findings.

First, it appears that by and large the correlation coefficients are high; that is, the relative positions of income levels of the various goods are quite similar in different years (although what is a "high" or a "low" correlation coefficient, in

---

[2] Some goods have been excluded not due to changes in classification but because the indexes constructed for them were obviously erratic and meaningless, fluctuating wildly from year to year and with data being very often absent altogether for one year or another. These are always goods in which world trade is very small, presumably largely accidental and hence highly irregular. Twenty-five goods have been dropped on this count, but their aggregate exports in 1970 amounted to less than 1% of total world exports.

[3] Rank correlations are preferable to correlations of the absolute levels of the indexes, for the present purpose, because they are less subject to the exaggerated impact of extreme observations. Correlations of the original levels of the indexes have also been calculated. By and large, they are very similar to the rank correlations, yielding inferences which are similar enough not to warrant their separate presentation.

Later on, when *trends* are established, the use of ranks rather than the original levels will be imperative. Since *average* income levels for all goods have changed over the years, and we are interested in *relative* positions, the inferences drawn from the use of original levels of indexes would be misleading – although, admittedly, standardization could be handled also in other fashions than ranking.

Table 8.1. Spearman's rank-correlation coefficients of income level series

A. Exports

	1952	1955	1960	1965	1970	1973
1952	1.000	0.681	0.617	0.542	0.539	0.447
1955		1.000	0.827	0.774	0.726	0.642
1960			1.000	0.853	0.811	0.695
1965				1.000	0.933	0.871
1970					1.000	0.905
1973						1.000

B. Imports

	1952	1955	1960	1965	1970	1973
1952	1.000	0.758	0.624	0.629	0.594	0.504
1955		1.000	0.769	0.754	0.645	0.580
1960			1.000	0.837	0.629	0.569
1965				1.000	0.802	0.734
1970					1.000	0.877
1973						1.000

any absolute statement, must necessarily be a matter of judgement). The main exception to this inference appears to be the series for 1952, the earliest year covered: in exports its correlation coefficients with any other series are consistently lower than the coefficients in any other equi-distant correlations between series of other years. This also holds for imports, but much more weakly. There may be two explanations for this phenomenon, the two being probably complementary rather than alternative. One is that the first few years following 1952 still manifested some of the rapid changes in trade structure that must, by casual observation, have taken place during the early post-war era. The proximity of the Korean war, with its own impact on trade patterns, might have been a contributing factor. The other explanation may lie not in the nature of trade, but in the quality of data. The year under consideration, 1952, is the first for which records appear by the SITC scheme, and the degree of universality of coverage at that time was substantially below what it became within a period of a few years later. Since the deficiency in coverage is presumably not unbiased – it concerned more the reporting of low-income countries than of others – this may be reflected in apparent changes in trade patterns and in the relative positions of goods following the improvement in the quality of data.

Other than 1952, it should be noted, no consistent difference appears to emerge among the observed years in the similarity of their patterns with those of other (equi-distant) years. That is, looking at table 8.1 – either part A or part B – any movement along a northwest to southeast diagonal does not reveal a consistent improvement, or deterioration, of the correlation coefficients (excluding, in such observation, the row of coefficients for 1952).

Second, it appears consistently that the closer are two years to each other, in time, the more similar their trade patterns; and the further apart they are, the more does dissimilarity grow. Looking, once more, at the aforementioned diagonals in the two parts of table 8.1, it is clear that the further is a diagonal from the main diagonal of unit-coefficients – the longer the distances in time represented by the diagonal – the lower the correlation coefficients. Differences in trade patterns thus seem to be greater the further apart are the years compared. This is probably not a surprising finding, but it is not devoid of meaning. It implies that changes over time, in trade structure, are not haphazard, incidental and reversible fluctuations. Rather, they must involve at least some degree of consistency and regularity in the patterns of change.

Another inference, drawn from the comparison of the two parts of table 8.1, is that as a rule the degree of similarity of patterns of various years is higher in exports than in imports. With the exception, again, of comparisons involving the series for 1952, all correlation coefficients between the patterns of any given pair of years are higher for exports than they are for imports. Sometimes the difference is substantial, while in other comparisons it is slight (in comparisons involving the series of 1955 the differences are smallest – excluding, again, the series of 1952 from this remark). Such a difference between exports and imports is again not surprising, particularly in view of the finding in the last chapter that various hypotheses of the possible origins of trade patterns seem to perform considerably better in explaining the structure of exports than in explaining imports. It is possible, of course, that alternative hypotheses, which have not yet been suggested and not tested, would explain import patterns as well as, or better than, export patterns. But with the evidence on hand now, an appropriate inference of the cross-section analysis would be that import patterns are less susceptible to explanation and generalization, and in this sense less "regular", than export patterns. If this is true, the degree of similarity between patterns in different points of time should be expected to be lower in the comparison of import than of export flows.

Finally, the Kendall Coefficient of Concordance has been used to evaluate the similarity of the complete set of observations, rather than of each pair of years separately.[4] This coefficient is found to be 0.770 for exports and 0.739 for imports. For observations ranging over a period of over 20 years these coefficients seem to be high enough to indicate a high degree of regularity – although, once more, this must be a matter of judgement.[5] Reinforcing the indications yielded by

---

[4] This coefficient is, in essence, similar in nature to the coefficient of rank correlation. But it refers simultaneously to the ranks in *all* the series covered (in the present case, six in number), whereas the ordinary rank-correlation coefficient (whether Spearman's as has been used here, or Kendall's) refers to just two separate series.

[5] Significance levels, here as in the correlation coefficients between pairs of series, are practically as high as desired (a level of 0.0001).

the comparisons of pairs of years, this appears to suggest that a "typical" pattern of export and import flows does exist, at least for the period covered by the series of the present study. Once more, this seems to hold more strongly for export than for import flows, but the difference is only slight.[6]

If, indeed, "typical" regular patterns seem to persist over time, than the use of averages for the period as a whole would be justified for a variety of purposes; and one such application will be made in the analysis of the terms of trade in the next chapter. It may be of particular interest, in the present study, to see whether the use of average indexes of income levels of exports and imports would have yielded roughly the same results, in the tests of various trade hypotheses, as the use actually made in the last chapter of the data of 1973 alone: the closer these two series, the more similar must be the inferences drawn from each of them alternatively. The rank-correlation coefficients between 1973 and the average 1952–1973 series (for only those 108 goods, of course, which appear in the latter series) are 0.876 for exports and 0.776 for imports. These coefficients are high enough, it seems, to expect the conclusions drawn from the use of 1973 alone to emerge also, by and large, from the use of average indexes. Hence, the use of the 1973 data must be reliable enough as a representation of a trade structure typical to a period of close to 20 years preceding this year. The observation (in table 8.1) of the high rank-correlation coefficients of the 1973 series with those of 1970 and 1965 (particularly for exports) suggests that this is even more true if patterns of the last decade preceding 1973, rather than two decades, are concerned.[7] Finally, the use of 1973 data (or of any other *single* year) implies the availability of income-level indexes for a larger number of goods than the use of average levels where, for the reasons specified earlier, this number is reduced. Thus, the application of the 1973 rather than the six-observation average indexes appeared to be preferable for the purpose on hand.

3. Trend movements of goods in the income ladder

As has just been seen, changes in the positions of income levels of goods over the years appear to be – at least in part – not just haphazard fluctuations, reversed from one observation to the other; rather, they are subject to some regularity or trend. To these trend changes we shall now turn.

---

[6]Excluding the series of 1952, the Coefficients of Concordance would become 0.843 for exports and 0.776 for imports. This supports the inference drawn before, namely, that the similarities in the system become much more pronounced if 1952 is excluded and that without 1952 the difference between exports and imports in the degree of regularity appears to be more substantial.

[7]Coefficients of rank correlation between the series for 1973 and 1970 have also been calculated for all goods (152) for which indexes of income level are available for these two years, rather than just the 108 for which observations exist for all the periods. These coefficients are 0.883 for exports and 0.809 for imports – just slightly lower than the respective coefficients shown in table 8.1.

The main device by which the trend movement of each good's position is examined is by fitting a (linear) regression to the six observations available for the good – the observations being presented again by rank positions rather than by absolute levels of the income-level index.[8] It would of course be a rare coincidence if any good is found, in this way, not to have changed its position at all (namely, to have a zero slope of the fitted regression line). Indeed, no such good is found. It is something else, however, to have a *significant* trend-line movement; this, evidently, cannot be expected in all cases. Requiring significance at the 5% level, only a minority of the goods are found to have demonstrated significant trend changes over time in their positions. These goods are presented in table 8.2: part A records the significant trends in exports, whereas part B shows similar changes in import positions.

Of the 108 goods covered in the present context, 38 appear to have manifested significant trend changes of their income levels of exports; in 23 of these, the relative income level has increased over time, whereas in the other 15 it has decreased.[9] In imports, the respective numbers are 28, for upward movements, and 16 for downward movements – a total of 44. The number of goods subject to this part of the investigation becomes hence substantially smaller than the total number covered thus far and this may be expected, naturally, to restrict the scope of inferences which may be drawn from these findings.

A first question which would seem to be of interest is the following: Is there any relationship between the movements of income levels of exports and of imports, of various goods? The "product cycle" interpretations of changes over time would be radically different with different directions of association. A *negative* association would mean that when a good's position in the ladder of income level of exports declined, the relative position of its income level of imports increased. That is, that richer countries have tended to export relatively less, and import more, of this good and vice versa for poorer countries. This would indicate a change in the nature of trade and specialization conforming with a factor-proportions prediction of trade patterns, or of anticipated changes in trade patterns following from technological changes. A change in a country's factor endowments, or in technology, would shift its pattern of specialization, leading it to export more of one good and import more of another.

A *positive* association of changes in export and import income levels would, on the other hand, be expected from a Linder's pattern of trade. In this scheme, we recall, countries of a given level of income exchange among them a certain range

---

[8] This is justified by the same reasons which applied earlier to the use of the ranked form in looking for similarities over the years. In ranking, the highest income level is assigned the value of 1 – the *lowest* value. Hence, a *negative* slope indicates an *upward* trend and a positive slope, a downward trend.

[9] Although the *average* ranking positions of the goods must always remain the same (with a given number of goods), there is no logical reason to expect the number of upward and downward movements to be equal. This is *a fortiori* true for the numbers of *significant* upward and downward changes.

Table 8.2. Goods with significant trend movements of income levels

A. Exports

	Increasing income level				Decreasing income level		
SITC	Slope	R^2			SITC	Slope	R^2
001	−0.101	0.939			053	0.144	0.620
012	−0.247	0.993			091	0.411	0.565
023	−0.131	0.629			121	0.243	0.603
024	−0.212	0.903			212	0.226	0.505
025	−0.141	0.853			242	0.215	0.781
032	−0.046	0.634			263	0.473	0.570
251	−0.375	0.913			276	0.187	0.508
266	−0.107	0.700			332	0.201	0.788
282	−0.481	0.645			341	0.530	0.519
321	−0.520	0.923			541	0.114	0.662
531	−0.426	0.762			611	0.072	0.588
561	−0.138	0.635			629	0.124	0.797
641	−0.126	0.502			631	0.075	0.581
653	−0.031	0.517			665	0.058	0.650
655	−0.110	0.930			682	0.122	0.716
666	−0.091	0.856					
681	−0.107	0.730					
685	−0.057	0.705					
711	−0.326	0.750					
733	−0.099	0.691					
861	−0.214	0.908					
862	−0.260	0.773					
864	−0.357	0.764					

of goods, whereas countries who share a different level of income would mainly trade by exchanging among them a different class of goods. When a good is found to have changed, over time, its origin of exports from richer to poorer countries, it should also be expected to change its import destination to poorer countries – hence a positive rather than a negative association of the income-level positions of exports and imports.

With the small number of observations available, drawing formal statistical inferences must become a futile attempt for the purpose on hand, and we would rather have to resort to more intuitive and casual observations. Looking at the two parts of table 8.2, it appears that neither negative nor positive associations emerge as anything close to a rule. First, of a total of 82 significant changes (38 in exports and 44 in imports), only 32 are common to the exports and imports of the same good, yielding thus just 16 goods in which significant changes have taken place on both the export and the import side. In the 50 other cases, a significant movement of the export position is not accompanied by a move of the import position, or vice versa. Thus, for the large majority of goods no association of

Table 8.2. (*Continued*)

B. Imports

Increasing income level			Decreasing income level		
SITC	Slope	R^2	SITC	Slope	R^2
011	−0.224	0.728	012	0.114	0.512
013	−0.350	0.584	061	0.237	0.580
024	−0.142	0.513	071	0.212	0.537
025	−0.184	0.878	074	0.136	0.551
043	−0.110	0.541	231	0.282	0.540
044	−0.048	0.644	266	0.533	0.686
051	−0.154	0.955	283	0.155	0.825
054	−0.203	0.893	421	0.078	0.682
055	−0.226	0.616	561	0.115	0.710
072	−0.171	0.689	641	0.326	0.962
112	−0.217	0.586	667	0.402	0.923
221	−0.114	0.696	685	0.446	0.805
271	−0.049	0.675	712	0.325	0.980
281	−0.217	0.760	734	0.195	0.648
282	−0.034	0.750	864	0.274	0.732
321	−0.139	0.763	892	0.070	0.644
332	−0.242	0.632			
341	−0.632	0.808			
611	−0.110	0.601			
629	−0.203	0.667			
711	−0.109	0.518			
714	−0.220	0.970			
732	−0.316	0.818			
735	−0.104	0.496			
821	−0.378	0.633			
841	−0.365	0.821			
851	−0.697	0.729			
861	−0.053	0.746			

movements can be established at all – a finding that would seem to be somewhat surprising, since one may have expected forces which affect exports of a good to also influence its imports, in one way or another. A reasonable interpretation of such finding would seem to be that such influences do exist, but that they are of more than one nature (that is, explained by more than one hypothesis of the origins of trade) and tend often to offset each other in the net outcome. Of the 16 goods for which significant movements over time are found for both exports and imports, in the majority – 10 cases – the association of the two is negative. But with the small numbers involved, the appearance of a majority of this size must be of a very limited value. Perhaps the only phenomenon worth noting is that in all cases in which the income level of imports has declined and the position of exports too has changed significantly – 6 cases altogether – the association is negative: the in-

Table 8.3. Average attributes of goods with trend changes

Trade flow by trend of income level	Capital per man ($thousands) (1)	Wages per man ($thousands) (2)	Index of scale economies (3)	Consumer goods ratio (4)	First-trade date (distance of year from 1970) (5)	Index of product differentiation (6)
Exports						
Increasing	18.4	6.0	0.062	0.351	25.1	0.77
Decreasing	12.0	5.6	0.026	0.467	26.7	0.61
Imports						
Increasing	13.3	5.7	0.027	0.537	28.5	0.67
Decreasing	16.2	6.1	0.092	0.306	23.4	0.70

come level of exports has tended to increase. But, once more, the numbers in-volved are too small to justify any generalization.

Next question, probably the most important in a study of a time path of the pattern of income levels, is: Are there any common attributes of goods whose in-come level of exports has tended to go upward vs. goods which have shown a downward trend of their income level? And similarly, may such common features be found in comparing the two categories in imports? The existence of any such features would express the nature of goods specialization in which has tended to shift from the rich to the poor, or vice versa.

To test the possibility of existence of such attributes, and their nature, resort will be made again to the variables quantified in Hufbauer's study, on which the tests performed in the last chapter have drawn.[10] Table 8.3 presents the (un-weighted) average values of each of the six variables: Capital per man; wages per man; an index of scale economies; the ratio of the good's use for direct consump-tion rather than as an intermediate input (or capital good) in the production pro-cess; a "first-trade date" (the higher the figure, the *older* the product); and an index of product differentiation.[11]

No two average values are similar, naturally, to each other. But the variance of the measures *within* each of the four groups examined is very high, so that most

[10] Hufbauer (1970), table A.2. The main element which one would probably wish to test and which is missing in these measures is the degree of technological innovation involved in the production of each good – a prominent element in "product cycle" hypotheses. See Posner (1961) and Vernon (1966).

[11] It will be recalled that the required data are provided in the source fully for goods in the major SITC categories 5–8 and only for a sample of goods included in the categories 0–4. Hence, data are missing for some of the goods covered in table 8.2. Table 8.3, thus, refers to the following numbers of goods; in exports, 16 (out of 23) in the group of upward-moving trend and 10 (out of 15) in the down-ward-moving group; and in imports, 14 (out of 28) in the upward-moving group and 12 (out of 16) of the other.

differences among the average sizes for the group are of very low significance. In comparing averages among the two groups in exports, differences in only two measures are found to be significant (at the 5% level), and these are *underlined*: the measure of scale economies and the ratio of consumer goods. The conclusions which emerge from this comparison thus seem to be that two common attributes of goods which have tended to become increasingly exported by richer countries may be identified. First, they are subject to a large impact of the factor of scale economies, relatively to goods whose exports have tended to shift from richer to poorer countries; and, second, the former goods are destined relatively little for final consumption, compared with goods increasingly appropriated by lower-income countries.

In comparison of the two groups of goods in *imports*, it is again precisely the same two variables in which significant changes among the averages appear. Higher-income countries thus are seen to have tended to increase their shares of imports of goods which are subject to a low impact of the factor of scale economies and which are destined heavily to final consumption, in comparison with goods which have tended to be increasingly imported by low-income countries.

It will be immediately apparent that these common attributes are in *opposite* directions in the export and import comparisons. That is, whereas high-income countries have tended to increase their shares in exporting "high-scale economies" goods, they have tended to decrease their shares in total imports of such goods. Likewise, exports of goods which are destined in a relatively high proportion for final consumption have become increasingly the domain of lower-income countries, whereas their imports have tended to shift to higher-income countries.[12] Such movements in opposite directions would be expected from "orthodox", factor-proportions hypotheses of determinants of patterns of trade, while a Linder-type hypothesis would predict that similar features should be shared by goods of which a given income-class of countries tends to both increase its export and its import shares in world trade.

As a further test of the role of the two attributes, correlations have been run between them and the *slopes* of the regression lines of the indexes of income level of exports and of imports (in the ranked form). This would show not only differences in *averages* of categories, but consistent patterns of effect. If, for instance, the larger the importance of the factor of scale economies, the more should its position of income level of exports rise over time, a correlation between these two variables should be found. The rank-correlation coefficients which have been calculated are presented in table 8.4, with significance levels in parentheses. They

---

[12] It should be noted that the averages presented are derived *partly* from the same goods; but in another part they refer to goods which appear only in one of the export groups but not in imports – or vice versa.

Table 8.4. Correlation between attributes and trends of exports and imports

Attribute	Exports	Imports
Scale economies	−0.240 (0.25)	0.150 (0.49)
Consumer goods ratio	0.191 (0.36)	−0.375 (0.08)

Rank-correlation coefficients with slopes of trend lines; significance levels in parentheses.

appear to show the same directions of impact as the calculations of averages,[13] but the significance levels are quite low – as might have been expected from the rather small number of observations available here. In a weak way, thus, these correlations support the inferences that the existence of a strong measure of scale economies in an industry leads to a tendency of the good's income level to increase over time, whereas a high ratio of sales for final consumption tends to contribute to a downward trend of the good's income level of exports. For imports, the reverse tendencies hold – with a particularly poor significance in the case of the impact of scale economies, but a relatively high level of significance when the factor of the ratio of sales for final consumption is involved.

The appearance of opposite signs in the relationship of attributes to changes in export vs. import patterns conforms, it should be noted, to the inferences drawn from the cross-section study of the last chapter. There, whenever a variable appeared to have a significant impact on the income level of exports, it would appear as a rule to have an opposite impact on the income level of imports. The two variables which are seen in the present analysis to have had a significant impact on *changes* appeared, in the cross-section study, to have had similar impacts on *positions* (although in that analysis several other variables have also been seen to have had significant influences). The degree of importance of the economies of scale factor thus seems both to contribute to a high-income level of exports, at a given time, and to a tendency over time to keep shifting to a higher-income level; and to opposite tendencies when the effect on the income level of imports is concerned. The higher the ratio of sales for final consumption of the good, on the other hand, the *lower* tends to be its income level of exports at a given point in time, and the more likely it is to be subject to a downward movement of this income level with time; while the opposite tendencies hold for imports. The results of the time series study and the cross-section study thus conform to each other both in their inferences about the impact of these two specific variables and in the

---

[13] It should be recalled that a *negative* slope (in the ranked form) indicates an *increasing* income level. Thus, the smaller (algebraically) is the slope, the more does the income level rise, or the less does it fall. Hence, the negative correlation found, for instance, between the measure of scale economies and the slope in exports, indicates that the more important the factor of scale economies, the stronger the tendency of the income level of exports to rise, and the weaker its tendency to fall.

support they give to expectations of trade patterns which would originate from "conventional" hypotheses of the determinants of trade and specialization.

Appendix

Table 8.A.1. Indexes of income level of exports, 1952–1973

SITC code	1952	1955	1960	1965	1970	1973	Average, 1952–1973
001	30.8	28.2	32.2	40.6	45.5	60.9	39.7
011	43.1	50.2	47.1	49.7	48.4	58.6	49.5
012	42.4	42.3	43.7	56.3	62.3	74.9	53.7
013	42.8	44.8	37.1	42.5	46.1	58.3	45.3
022	51.1	59.0	57.3	62.5	55.2	70.1	59.2
023	36.2	44.8	48.3	54.0	52.6	69.1	50.8
024	33.1	38.7	44.2	50.8	53.3	71.7	48.6
025	41.5	35.2	36.7	46.7	48.3	69.4	46.3
031	43.0	40.7	30.0	43.5	43.3	46.8	41.2
032	36.2	16.4	18.2	27.1	36.9	52.0	31.1
041	83.6	75.8	80.6	70.8	78.6	88.3	79.6
042	72.9	21.0	32.8	42.1	48.2	53.2	53.3
043	69.1	76.6	75.0	65.3	63.1	78.4	71.3
044	96.9	92.3	64.2	75.3	65.1	81.7	79.3
045	77.6	65.9	80.4	81.7	71.1	76.0	75.5
046	69.4	71.9	83.5	70.7	58.8	72.2	71.1
048	52.4	35.1	38.8	48.8	52.3	71.1	49.8
051	30.7	25.5	30.1	28.7	30.3	30.8	29.4
052	40.3	63.3	49.2	25.1	19.9	40.1	39.7
053	52.7	52.1	53.6	43.1	41.4	43.9	47.8
054	44.5	39.6	41.4	38.7	41.2	47.5	42.2
055	47.3	15.5	17.9	20.8	29.3	44.5	29.2
061	35.9	27.7	26.1	21.9	22.8	24.7	26.5
071	11.8	6.9	9.0	7.0	8.9	11.4	9.2
072	29.1	8.7	12.4	10.1	10.3	16.8	14.6
074	16.4	5.5	4.0	4.0	3.8	10.1	7.3
081	49.3	35.7	36.0	50.1	54.5	58.5	47.4
091	76.6	75.0	33.5	40.9	44.7	68.1	56.5
112	41.4	40.9	41.4	47.9	44.9	54.3	45.1
121	69.0	59.1	69.3	49.4	61.0	54.9	60.5
122	63.9	67.3	73.4	67.6	66.4	71.7	68.4
211	50.7	37.9	33.9	47.8	48.4	60.7	46.6
212	66.5	74.4	45.2	52.0	47.0	69.3	59.1
221	75.6	47.3	52.2	56.4	72.6	73.9	63.0
231	84.4	12.1	18.2	24.6	24.8	29.9	32.3
242	63.5	44.7	26.6	36.7	40.5	37.4	41.6
243	62.4	51.8	54.2	57.4	63.5	69.6	60.0

Table 8.A.1. (*Continued*)

SITC code	1952	1955	1960	1965	1970	1973	Average, 1952–1973
251	59.9	59.5	64.2	68.4	77.0	80.8	68.3
262	46.0	49.0	47.1	47.3	48.6	58.3	49.4
263	81.4	38.3	62.8	31.6	24.9	33.6	45.4
264	3.9	3.0	3.4	3.0	3.8	9.7	4.5
265	32.8	22.1	29.2	18.9	15.4	31.8	25.0
266	38.7	40.3	42.1	43.4	49.8	68.0	47.1
267	53.4	30.0	34.0	36.9	58.3	79.7	48.7
271	58.4	13.9	7.2	15.1	6.7	32.1	22.2
276	59.1	64.7	52.2	39.7	46.8	60.2	53.8
281	50.2	49.6	49.1	46.3	43.2	51.5	48.3
282	46.6	79.8	73.6	73.1	79.8	84.1	72.8
283	43.2	33.1	25.8	37.9	46.9	39.6	37.8
284	60.8	78.7	86.8	63.8	69.7	75.3	72.5
285	74.4	71.4	70.2	59.1	71.7	59.5	67.7
292	40.4	27.9	27.9	33.5	35.3	53.4	36.4
321	59.3	59.2	61.7	68.1	78.4	85.1	68.6
331	52.1	33.1	47.1	19.1	21.5	23.5	32.7
332	60.7	47.8	54.3	46.6	38.9	38.5	47.8
341	74.8	100.0	84.0	68.0	67.5	65.7	76.7
411	70.9	80.9	75.1	79.2	82.3	80.5	78.2
421	57.2	43.0	69.7	61.1	48.9	50.5	55.1
512	65.1	60.9	61.3	63.7	65.7	75.0	65.3
513	51.5	52.5	62.5	57.6	62.5	69.2	59.3
531	47.0	35.2	50.3	57.5	61.8	81.1	55.5
533	64.0	75.9	67.3	59.5	55.1	71.0	65.5
541	68.5	64.0	60.8	60.2	60.6	71.3	64.2
561	43.3	46.7	46.9	54.2	63.4	68.3	53.8
599	61.1	65.9	76.2	62.7	64.1	72.8	67.1
611	47.1	43.2	31.3	34.5	29.0	44.7	38.3
629	62.7	57.0	60.9	53.9	53.8	65.6	59.0
631	51.5	47.2	32.6	36.8	43.9	50.9	43.8
641	65.4	62.3	57.1	64.3	69.1	76.6	65.8
642	59.9	32.7	45.0	49.6	54.6	68.9	51.8
651	38.7	36.8	42.7	44.9	47.8	56.5	44.6
652	44.5	40.2	36.3	37.1	38.9	47.1	40.7
653	41.9	39.1	35.6	43.8	45.3	56.9	43.8
655	43.0	40.0	37.2	46.5	52.4	68.5	47.9
656	52.0	29.3	15.9	41.9	16.7	40.5	32.7
657	39.2	42.6	39.4	35.4	39.9	56.2	42.1
661	41.1	34.9	27.7	30.8	32.6	46.5	35.6
662	52.1	22.3	43.9	38.7	47.6	62.2	44.5
664	49.2	57.2	44.2	63.5	53.8	70.7	56.4
665	57.0	56.2	46.2	49.9	50.7	66.1	54.4
666	31.5	29.8	27.8	40.3	42.0	61.5	38.8

Table 8.A.1. (*Continued*)

SITC code	1952	1955	1960	1965	1970	1973	Average, 1952–1973
667	40.1	36.5	35.0	40.9	41.1	50.5	40.7
681	38.5	30.5	22.8	48.3	45.3	62.3	41.3
682	55.6	40.2	45.2	42.9	38.3	43.0	44.2
683	64.6	63.7	54.8	64.5	68.8	74.2	65.1
684	58.9	57.4	63.0	61.7	66.7	69.9	62.9
685	38.9	35.4	34.9	45.7	44.8	57.6	42.9
686	55.0	48.4	49.9	48.7	56.9	64.5	53.9
687	33.2	23.1	23.3	20.0	10.0	19.1	21.5
711	55.1	55.0	57.1	68.5	70.0	76.9	63.8
712	71.0	70.4	74.7	71.6	68.3	75.9	72.0
714	67.9	62.7	62.3	68.4	70.8	75.5	67.9
715	60.9	75.5	66.1	63.1	63.7	77.4	67.8
731	50.9	55.4	65.4	63.3	65.3	69.8	61.7
732	65.5	65.3	57.7	61.5	66.1	76.2	65.4
733	42.6	38.4	42.2	52.6	51.1	66.8	49.0
734	56.8	91.4	87.6	79.0	85.1	87.2	81.2
735	44.4	48.1	43.9	46.0	52.8	66.8	50.3
812	59.2	85.8	79.4	61.9	54.9	67.8	68.2
821	54.6	42.2	39.9	50.7	54.6	67.9	51.7
841	48.7	38.2	36.7	44.2	42.3	45.3	42.6
851	48.8	25.4	26.3	35.5	36.0	41.1	35.5
861	50.5	52.0	57.7	63.1	65.3	75.1	60.6
862	57.8	61.0	69.1	68.3	71.3	76.8	67.4
864	47.5	34.1	53.0	60.6	59.7	79.7	55.8
891	49.0	56.1	43.9	54.9	55.4	66.8	54.4
892	56.4	58.9	60.8	61.0	60.8	67.6	60.9
899	86.1	48.0	18.8	32.5	33.6	56.5	45.9

Table 8.A.2. Indexes of income level of imports, 1952–1973

SITC code	1952	1955	1960	1965	1970	1973	Average, 1952–1973
001	39.1	36.5	37.9	49.9	45.7	49.6	43.1
011	39.2	43.2	52.5	52.0	58.1	63.6	51.4
012	54.5	43.4	48.0	51.0	43.8	49.6	48.4
013	53.4	63.0	66.7	71.3	72.5	70.9	66.3
022	39.4	9.3	15.1	15.0	17.5	34.9	21.8
023	39.2	42.2	47.2	47.0	41.0	51.4	44.7
024	45.4	46.9	42.6	46.5	49.5	64.8	49.3
025	34.6	23.7	40.7	48.7	48.0	61.0	42.8
031	65.5	58.9	63.5	63.9	63.9	67.7	63.9

Table 8.A.2. (*Continued*)

SITC code	1952	1955	1960	1965	1970	1973	Average, 1952–1973
032	56.4	71.8	67.4	59.7	62.2	62.2	63.3
041	33.2	28.8	26.7	22.7	28.5	30.0	28.3
042	15.6	9.9	7.6	11.5	9.3	16.8	11.8
043	34.3	39.9	43.6	39.6	51.0	56.4	44.1
044	37.0	33.5	35.9	37.6	40.0	51.3	39.2
045	47.5	37.8	40.2	36.7	39.1	54.9	42.7
046	8.0	8.0	8.2	9.0	7.7	12.1	8.8
048	40.8	8.5	23.5	17.5	21.3	49.3	26.8
051	51.2	50.0	51.0	56.0	58.0	66.7	55.5
052	43.1	33.2	44.2	23.2	15.4	54.4	35.4
053	58.9	58.0	46.1	53.1	56.5	67.7	56.7
054	45.7	39.6	42.9	52.4	56.5	63.3	50.1
055	49.8	49.0	48.5	47.8	61.8	68.1	54.2
061	61.2	60.0	63.5	54.1	58.1	52.2	58.2
071	80.8	76.5	76.2	73.7	71.5	76.8	75.9
072	60.9	59.9	59.9	62.5	67.8	69.3	63.4
074	48.2	47.9	48.4	47.7	33.1	40.3	44.3
081	56.7	38.3	42.5	48.5	49.5	59.2	49.1
091	32.0	19.1	10.4	48.9	20.4	44.5	29.2
112	56.6	56.7	60.4	66.2	67.7	68.2	62.6
121	46.0	44.9	52.4	52.1	45.8	59.7	50.2
122	43.1	12.8	15.8	36.7	20.1	43.2	28.6
211	43.5	45.2	47.6	50.2	39.4	52.1	46.3
212	65.1	68.6	69.2	67.1	56.0	70.9	66.2
221	41.6	37.9	40.6	44.1	46.0	60.5	45.1
231	66.3	52.0	42.2	46.2	51.2	53.0	51.8
242	45.5	41.9	35.0	35.8	39.8	53.4	41.9
243	51.9	52.9	53.7	55.3	54.4	65.6	55.6
251	54.3	54.3	56.6	57.1	55.3	61.9	56.6
262	50.0	48.2	45.1	49.6	42.8	55.6	48.6
263	30.6	32.9	30.4	35.0	36.7	43.9	34.9
264	38.6	41.4	41.3	31.0	37.4	42.8	38.8
265	59.7	40.2	43.7	29.1	11.4	55.3	39.9
266	67.2	69.9	33.8	26.4	37.1	46.3	46.8
267	51.8	20.5	21.0	20.8	29.7	38.6	30.4
271	38.5	24.8	32.8	38.2	38.7	51.7	37.5
276	55.5	83.2	74.4	60.0	51.9	58.7	64.0
281	41.8	50.9	53.7	54.9	55.1	67.6	54.0
282	30.9	30.8	24.9	33.0	35.6	45.6	33.5
283	64.2	65.2	60.7	57.3	56.6	64.8	61.5
284	46.4	48.4	30.2	42.9	50.7	64.8	47.2
285	54.8	61.8	64.1	54.2	45.1	71.9	58.7
292	55.8	56.3	56.8	57.5	57.7	64.7	58.1
321	37.1	37.4	43.1	45.0	46.8	60.4	45.0
331	48.0	48.9	56.0	49.2	48.4	55.5	51.0

Table 8.A.2. (*Continued*)

SITC code	1952	1955	1960	1965	1970	1973	Average, 1952–1973
332	47.0	39.4	57.9	54.6	56.4	67.7	53.8
341	41.3	31.2	22.8	64.4	67.6	73.0	50.1
411	37.4	26.1	31.6	35.1	21.8	44.6	32.8
421	44.6	42.1	37.7	29.9	32.8	41.1	38.0
512	47.6	40.1	42.1	46.7	48.5	53.5	46.4
513	49.4	45.8	61.7	47.9	53.9	56.2	52.5
531	37.0	8.2	8.2	20.3	25.3	45.2	24.0
533	38.9	24.1	26.6	26.3	44.1	48.2	34.7
541	34.2	28.4	28.8	34.5	35.8	41.9	33.9
561	50.8	39.5	40.5	34.3	38.6	37.4	40.2
599	43.4	36.8	34.4	35.6	39.5	46.3	39.3
611	45.6	42.2	44.9	47.2	49.4	62.2	48.6
629	41.4	16.7	27.2	37.2	53.8	62.1	39.3
631	56.2	67.2	71.8	74.2	64.7	67.4	66.9
641	73.2	66.3	61.3	60.1	56.5	60.4	63.0
642	45.5	10.5	15.9	22.4	41.9	53.8	31.7
651	37.8	30.8	35.0	40.2	46.2	49.5	39.9
652	42.5	30.0	34.9	39.4	42.2	53.5	40.4
653	61.2	45.2	49.3	54.5	51.0	55.2	52.7
655	56.9	20.8	29.7	43.1	48.0	57.2	42.6
656	50.0	21.7	20.8	28.1	36.8	50.0	34.6
657	59.6	52.8	50.4	55.2	60.2	72.0	58.4
661	38.0	11.8	16.3	20.8	34.7	51.4	28.8
662	45.5	44.0	41.8	40.5	49.7	59.9	46.9
664	51.0	71.7	69.7	61.8	61.7	61.8	63.0
665	47.2	52.6	18.9	34.7	38.6	55.7	41.3
666	66.9	81.3	90.7	88.5	89.5	68.5	80.9
667	74.1	69.5	66.7	61.0	54.9	62.6	64.8
681	56.3	57.0	24.0	45.9	60.8	72.0	52.7
682	56.3	53.5	48.4	54.4	54.2	63.3	55.0
683	75.0	75.3	68.9	72.7	70.4	80.1	73.7
684	53.1	53.8	50.6	57.3	53.6	60.5	54.8
685	73.9	59.0	61.3	55.2	39.9	55.6	57.5
686	49.1	57.4	47.9	48.1	54.5	62.9	53.3
687	80.7	74.7	55.9	62.2	71.7	66.9	68.7
711	46.4	36.2	34.5	44.8	53.7	59.3	45.8
712	64.1	59.8	55.3	50.6	48.5	50.9	54.9
714	40.9	43.0	46.5	52.0	56.4	64.3	50.5
715	51.6	39.0	32.4	43.5	50.6	49.7	44.5
731	36.4	29.8	11.6	10.6	12.9	29.6	21.8
732	45.6	39.4	45.9	49.5	62.9	67.8	51.9
733	47.1	44.7	14.1	23.2	56.3	68.9	42.4
734	61.9	55.0	43.3	50.8	52.3	55.5	53.1
735	34.1	35.4	44.2	43.4	42.2	57.4	42.8

Table 8.A.2. (*Continued*)

SITC code	1952	1955	1960	1965	1970	1973	Average, 1952–1973
812	42.1	41.7	18.8	39.1	48.2	58.3	41.4
821	56.2	46.8	37.3	59.0	65.2	72.6	56.2
841	56.3	53.2	58.1	61.2	65.1	73.2	61.2
851	55.4	26.1	70.2	63.3	73.4	78.8	61.2
861	49.0	49.1	46.8	52.3	54.4	60.0	51.9
862	42.5	58.4	30.0	45.3	49.4	57.7	47.2
864	62.6	60.3	58.1	61.5	50.6	54.7	58.0
891	56.0	62.6	36.4	68.2	66.4	68.2	59.6
892	57.1	55.2	51.4	52.6	55.1	61.3	55.5
899	58.0	35.2	14.5	20.1	64.0	62.1	42.3

CHAPTER 9

THE TERMS OF TRADE BETWEEN POOR AND RICH NATIONS

The long-term movement of the terms of international trade between poor and rich countries has certainly been one of the most important issues, and perhaps most controversial, in both national and international economic policy debates in the post-war era. It is probably one of the very few in which deliberations by economists have contributed materially – for better or for worse – to the shaping of national economic policies; in particular to policies which determine whether the economy would have an "inward" or "outward" looking nature. Much of the operation of the United Nations Organization in the economic sphere has concentrated around this issue. And, to cite a central topic of recent years, the celebrated "New International Economic Order" is essentially again a scheme, or a plan, concerned with the terms of trade between rich and poor.

In the present chapter, the concepts and measurements developed thus far in this part of the study will be applied to the terms-of-trade issue. Before performing the main task of the analysis, however, some mention of the major elements of the debate is in order. Thus, in the chapter's first section, popular theses concerning the movement of the terms of trade will be surveyed briefly and the nature of the statistical measures employed to support, or test, these theses will be critically examined. In the second section, the alternative measure will be proposed, and its nature and method of estimation discussed. The third section shall present the basic data constructed for the purpose and draw the salient inferences. Then, in the final section these will be contrasted with the inferences drawn by traditional methods and from the existing empirical literature. An appendix will provide some discussion of the nature and quality of the price data constructed for this study.

1. The terms-of-trade issue

The terms-of-trade argument, as it has been put forward in much of the economic literature, has two main strands, not necessarily related to each other: One is concerned with the *movement* of the terms of trade, over time, whereas the other involves their *position* at a given point of time.

The first version states that the terms of trade have manifested a long-term trend favoring the rich nations in their trade with the poor. This may be based either on statistical investigations of past development and their extrapolation into the future, or on a priori reasoning leading to expectations of this nature, or both. From this should follow certain national and international policies, in the direction of changing this presumed movement of relative prices, changing the structural pattern of specialization of economies, or making the gainers from the presumed movement compensate the losers.

The second variety consists of the argument that at any given point of time, the terms of trade are in some sense "unfair" to the poor nations. The nature of this "unfairness" may, again, vary in different arguments. It may mean that the gains from trade and specialization are appropriated overwhelmingly – or at least in an "excessively" large measure – by the rich partners. Sometimes this is extended to the point where it is argued that not only do the poor nations gain little, but they may actually be losing from international trade. In other versions, the "unfairness" may be based on something like the double-factoral terms-of-trade concept, but in a static sense. Specifically, it is argued – or implied – that a unit of labor invested in the rich country's production buys, through trade, much more than a unit of labor's product of the poor nation. The policy implications from this strand of argument call, again, primarily for schemes of intervention in the market determination of prices and for compensation. This line of reasoning is sometimes extended to movements over time – thus blending with the previous strand. That is, the "unfairness" is interpreted in the sense that the double-factoral terms-of-trade change continuously against the poor.

The present study will be concerned solely with the first version of the topic, that is, with changes over time in the international terms of trade rather than with the degree of their "fairness". And it will involve – along with the overwhelming part of the empirical literature on the issue – the "commodity" terms of trade, rather than the "factorial" terms.

The "terms-of-trade" debate in a sense has been played only on one half of the field. There seem to be several popular arguments leading to a priori expectations of a *downward* trend of the terms of trade of the poor and various empirical pieces of evidence offered to support this expectation. Counter arguments are then presented to refute the a priori analysis; and to deflate the empirical support. But there is apparently no widely-accepted analysis, or empirical evidence, leading to a general expectation of a favorable trend of the terms of trade of the poor.

The popular theses of a long-term deterioration of the poor nations' terms of trade are of three varieties, with some similarities and overlap of the three (besides, of course, their common inferences).[1] First, most widely held, and apparently the

---

[1] For a critical survey, as well as a development of a complete model of his own, see Findlay (1980).

one with the most substantial impact on policy, is the Prebisch–Singer thesis.[2] This identifies, implicitly or explicitly, the income level of countries with given structures of trade: poor nations export primary goods and import processed, manufactured goods, whereas rich nations export manufactures and import primary goods. For a variety of reasons, in turn, the relative price of primary goods vs. manufactures is expected to fall. The empirical support offered is based on changes in the relative price of primary goods vs. manufactures from about 1870 to World War II. These, in turn, are inferred in the most widely publicized version of the thesis – that of Prebisch – from the terms of trade of Britain during that period.

The second thesis is that of Lewis (1954). It still assumes, implicitly, that poor nations export primary goods, but its argument is not concerned with the relative price of primary goods. Rather, it is related directly to the country. It argues, in essence, that a combination of foreign investment in the export branches of the underdeveloped economy and the existence in it of an excess supply of factors (specifically of labor) leads to an infinitely elastic supply of its exported goods, whereas supply elasticities of the developed nations are finite. Hence, a general expansion is expected to lead to a deterioration of the terms of trade of the poor.

Finally, a more recent version – yet again, apparently very popular – is the "unequal exchange" thesis of Emmanuel (1972). The thesis appears to be a mixture of the static, "unfairness" argument with the expectation of a time trend of deterioration of the terms of trade of the poor. In caricature, this thesis is based on the notion that rich countries enjoy favorable terms of trade simply because they are rich; and the poor, inversely, suffer from unfavorable terms because they are poor (partly this involves an element similar to the Lewis type "unlimited supply" of labor – or, better, the Malthusian subsistence level of wages). The richer the nation becomes, therefore (relative to its poor partner), the more favorable become its terms of trade. The income position of the country rather than its pattern of specialization and trade, as a source of its expected trend of terms of trade, is strongly emphasized in this thesis. Moreover, as an extension, a dynamic "reverse Midas touch" element is incorporated into this thesis, namely: Any good which enjoys favorable terms of trade while being in the production and export domain of the rich nations is expected to have the terms of trade trend reversed once its production and export are taken over by the poor.[3]

---

[2] Prebisch (1950) and Singer (1950).

[3] "... A study of the specific nature of the products concerned ... fails to provide us with a key to the explanation of century-long tendencies in the terms of trade ... There is a very simple reason for this failure, namely, that there is no such tendency characteristic of certain products or certain categories of products. The worsening of the terms of trade for primary products, is an optical illusion. It results from a mistaken identification of the exports of the rich countries with the export of manufactured goods and of the exports of the poor countries with the export of primary products.

The copper of Zambia or the Congo and the gold of South Africa are no more primary than coal, which was only yesterday one of the chief exports of Great Britain; sugar is about as much 'manufactured' as soap or margarine and certainly more 'manufactured' than Scotch whisky or the great wines

The empirical evidence found in the literature is, by and large, confined to the first thesis, that is, it explores changes in the relative price of primary goods to manufactures. Critical examinations of this evidence abound and I do not intend to repeat them here.[4] Some basic points should be mentioned, however, before proposing what appears to me to be an adequate approach to the empirical study.

It is by now generally recognized – and well borne out by the findings of the present study – that the identification of "primary goods" with "exports of poor nations" is misleading. Hence, the relative price of primary goods to manufactures is likely to deviate substantially from the relative price of the trade of the poor vs. the trade of the rich; it might possibly not only give the wrong answer so far as size is concerned, but also yield the wrong sign.

To correct it, it has often been suggested that primary goods should be subdivided into those which are the domain of the poor and those which are exported by the rich. Similarly, presumably, manufactures would have to be so subdivided – although this would be much more difficult, since rarely do the poorer nations export the lion's share of any manufactured good (provided the "good" is not so narrowly classified as to make almost each country's exports a separate "good"). Such a procedure would certainly yield some improvement, and probably help to at least avoid a totally misleading answer. But it would still be highly deficient. How are goods to be classified into the sub-categories? Would it be simply a 50% rule – any good more than half of its exports originate in poor countries be classified in one sub-category, other goods in its alternative? If so, does that imply that the relative price of a good fifty-one percent of which are exported by the poor carries the same significance for the terms of trade of the poor nations as the price of a good of which they export ninety-nine percent of the world total? Obviously this again would be misleading. One would appropriately have to carry the subdivisions further; namely, not into just two major sub-categories (four in all – two "primary" and two "manufactured" categories), but to several such groups and the more, presumably, the better (that is, the closer the approximation of the result to the terms of trade of poor vs. rich). But this leads, eventually, to

---

of France ... And yet the prices of the former decline while those of the latter rise, and the only common characteristic is that they are, respectively, the products of poor countries and the products of rich countries.

Textiles were formerly among the pillars of the wealth of the industrialized countries and Britain's warhorse; since they have become the specialty of poor countries, their prices hardly suffice to provide a starvation wage for the workers who produce them and an average profit for the capital invested in their production, even where the technique employed is the most up-to-date.

Are there really certain products that are under a curse, so to speak; or is there ... a certain category of countries that, whatever they undertake and whatever they produce, always exchange a larger amount of their national labor for a smaller amount of foreign labor?" (Emmanuel, *Ibid.*, pp. xxx–xxxi.)

[4] For an excellent recent discussion, see Spraos (1980).

the conclusion that each good should be looked at separately, according to the share of poor vs. rich countries in its trade – an approach which is indeed incorporated in the measure which will soon be submitted.

Another approach, more direct (and, in that sense, relevant to the Emmanuel version rather than to the Prebisch–Singer thesis) is to measure changes in relative levels of prices of categories of *countries*, rather than of goods. In the simplest way, countries would be classified into two categories, "poor" and "rich", and the relative price of the two should be studied. This is done, for instance, in the U.N. measure of the terms of trade of "developing" vs. "developed" countries. While this is an improvement over the former procedure, it is still inadequate. Again, how should we proceed to classify (*countries*, in this case, rather than goods)? Should we – as is the actual practice – have just two divisions, "poor" and "rich" ("developing" and "developed"), using some (necessarily arbitrary) dividing line? But if that is what we do, the necessary implication would be that the change in the relative price of the poorest country (or the richest country) has the same significance as the change in the terms of trade of a country which is just below (just above) the dividing line. If our concern is that of the relative position of "poor" vs. "rich", any conclusion involving such implication must be misleading. As in the case of commodities, thus, we would have to resort to finer classifications of countries, according to the degree of "poorness" or "richness", and the finer (that is, the closer is each division to a given income level, without a dispersion within the group), the better is the measurement. This distinction, it should be remarked – between one degree of "poorness" or of "richness" and another – should have been applied also to the classification of *goods*. That is, the position of each good should be determined not only by the fraction of its trade conducted by "poor" or by "rich" countries in a general way, but by the degree of such richness or poorness of each of the trading nations.

2. Measurement of terms of trade through income levels: The approach

This, precisely, is the nature of the index of income level of trade – the basic tool applied in the present part of the study. A good's index of income level of exports will be higher, we recall, the richer are the countries which export it, the degree being determined by two elements: the higher the proportions of rich countries in total exports of the good and the richer these countries are. The index thus incorporates the elements argued earlier to be necessary in order to indicate the "richness" or "poorness" of the exporting countries of any given good; similarly, this is done for imports. In its formulation, the index of income level of trade grants the two elements equal weights.

If, now, the change in price of each good over time is found, we will be able to determine the terms of trade of poor and rich nations. A relative increase in the price of a good with a high-income level of exports indicates an improvement of the terms of trade of the rich countries, whereas an increase in the price of a good with low-income exports level favors the poor countries. Similarly, an increase in the price of a good with a high-income level of *imports* is a deterioration of the terms of trade of the rich, whereas an increased price of a good with a low-income level of imports works against the poor nations.[5]

It will be recalled, from the analysis of the last chapter, that while changes in the relative positions of goods have taken place over the years, a very high degree of regularity seems to have existed in the system all throughout. The *averages* of the levels of each good, over the six observations, thus appear to be meaningful – dispersions around the averages being rather modest. It is hence these averages which will provide, in the present analysis, the first element required for the calculation of the terms of trade.

The other necessary ingredient is the computation of changes, over time, in the price level of each good. "Goods" are obviously defined, for this purpose, in the same way as in the computation of indexes of income levels and the years selected for the calculations are also the same, except that the latest year handled for this purpose has been 1970.[6] A somewhat more elaborate description of the method of derivation of the price data, and a discussion of the extent of reliability which may be attributed to them, will be found in an appendix to this chapter. Only a few essential elements will be pointed out here.

Basically, price changes have been calculated by means of the unit-cost changes, yielded by the division of values by quantities (where values have always been expressed in U.S. dollars, either in the original data or by use of conversion factors). This method is subject to deficiencies which are only too well known, especially when highly processed goods are concerned. Yet, for a comprehensive study of the present nature, it appears to be the only feasible method.

Since price calculations are made for "goods" defined by a given scheme of classification (the SITC), they can naturally be carried out only for that period for which records of trade following this scheme are available. This rules out any time prior to the 1950s. Hence, the results of the present study cannot be compared or contrasted with the inferences offered as evidence in the controversy over the long-term historical trend of the terms of trade. The *method* of investigation proposed here, it should be emphasized, is capable in principle of being used for such long historical stretches, but the availability of comparable data would be quite restricted.

[5]But more precise definitions will be discussed in the next section.

[6]Ending the coverage of the study of prices with 1970 has the virtue of defining a time period which is as "normal" and free of violent fluctuations as one can find in the last two generations – avoiding the tremors of the early post-war and Korean war years, on the one hand, and of the strong cyclical changes of commodity prices in the 1970s, on the other. The trends indicated in this study are therefore subject less severely than usual to the impact of the selection of specific beginning and end years.

Price changes in the present study have been calculated for the periods between each of the points of observation noted in the last chapter; that is, from 1952 to 1955, from 1955 to 1960, and so on. These periodical changes have then been chained, to get the price movement of each good from 1952 to 1970. The period covered in this study of the terms of trade ranges thus over eighteen years – about half of the post-war era.[7]

For 15 of the 108 goods for which income-level indexes are available the computation of price changes could not be adequately carried out – primarily due to changes in classification – leaving thus 93 goods for which both income-level indexes and price indexes have been constructed. Total exports of these goods in 1970 amounted to 56.4% of world exports.

3. Estimates and inferences

The stage is now finally set for the study of the changes in the terms of trade. The basic indexes constructed, of the average income levels of exports and imports of each good and of the price changes of the individual goods, are presented in table 9.1, columns (1) and (2) of which draw the data from, respectively, tables 8.A.1 and 8.A.2 of the last chapter. Almost all of the following analysis is based on these findings.

In interpreting the data and drawing inferences, it will be immediately apparent that the concept of the "terms of trade" is not unique: the development of these terms is appropriately described by more than the change in one ratio. The various ratios involved are presented in table 9.2, where we would have to read both along columns and along rows.

First, one may look at exports, and ask: Have exports of the poor fared better, or worse, than exports of the rich? Dividing all goods into two approximately equal-sized categories (using for that the shares in 1970 total-world exports), we see in table 9.2 that the price level of the high-income-level goods increased, from 1950 to 1972, by 1.189; and the price of the low-income group, by an average of

---

[7] The selection of beginning and end years may, as is well known, bias any inferences concerned with trends of price changes. In principle, it would have been desirable to experiment with alternative intervals. Data limitations do not make this procedure feasible, in the present context; changing either the beginning or the end year – and definitely both – would make the period covered very short and the data themselves less reliable. The end year, 1970, is by all evidence a rather "normal" one, so far as general market conditions are concerned. The start year, 1952, is one in which the Korean boom, which led to a substantial increase of relative prices of primary goods, is still reflected. Hence, the selection of the range between 1952 and 1970 may probably be expected to contain some bias in indicating a decline of relative prices of primary goods.

Table 9.1. Income levels and price changes

| SITC code | Income-level index | | Price Ratio | Percentage in 1970 world exports |
	Exports	Imports	(1970/1952)	
001	39.7	43.1	2.704	0.5
011	49.5	51.4	1.655	1.3
012	53.7	48.4	1.122	0.1
013	45.3	66.3	1.378	0.3
022	59.2	21.9	0.980	0.2
023	50.8	44.7	0.839	0.2
024	48.6	49.3	1.542	0.2
025	46.3	42.8	1.076	0.0
031	41.2	63.9	2.499	0.7
032	31.2	63.3	1.260	0.2
041	79.6	28.3	0.761	1.1
042	53.4	11.8	0.772	0.3
043	71.3	44.1	0.761	0.2
044	79.3	39.2	0.754	0.7
045	75.5	42.7	0.930	0.1
046	71.1	8.8	0.804	0.1
048	49.8	26.8	0.926	0.1
051	29.4	55.5	1.845	1.2
052	39.7	35.4	1.906	0.0
053	47.8	56.7	1.122	0.3
054	42.2	50.1	1.704	0.7
055	29.2	54.2	1.284	0.2
061	26.5	58.2	0.973	1.0
071	9.2	75.9	0.978	1.2
072	14.6	63.4	1.203	0.3
074	7.3	44.3	0.924	0.2
081	47.4	49.1	1.442	0.8
091	56.5	29.2	1.015	0.0
112	45.1	62.6	3.277	0.9
121	60.5	50.2	1.474	0.4
122	68.4	28.6	3.015	0.1
211	46.6	46.3	1.120	0.2
212	59.1	66.2	3.063	0.1
221	63.0	45.1	0.968	0.8
231	32.3	51.8	0.761	0.7
243	60.0	55.6	1.580	1.0
251	68.3	56.6	0.895	1.0
262	49.4	48.6	0.670	0.7
263	45.4	34.9	0.648	0.9
264	4.5	38.8	0.765	0.0
265	25.0	39.9	0.640	0.0
266	47.1	46.8	1.159	0.3
267	48.7	30.4	0.658	0.0
271	22.2	37.5	1.074	0.2
282	72.8	33.5	0.864	0.3
283	37.8	61.5	6.364	1.3

Table 9.1. (*Continued*)

SITC code	Income-level index		Price Ratio	Percentage in 1970 world exports
	Exports	Imports	(1970/1952)	
284	72.5	47.2	2.599	0.2
292	36.4	58.1	3.284	0.4
411	78.2	32.8	0.983	0.1
512	65.3	46.4	0.607	1.7
531	55.5	24.0	1.180	0.2
533	65.5	34.7	2.100	0.2
541	64.2	33.9	1.691	1.0
561	53.8	40.2	0.890	0.5
599	67.1	39.3	1.161	1.0
611	38.3	48.6	1.156	0.1
629	59.0	39.7	1.024	0.6
631	43.8	66.9	1.393	0.4
641	65.8	63.0	0.892	1.7
642	51.8	31.7	1.232	0.2
651	44.6	39.9	0.979	1.1
652	40.7	40.4	2.761	0.6
655	47.9	42.6	1.684	0.3
656	32.7	34.6	1.161	0.1
657	42.1	58.4	1.134	0.2
661	35.6	28.8	1.354	0.1
662	44.5	46.9	2.849	0.2
664	56.4	63.0	1.675	0.3
665	54.4	41.3	1.820	0.1
666	38.8	80.9	1.747	0.1
682	44.2	55.0	1.959	2.1
683	65.1	73.7	2.879	0.4
684	62.9	54.8	1.140	0.8
685	42.9	57.5	0.976	0.0
686	53.9	53.3	0.773	0.1
687	21.5	68.7	1.519	0.1
711	63.8	45.8	2.467	1.7
712	72.0	54.9	1.632	0.9
714	67.9	50.5	2.801	1.6
715	67.8	44.5	1.205	1.5
731	61.7	21.8	2.474	0.2
732	65.4	51.9	1.281	7.6
733	49.0	42.4	1.582	0.2
812	68.2	41.4	1.776	0.2
821	51.7	56.2	1.523	0.5
841	42.6	61.2	1.339	2.0
851	35.5	61.2	1.716	0.7
861	60.6	51.9	1.401	1.3
862	67.4	47.2	1.283	0.2
864	55.8	58.0	0.924	0.2
891	54.4	59.6	1.845	0.6
892	60.9	55.5	1.171	0.6
899	45.9	42.3	1.095	0.4

Table 9.2. Price levels
by groups of income levels (weighted averages, ratio of 1970 to 1952)

Ranking by income level	Exports (1)	Imports (2)	Exports/Imports (= (1)/(2)) (3)
All goods	1.256	1.256	1
(a) Upper half	1.189	1.393	0.854
(b) Lower half	1.334	1.124	1.187
(b)/(a)	1.122	0.807	1.390
Top quintile	1.115	1.506	0.740
2nd quintile	1.221	1.374	0.889
3rd quintile	1.256	1.364	0.921
4th quintile	1.250	1.122	1.114
Bottom quintile	1.508	1.026	1.470

1.334.[8] A relative *improvement* in the position of low-income exports has thus taken place: the ratio of the latter increase to the former is above unity – it is 1.122.

In the same way, one may ask what happened to imports. We see, from the imports column in table 9.2, that the average price of the high-income-level imports increased by 1.393, whereas the price of low-income-level imports increased by 1.124. The ratio of the latter to the former is below unity at 0.807. This is again, a relative *improvement* in the position of poor countries: goods imported by low-income countries manifested a smaller price increase than goods imported by high-income countries.

These comparisons refer, strictly speaking, not to the "terms of trade" – although they are often used in this context. They provide answers, we recall, to the question whether poor nations have fared better or worse than the rich in changes of export prices of the two groups of countries, or of import prices. But these answers do not necessarily indicate the nature of price changes in trade *between* these two groups of countries. If high-income-level exports are also high-income-level imports – that is, if high-income countries export and import the same range of goods, in similar proportions – a relative decline in the price level of these goods (relative, that is, to the price level of other goods) does *not* lead to a deterioration in the position of these countries, since they themselves both export and import the goods whose prices have relatively declined. And the same holds for the apparent improvement in the position of the poor countries. We may then change our question, and ask: In the trade of the rich countries, have export prices risen more, or less, than prices of imports? And similarly, in the trade of the poor.

[8] In all weighted averages, the shares of goods in 1970 total-world exports of goods served for weights. Since end-year values were thus used, harmonic means were calculated.

We see, from line (a) of the third column, that the relative price in the rich countries trade has deteriorated – the terms of trade changed against these countries: the ratio of the export price change to the import price change, for goods in the top half (which are different for exports and imports!), is below unity at 0.854. Similarly – this is now self-evident – the terms of trade of the poor nations have *improved*: the ratio under consideration is 1.187, a relative increase of the price of exports over imports.[9] Dividing the latter ratio by the former, one gets the factor by which the terms of trade of the poorer have improved in relationship to the terms of trade of the richer nations. This factor appears to be 1.390 – a relative improvement of the poor by close to 40%.

All these ratios were based on comparisons of the top half income-level goods with the bottom half (in exports and imports). We may go further to see whether the inferences thus drawn apply also for finer distinctions and whether a consistency, or regularity, appears in the pattern. This is done in two ways. First, still in table 9.2, goods are separated not just into two halves but into quintiles (of roughly equal values, still using for that the 1970 shares in world exports). The pattern noted before appears to be reinforced here and to reflect rather consistent tendencies. With almost no exception, the further down is the export income-level category of the goods, the more has its price level risen; and the further down the income level of imports of a category the less has its price increased. Furthermore, the further down the categories compared, the more has the price of exports increased in relation to the price of imports. In the extremes, the contrast is striking. For the top quintile a substantial deterioration appears: the relative price of exports to imports has fallen to 0.740. For the bottom quintile, on the other hand, the improvement of the terms of trade is just as remarkable: the relative price of exports to imports has risen to 1.470. The ratio of the latter to the former is almost 2, in comparison with about 1.4 when goods were divided into just two categories.[10]

---

[9] In principle, the product of the two ratios (0.854 and 1.187) should be unity. In fact, it is 1.014 – the slight discrepancy being due to rounding and to the fact that the two categories of goods, presumably two "halves", differ slightly in size.

[10] The finer the classification, and the smaller the categories, the more is each category likely to be affected by extreme cases. In the classification into quintiles, the impact of one such extreme good is substantial. This is SITC No. 283 – non-ferrous metal ores – a good whose price recorded more than a six-fold increase. This good is included in the bottom quintile for exports and in the top one for imports. If this good is taken out altogether all the former inferences would still hold, but the sharpness in the positions of the top and bottom quintiles would disappear. Without this good, the price level for the bottom export quintile would be 1.364 (instead of 1.508), and the price for the top import quintile, 1.370 (rather than 1.506). The export to import price ratio would become 0.814 (instead of 0.740) for the top quintile, and 1.329 (instead of 1.470) for the bottom one. Finally, the ratio of the relative price change in the bottom group to that of the top would become the still impressive, but less spectacular figure 1.633 (rather than 1.986).

But the division into quintiles too, although tending to reinforce the former inferences and to show regularity, is still arbitrary. In addition, therefore, regressions of the price changes of the goods have been drawn on the export and import income levels of each good. This has been done for both the original income level and price data and for the rank positions (to diminish the effect of extreme values). The results are about the same in both forms. They support the impression gained so far, although not in an overwhelming way. The relationships appear to be somewhat stronger when the ranked rather than the original-values form of the regressions is used. For exports, the signs of the regression coefficients are negative – that is, the higher the income level of exports, the lower the price increase – but the correlation coefficients are very low, and the results are not reasonably significant (the t values are, respectively, for the original values and the ranks -0.113 and -0.709). On the import side, the coefficients are positive: the higher the income level of the good's imports, the more does its price tend to increase. The correlation coefficients (rs) are still rather low (0.256 for the original values and 0.310 for the ranked form), but the outcomes are significant at the 1% level or better. When, however, *weighted* regressions are calculated, the results appear to be more conclusive on the exports side as well. The correlation coefficients of the export regressions are then -0.168 for the original values, and -0.190 for the ranked form, and both are significant at practically any level. In the imports regressions, the correlation coefficients are, respectively, 0.243 and 0.298; and are also significant at any desired level.

It thus appears that the tendencies of goods to manifest a higher price increase the lower their income level of exports and the higher the income level of imports are indicated by the regressions, but far from any universal empirical law is established. The unmistaken tendencies inferred before, of a deterioration of the terms of trade of the rich and an improvement of the poor nations' position, are thus less the result of a universal pattern of price changes; they are largely the outcome of the price movements of specific, relatively important, exported and imported goods.

I turn now to the verification of the extended Emmanuel thesis (to which I have referred before as the poor's "reverse-Midas touch"). It states that whenever goods are "downgraded" – their exports pass from the rich to the poor – the terms of trade move against them; whereas when exports change their income level of origin upwards – they are becoming the domain of the rich rather than of the poor – the terms of trade tend to favor them. Apparently this variant of the terms-of-trade argument has never been tested, beyond the mention of casual observations as in Emmanuel's own argument. With the availability of the measure of income level of exports, such a test may be readily performed – albeit for the relatively short period to which the present study is confined.

The crucial element for such an examination has been provided by the analysis of the last chapter. There "upward" and "downward" moving goods, in exports and imports, have been distinguished, where an upward movement indicates a tendency of the good's origin or destination, respectively, to move from poorer to richer nations. The findings of that analysis were presented in table 8.2 in the last chapter (ch. 8). For the present purpose, the export data (part A) are the elements required. Of the 38 goods recorded there as having shown a significant upward or downward movement of the index of income level of exports, price data are available (in table 9.1) for 31 goods: 20 goods with an upward movement and 11 goods with a downward trend.

The weighted average price ratio (of 1970 to 1952) of the upward-moving group is 1.226 (the unweighted average is 1.324). The weighted average for the down-ward-moving goods is slightly higher at 1.293 (the unweighted average is 1.488), but the difference appears to be small enough to treat the two averages as roughly equal. By this evidence, thus, the thesis under consideration is refuted, although its reverse would not be established either. The evidence, to repeat, is necessarily weak: besides being applied to a smaller number of observations, over time, covering a relatively short period, it also applies to a drastically reduced range of goods. But it is, apparently, the only evidence produced thus far.

4. Contrasting inferences of alternative approaches

The upshot of the previous section was that by all interpretations of the concept, the terms of trade of the poor nations have improved over the period under con-sideration, and the terms of trade of the rich have deteriorated. It should be inter-esting to compare and contrast this main inference with that which would be yielded by the popular, conventional methods of estimating changes of the terms of trade of the two halves of the world. This will be undertaken in the present section.

To start with, we may use the price estimates made in the present study for individual goods, but apply them in a traditional measurement of the terms of trade. The most popular measure – the yardstick for the Prebisch–Singer thesis – has been the relative price of primary goods to manufactures. This may be derived from table 9.3 (where all averages are, as elsewhere in this study, harmonic means weighted by 1970 export values). It is seen that the price level of all primary goods was, in 1970 (in relation to 1950), 1.180, whereas the price level of all manufactures was 1.307. The ratio of the former to the latter is 0.903.[11] This mea-sure would then show a deterioration of the terms of trade of the "poor" (repre-sented by exports of primary goods) vs. the "rich" (represented by manufactures).

[11]"Primary goods" are defined here as categories 0–4 of the SITC, excluding goods 091 (margarine, shortening), 122 (tobacco manufactures), 266 (synthetic, regenerated fiber) and 267 (waste of textile fabrics). Adherence to the definition used in the U.N. publications, where "primary goods" constitute simply of categories 0–4 (with no omission or addition) would have led to practically no change.

Table 9.3. Price changes, by categories of goods
and of income levels
(Weighted averages, ratio of 1970 to 1952)

	Exports (1)	Imports (2)
Primary goods		
All goods	1.180	1.180
Upper half	1.102	1.433
Lower half	1.266	1.001
Manufactured goods		
All goods	1.307	1.307
Upper half	1.187	1.350
Lower half	1.448	1.271

A sub-division of primary goods, into those exported by the poorer vs. those originating in the richer nations, would go a long way in explaining the contrast between such inference and the tendencies indicated in the present study. It is seen from table 9.3 that the price ratio of the primary goods which, by their indexes of income level, belong to the top half, was only 1.102 – substantially below the average, either for primary goods or for all goods; whereas the price ratio of the lower half was 1.266 – about the same as the average for all goods. A similar relative change took place within the sector of *manufactures.* The price of manufactures belonging to the top half income-level group has increased by 1.187, whereas manufactures belonging to the lower half witnessed a price increase of 1.448. Relative-price changes between poor and rich countries' exports *within* each sector have tended thus to reinforce each other.

But this does not exhaust the difference – the comparison thus far has neglected the *imports* side. Looking at imports of primary goods, we see again a relative improvement in the position of the poor: the price level of the top half income-level imports – that is, imports of the richer countries – increased substantially, the 1970 to 1952 price ratio being 1.433; whereas the price of the lower-half imports remained virtually unchanged and the ratio was 1.001. In the imports of manufactures, the relative change was in the same direction, although it was only mild: the price level of the top-half income level increased by 1.350, while the price of the lower half increased by 1.271. Relative-price changes in each category when distinctions are made among richer and poorer importers thus help to explain why the simple comparison of the price of primary goods to the price of manufactures cannot convey the true impression about the change in the terms of trade of the poor with the rich nations.

Let us now turn to a comparison with the conventional findings provided by the prime source of data on sectoral terms of trade – the United Nations' esti-

Table 9.4. Price indexes, by areas or categories of goods
(ratio of 1970 to 1952 price)

(1) Price level of primary goods	0.958
(2) Price level of manufactured goods	1.215
(3) (= (1)/(2)) Relative price of primary goods	0.788
(4) Price level of exports of developing areas	0.939
(5) Price level of exports of developed areas	1.129
(6) (= (4)/(5)) Relative price of developing areas	0.832
(7) Terms of trade of developing areas	0.942
(8) Terms of trade of developed areas	1.095
(9) Price level of primary-good exports of developing areas	0.915
(10) Price level of primary-good exports of developed areas	0.987
(11) (= (9)/(10)) Relative price of developing areas' primary goods	0.927

Source: Calculated from U.N. *Yearbook of International Trade Statistics* (1961, 1977)

mates. Table 9.4 is based on the *U.N. Yearbook of International Trade Statistics*[12] and presents various measures related to the concept of terms of trade of poor vs. rich nations.

These measures are provided in lines (3), (6), (7) and (8). The first is, again, the commonly-used relative price of primary goods. It shows a decline, from 1952 to 1970 to an even larger extent than the previous use of the present study's price data would indicate. If this were to be taken as the representation of the terms of trade of the poor nations, it would thus show a significant *deterioration*. Line (6) is also derived from the relationship of two sectoral price levels, the two sectors being now not the exports of two categories of goods but those of two categories of countries. This measure indicates again a substantial decline in the relative price of the exports of the poorer countries. Lines (7) and (8) are the most direct measure of the terms of trade, provided from this source. They express the change in the relative price of the *bilateral* trade flows of the two sectors of nations: the price of exports of one to the other vs. the price of its imports from the other.[13] This measure shows again a deterioration of the terms of trade of the poor sector, and an improvement of the terms of trade of the rich – although the change is considerably smaller than those that would be inferred from the previous measures. Thus, instead of the clear indication of improvement yielded by the concept offered in the present study, we get here a consistent inference of a deteriorating position of the poor nations.

[12] The data are drawn from the 1961 and 1977 volumes, but are not specific to these volumes, nor indeed in part to this publication.
[13] The product of lines (7) and (8) should presumably be unity – one is the inverse of the other. In fact, it is close enough at 1.031.

It is interesting to note that a strong contrast between the two alternatives appears when price movements within the sector of primary goods are concerned. In the present study (table 9.3), a substantial *improvement* of the position of exports of poorer countries has appeared; whereas in the data examined now, as can be seen from lines (9) to (11), a relative *deterioration* – albeit slight – appears to have taken place.

Finally, it would have been most useful to apply the prices of *individual* goods from which the U.N.'s sectoral price estimates were derived to the conceptual procedure followed in this study. This would have separated out the effect of using different price data from the effect of adopting a different approach to the study of the terms of trade. Unfortunately, this cannot be carried out, since U.N. price data for individual goods are not available. While the U.N. does calculate individual prices (in a fashion which could be easily transformed into the scheme of the

Table 9.5. Price levels
of primary goods, by groups of income levels (using U.N. individual-prices data)

	Exports (1)	Imports (2)	Exports/Imports (= (1)/(2)) (3)
Ranking by income level			
All goods	1.043	1.043	1
(i) All goods classified into halves			
(a) Upper half	1.014	1.196	0.848
(b) Lower half	1.073	0.940	1.141
(b)/(a)	1.058	0.786	1.346
(ii) All goods classified into quintiles			
Top quintile	0.963	1.143	0.843
2nd quintile	1.090	1.245	0.876
3rd quintile	1.191	1.000	1.191
4th quintile	1.049	1.039	1.010
Bottom quintile	0.884	0.802	1.102
(iii) Goods common to both price sets,[a] U.N. prices			
(a) Upper half	1.042	1.270	0.820
(b) Lower half	1.096	0.877	1.250
(b)/(a)	1.052	0.691	1.522
(iv) Goods common to both price sets,[a] present-study's prices			
(a) Upper half	1.007	1.400	0.719
(b) Lower half	1.231	0.814	1.512
(b)/(a)	1.222	0.581	2.103

[a] This excludes, from the goods covered in (i) and (ii), SITC groups 281, 321, 331 and 421.

3-digit level of the SITC) for most primary goods, and in turn uses these prices in the construction of sectoral-price indexes, no individual U.N. prices exist for manufactures.[14] As a partial substitute, I have applied only the available U.N. prices – namely, prices of primary goods – to the conceptual procedure proposed here.[15] This is presented in table 9.5, which is similar in nature to table 9.2, except that it treats the group of (primary) goods covered by the U.N. individual-price data as if it were the universe of all goods.

From parts (i) and (ii) of table 9.5 it appears that the application of the U.N. prices leads to inferences similar to those found in the present study, although in a less consistent manner: In the international exchange of primary goods, the terms of trade of the poor nations improved during the period under consideration. This indication is similar to that derived earlier from table 9.2. Regressions of U.N. price data on the income-level indexes of exports and imports also yield roughly similar inferences to those reached earlier. The correlation coefficients in exports are mostly negative, but have a very low significance. In imports, all four correlation coefficients (in the original data and the ranked forms, weighted and unweighted) are positive. They are slightly above or slightly below 0.4 and are all significant at the 1% level. Thus, for these goods and using this set of price indexes, the price of imports appears to tend to increase more the richer the importing nations.

In order to isolate completely the effect of the use of different price data, parts (iii) and (iv) of table 9.5 refer only to those primary goods for which price data are available in *both* the U.N. source and the present study. Qualitatively, it appears, the inferences of comparisons derived from the two alternative price sets would be essentially similar, but the improvement in the terms of trade of the poor appears to be more dramatic when the present study's set of prices is used than when the U.N. prices are applied. Thus, it is probable that part – but it could be only a minor part – of the contrast between the inferences of the present study and the indications provided by the conventional, U.N. yardsticks might be due to differences in individual price estimates.[16]

---

[14] In the sector of manufactures, the U.N. estimates are apparently based on the following procedure: Unit-cost calculations are made for a sample of goods (classified at the 5-digit, or even the 7-digit level). These are then aggregated, using some weighting scheme, into the price level of "manufactures" as a whole – with no intermediate stages of aggregation (such as at the 3-digit, or even the 2-digit SITC level).

[15] These individual prices are described in the appendix.

[16] Even so far as the average price change for the category of primary goods as a whole is concerned, differences between the present study's and the U.N.'s individual prices for goods which are commonly covered seem to be less important than differences in *coverage* of this category. For sixteen goods, representing in combination a substantial weight, price estimates are available in the present study but not in the U.N. sources. The weighted average 1970 to 1952 price ratio for these goods is 1.777 – materially higher than the study's average (1.180) for all primary goods. This is substantially affected by one good (SITC 283) – non-ferrous base metal – but even without it the average for the fif-

5. Conclusions

The findings of this analysis have shown an obvious improvement of the terms of trade of the poor nations vs. the rich, during the period from 1952 to 1970. This is contrasted with conventional forms of measurement, which indicate a deterioration of the poor nations' position.

The purpose of this chapter has not been, however, to attempt an establishment of any long-term tendencies of the movement of the terms of trade. The period covered would in any case be much too short for that, and no a priori justifications are offered here which would lead one to expect a long-term tendency of the nature revealed for the period of the study. The main message of this analysis is that verification of the theses suggested for terms-of-trade movements requires an adequate conceptual approach to the estimate. Such an approach is suggested here. That it leads to inferences which are radically different from those yielded by conventional, traditional methods of evaluation only serves to demonstrate the significance and concreteness of the issue. Hopefully, this may contribute to the establishment of badly-required firmer ground for the important discussion of the plight of the poor nations in their trade with the rich.

Appendix: The construction and reliability of price data

As was mentioned in the text, all the price data used in the present study were constructed through unit-cost derivations: values were divided by quantities to yield the price per unit. This was done for all goods, classified by the 3-digit level of the SITC.

The unit-cost calculations are as inclusive and universal as they could be made. They have been carried out separately – for each good – for each country for which any trade in the good was recorded. The results for individual countries were then averaged, using the share of each country in world trade in the good, to yield the general price change for the good in question for the period under consideration. For each good, this unit-cost calculation was made twice: once for exports of the good, once for its imports.

Four periodical price changes were thus calculated: From 1952 to 1955, from 1955 to 1960, from 1960 to 1965 and from 1965 to 1970. The price change of each good between 1952 and 1970 was derived by chaining these periodical changes.

---

teen other goods would be 1.433. On the other hand, the U.N. sources cover four goods for which price data are absent in the present study. Their aggregate weight is also substantial, particularly because they include oil. But the weighted average of their price ratio is 1.053 – quite similar to the average (1.043) for all primary goods (using the U.N.'s set of prices). Hence, this part of the difference in coverage does not contribute to the differences among *averages*.

It would be enough, of course, for one link in the chain (that is, for one periodical price change) to be missing to make the construction of a price change for the good in question impossible. Two reasons have led to such incidents, and hence to the exclusion of 15 out of the 108 goods for which income-level indexes could be derived. One is changes in the classification scheme: in a few instances, a proper matching of the two classification schemes used (the original and the "revised" SITC) made it possible to construct the long-term series of the index of income level of trade of the good, yet, the unit-cost calculation was then still impossible (without, that is, an unduly large amount of work). Second, in a few cases the unit-cost calculations yielded an obviously absurd result. In one or two cases, this may probably be assigned to computational errors. But by and large, this happened in goods for which the unit-cost method might be expected, a priori, to be particularly deficient. Two goods, aircraft and ships, are the most obvious and most important such cases. Of the close to 20% of total-world exports thus excluded, over half are in the oil group (category 3 of the revised SITC). For obvious reasons, these goods are most often separated out, for studies of the terms of trade of poor vs. rich; their exclusion from the present study is thus not a great loss. Other goods excluded, on the other hand, are mostly manufactures, and the reduction of representation of such goods in the study would tend to add an element of tentativeness to the interpretation of its findings.[17]

As mentioned, two indexes of price changes were calculated for each good; one derived from the unit-cost of exports, the other from the imports side. In principle, since world exports of the good are equal to world imports, the two indexes should be identical. For well-known reasons, however, they would be expected to differ in any concrete estimation. To mention these reasons briefly, they are mainly: (a) Exports are recorded f.o.b., and imports c.i.f. A relative change (relative, that is, to the f.o.b. price of the good) in the costs of transportation would create a divergence of the two indexes. (b) The timing of recording the exports of the good (in one country) and its imports (in another country) must be different, leading to another source of divergence. (c) Beside timing, incomplete (or sometimes, an exaggerated) recording of exports and imports is quite prevalent. This would lead to particularly deficient results – and, potentially, particularly large divergences between the export and import price indexes – when quantities are recorded correctly, but not values, or when it is the other way around (and, as can naturally be expected, inappropriate recordings in the exporting and importing countries do not match). (d) Finally, different valuations in different countries' records may be

---

[17]Other than the ships and aircraft, mentioned before, the exclusion of various manufactured goods was mainly due to the changes in the classification system. The major revision in the scheme was undertaken in category 7 ("machinery and transport equipment" – to which, of course, ships and aircraft too belong). The representation of this category has thus suffered most, whereas in all other categories (save 3 – "mineral fuels") the coverage of the present study would seem to be quite adequate.

expected in general (beyond the intentionally misleading recordings). This problem is compounded when different currencies are used in the individual country's recordings, and conversion factors have to be applied.

Indeed, the results yielded by the two alternative calculations, from the exports and imports recordings, diverge substantially from each other. In the individual periods, the relationship of the two alternative series to each other is quite weak. In the series of price changes from 1955 to 1960 and from 1960 to 1965 the correlation coefficients of the two series are practically zero. For the changes from 1952 to 1955 and from 1965 to 1970 the relationship is of the expected sign, and is highly significant, but the correlation coefficients are still not high: 0.214 and 0.351, respectively. The relationship of the two alternative series for the period surveyed as a whole, however–namely, for the price change from 1952 to 1970–is much stronger:[18] a (linear) regression of the price indexes derived from imports on the indexes derived from the exports side has a slope of 0.948, and an adjusted R^2 of 0.588 (with a t value of 8.99). The slope thus appears to be very close to unity (as it would be had the two series been identical),[19] and the coefficient of determination, too, to be moderately high–certainly high enough to indicate a strong resemblance of the two alternative series. Apparently, large deviations of the series from each other in any given period tend to be *offset* – rather than reinforced – by opposite deviations in another period. This may have been expected on one score–the divergences due to different *timing* of recording the transactions–but not necessarily on the others.

The reasonably high similarity of the two alternative series justified the conduct of further work by the use of *averages*, rather than a separate work with the two alternatives. This, indeed, has been the procedure followed: the average of the two alternative indexes, for each good (for the total period covered – 1952 to 1970) is used as the single index of the change in the price level of that good.[20]

The unit-cost estimates could, on well-known grounds, at best be reasonable approximations of the true price changes. How adequate are the data derived in this way in the present study? A full test cannot, obviously, be carried out: it would require knowledge about the "true" price indexes which, were it available, would have been used to start with. But a few partial checks may give some indications.

For the majority of primary goods, price quotations are available. In principle, they should be much superior to unit-cost estimates, although problems of weight-

---

[18] This correlation refers to those goods for which export and import price indexes exist for all (4, that is) periodical calculations, whereas the correlations for each individual period (namely, from 1952 to 1955, and so on) were made for those goods (larger in number, of course) for which the two indexes for *that* periodical comparison are available.

[19] A hypothesis that the slope is different from unity has a t value of 0.5, and must hence be rejected.

[20] This statement is true for most cases. Sometimes, however, one of the measures – the export or the import price index – in a given period, would look obviously improbable. In that case, and for that period, only the other measure would be included.

ing and aggregation of many quotations for a single "good" still make them less than perfect descriptions of the "true" price changes. Such price-quotation indexes may be used as a yardstick with which the present study's price indexes, for the same goods, could be matched.

Table 9.A.1 presents market quotations from two sources. Column (2) shows the price set derived from the U.N. source, which has been discussed in section 4 of the text;[21] whereas column (3) presents prices – again, market quotations – provided in the I.M.F.'s *International Financial Statistics*.[22] Along with these, the set of prices used in the present study for these goods is presented in column (1).

Since coverage of the U.N. set of prices is considerably wider than that of the IFS, it is probably more instructive for the purpose on hand. A comparison of this set with that of the present study shows a large degree of resemblance. The (weighted) average price ratio of the 35 goods shown is, in the U.N. set, 1.036. In the present study's set, the average level is 1.158. The latter is higher than the former, as might be expected in a comparison of unit-cost calculations with market quotations, but the difference is modest. More important, the *order* of these two alternative series is highly similar. The largest deviations between rankings in the two orders occur in goods which are mostly of no quantitative significance. Thus, while the unweighted (Spearman) coefficient of rank correlation between the two series is 0.764, the weighted coefficient is 0.929.

A comparison with the IFS price set gives a similar impression. For the 16 goods covered by both this set and that of the present study, the (weighted) average level of the IFS prices is 0.931, whereas the average level of the study's price estimates is 0.966 (for the same goods, the average level of the U.N. prices is only 0.911). The unweighted rank-correlation coefficient of the study's and the IFS prices is 0.843, and the weighted coefficient is 0.889.

By these yardsticks, thus, the set of price estimates used in the present study for most primary goods appears to be rather reliable, and close to the "true" prices insofar as these are adequately represented by market quotations. Quite little in the inferences drawn in this study would have changed had the unit-cost estimates employed in the study been replaced by market quotations whenever the latter are available.

---

[21] Only goods for which price estimates are also available in the present study are shown. In addition, the U.N. source provides prices for goods number 281, 321, 331 and 421.

[22] The original data are not classified by the SITC, but identification of goods with the appropriate 3-digit SITC group is mostly straightforward. Data about the U.N. prices are drawn from the United Nations, *Methods Used in Compiling the United Nations Price Indexes for Basic Commodities in International Trade* (1979). In this source, the various price quotations for each good are weighted, and a single index appears for the good. The IMF data are drawn from the 1980 *Yearbook of International Financial Statistics*. Here, most often more than one price quotation appear for a single good, and the various quotations have been represented in table 9.A.1 by using, arbitrarily, unweighted means. The *IFS* source provides, on many occasions, unit-cost estimates in addition to price quotations, but these have been ignored for the present purpose.

Table 9.A.1 Alternative price series for primary goods
(ratio of 1970 to 1952 prices)

SITC code	Study prices (1)	U.N. prices (2)	I.F.S. prices (3)
011	1.655		
012	1.122	{1.714	
013	1.378		
022	0.980	1.025	
023	0.839	0.829	
024	1.542	2.829	
025	1.076	0.638	
031	2.499	{1.892	
032	1.260		
041	0.761	0.771	0.682
042	0.772	0.827	0.870
043	0.761	0.854	
044	0.754	0.746	
046	0.804	0.771	
061	0.973	0.905	0.883
071	0.978	1.000	1.013
072	1.203	0.922	0.898
074	0.924	1.061	1.074
081	1.442	1.107	
112	3.277	1.447	
121	1.474	{1.258	1.579
122	3.015		
211	1.120	0.831	0.872
221	0.968	0.919	1.110
231	0.761	0.590	0.566
243	1.580	1.085	
251	0.895	0.837	
262	0.670	0.631	0.611
263	0.648	0.614	0.693
264	0.765	1.358	
265	0.640	0.963	
411	0.983	1.164	
561	0.890	1.063	
682	1.959	1.932	2.183
683	2.879	2.385	
684	1.140	1.479	
685	0.976	0.839	0.883
686	0.773	0.769	0.826
687	1.519	1.385	1.379

Source: See footnote 22.

The proximity of the study's unit-cost estimates to the true indexes is probably weaker for those primary goods for which no market quotations are generally available: presumably, the absence of such data reflects a larger degree of heterogeneity of the good, and the larger the heterogeneity, the less adequate are unit-cost calculations likely to be. This is probably even more true, on average, for manufactures, where no market quotations may be found at all (nor, indeed, any other price estimates equivalent to those of the present study). Two very partial and limited tests will be presented here, but the indications yielded by them must be extremely restrictive.

First, I have calculated for the years from 1953 to 1970 – roughly the period covered in the present study – the weighted average of the increase in the indexes of wholesale prices of the major developed economies, using the *countries'* shares in 1970 world exports for weights.[23] Together, the exports of these countries amounted to slightly over two thirds of world exports in that year. The ratio of the (weighted) average wholesale price level in 1970 to that of 1953 is 1.312. The weighted exchange rate – price of currencies in U.S. dollars – using again the same weights, was 0.975 in 1970 (taking 1953 as unity).[24] The product of these two changes yields an average index of wholesale prices, expressed in dollar terms, of 1.279 (that is, an increase of 27.9%). In view of the slight price decline between 1952 and 1953, this indicates an average price increase from 1952 to 1970 of roughly 25%.

The average price increase yielded by the present study's estimates, for all goods covered, is of the same order (the 1970 to 1952 price ratio is 1.256). The average price increases of the upper-half goods (ranked by income level), which are probably more representative for the group of countries under consideration, were about 10% for exports and 43% for imports; since both prices of exports (or exportables) and imports (or importables) must heavily affect a country's wholesale price index, these price changes seem together not to be grossly inconsistent with a wholesale price increase of 25%. The average price increase of all manufactured goods covered in the present study is roughly 30%, and these goods, again, must be more relevant (on average) to the group of countries under consideration than prices of other goods. This price increase is again quite similar to the average rate (25%) of increase of wholesale prices.

---

[23] 1953 rather than 1952 was taken here because this is the starting year in the source in which these data are readily available – the U.N. *Statistical Yearbook*. In general, changes in wholesale prices from 1952 to 1953 appear to have been only slight (roughly, from partial evidence, a decline of 2%–3%). The countries included are: Austria, Belgium, Canada, Denmark, Finland, France, Germany, Italy, Japan, Netherlands, New Zealand, Norway, Sweden, Switzerland, the U.K. and the U.S.

[24] This includes, of course, the appropriate weight for the U.S. exports, with the price of the dollar for this trade flow remaining by definition unity. Excluding the U.S. – that is, the price in U.S. dollars of *other* currencies, weighted by countries' shares in world exports – the ratio is 0.968.

By this comparison, the *average* price levels constructed in this study, for all goods in general or for manufactured goods in particular, seem to be at least not widely off the mark. But this does not, it should be emphasized, provide any check of the price estimates for *individual* goods.

For some manufactured goods, reliable price estimates are available in the thorough study of Kravis and Lipsey (1971) – apparently the only source of such data. Unfortunately, only 8 goods are common to that source and to the present study; in addition, the Kravis–Lipsey investigation refers to price changes between 1953 and 1964, whereas the present study refers to the period from 1952 to 1970. In order, however, to enable some comparison, I have calculated from the present study's data price changes for the 8 relevant goods for the period from 1952 to

Table 9.A.2. Alternative price estimates for a few manufactured goods

SITC code and description	Study prices (ratio of 1965 to 1952) (1)	Kravis–Lipsey prices (ratio of 1964 to 1953) (2)	
711: Non-electric power machinery	2.451	U.S.	1.277
		U.K.	1.233
		Germany	1.207
712: Agricultural machinery	1.381	U.S.	1.241
		U.K.	1.207
		EEC	1.214
		Germany	1.202
714: Office machines	1.884	U.S.	1.000
		U.K.	0.989
		EEC	0.828
		Germany	0.840
715: Metal-working machinery	1.283	U.S.	1.268
		U.K.	1.436
		EEC	1.411
		Germany	1.386
731: Railway vehicles	1.843	U.S.	1.229
		EEC	1.373
		Germany	1.367
732: Road motor vehicles	1.069	U.S.	1.101
		U.K.	1.147
		EEC	1.079
		Germany	1.110
861: Scientific instruments	1.220	U.K.	1.395
891: Musical instruments	1.509	EEC	1.385
		Germany	1.447

Source: See text.

1965 (that is, omitting the last change in the chain, between 1965 and 1970). The results, along with the Kravis–Lipsey data, are presented in table 9.A.2.

By this test, the showing of the study's data is quite poor. The unweighted average price ratio, using the study's data, is 1.580; in the Kravis–Lipsey data, it is only 1.248.[25] The gap between the weighted average levels (which are of some significance, since trade in the 8 goods on hand was over 40% of the 1970 aggregate of all manufactures covered in this study), is smaller: the respective ratios are 1.278 and 1.157. What is probably more meaningful is the fact that there is no similarity in the *order* of price levels in the two alternative series (the unweighted rank-correlation coefficient is negative, and the weighted coefficient is positive, but both are very low.) This may be a "worst case" comparison: The number of items is very small, assigning a large potential role to chance deviations; the period considered is not entirely equal in the two series, and is particularly short (it will be recalled that the shorter the period and the smaller the number of "chains", the less accurate are the calculations likely to be); and, in particular, the goods considered, mostly machinery of various types, are among the most heterogeneous, and unit-cost calculations are likely to lead to most inaccurate inferences when these goods are involved. Yet this comparison would at least suggest that the price estimates for manufactured goods in the present study cannot be more than very rough approximations, and that inferences drawn from them may not be regarded as more than tentative.

[25] For these comparisons, the price index for each good in the Kravis–Lipsey data is represented by the mean of the various price ratios provided in the source.

CHAPTER 10

THE INCOME LEVEL OF EXPORTS AND TRADE BARRIERS

An issue of trade relationships between poor and rich nations which also concerns the terms of trade between the two groups is that of commercial *policies* applied to this trade, in particular policies followed by the rich countries. The issue has gathered momentum in recent years, forming a central element in the clamor for a "new international economic order", an important part of which would presumably be more favorable terms of trade for the less-developed countries (the LDC's) in their transactions with the developed countries (the DC's); this improvement would presumably be achieved, to a large extent, by more favorable tariff treatment on the part of the developed countries. A contributing factor to the eminence of the issue has been the recent astonishing growth of the exports of many LDC's to the DC's – particularly exports of manufactures. With this growth came an increasing resentment in at least some DC's or some sectors to imports from LDC's, and a mounting suspicion that a further rapid rise of exports from LDC's to DC's is likely to meet an increased level of barriers to this trade.

The tariff-level issue – or, more generally, the issue of the level of trade barriers – may be separated into two parts: the "positive" and the "normative" aspects. First, it is often argued that the existing structure of trade barriers discriminates against the trade of LDC's, this discrimination being one of the causes of the unfavorable, or "unfair", terms of trade of these countries. The normative aspect of the issue has been the argument that discrimination in favor of the trade of LDC's should be explicitly introduced into tariff treaties and into the network of tariffs and non-tariff barriers to trade. This argument has, in fact, been accepted in principle by the highly-developed countries, an acceptance that has led, *inter alia*, to the introduction into the GATT scheme of the "generalized system of preferences", by which developed countries are entitled to grant special tariff concessions to the LDC's.

The present chapter is confined to the first aspect, overlooking entirely the second. It does not ask whether tariff discrimination in favor of LDC exports should take place, or what are the pros and cons of such policy. Rather, it tries to reveal whether the existing system of tariffs and non-tariff barriers discriminates in favor, or against, the trade of LDC's. It will also inquire whether the nature of this trade would lead to the anticipation of future discrimination, in one direction or another.

In trying to establish whether any discrimination is involved in the trade-barriers system, it will be assumed that *no discrimination*, either way, is applied to the trade of specific *countries*. This assumption determines, indeed, the nature of the present inquiry, and should it grossly violate the facts, the findings of this study would lose much of their meaning. It is assumed, thus, that any non-uniformity in the level of tariffs and other trade barriers is expressed in varying levels of barriers to the flows of different *goods*. Discrimination against or in favor of a country is due only to its pattern of specialization: if it specializes in goods which face high barriers in international trade, it is confronted with a high level of barriers in general, and may thus be said to be discriminated against – although not by design specifically aimed at this country. And, in contrast, a country whose exports happen to be primarily concentrated in goods which face low trade barriers, enjoys discrimination in its favor.

The investigation, moreover, does not apply to the trade of specific countries, but to the trade of LDC's in general.[1] Its subject matter may thus be defined as follows: Does the system of the tariff and non-tariff barriers, in the highly-developed part of the world, discriminate against, or in favor, of goods in which low-income countries tend to specialize?

1. Discrimination in commercial policies: A study through income levels

Thus presented, the inquiry appears immediately to lend itself to the application of the basic tool used throughout this part of the study, namely, the index of income level of trade. A good exported mostly by low-income countries – the LDC's – will have a low index of the income level of exports. A knowledge about the tariff and non-tariff barriers to which this good is subject in the imports of the rich countries, in comparison with the treatment of high income-level goods, would thus provide the basis for an answer to the question posed.

Two sets of data are thus required: the indexes of income level of exports of individual goods and the levels of trade barriers faced by the exports of each good. The first set will be drawn from the data developed in chapter 6; that is, the indexes of income level of exports in 1973, for the 174 goods classified by the 3-digit level of the SITC. These data are presented in table 6.1 of that chapter.

The other set of data refers to six series of indicators of barriers to trade: Nominal tariffs; effective rates of protection; and indexes of the level of non-trade barriers (NTB's) – each of these for the United States and, separately, for a group of countries consisting of the six original members of the E.E.C., the U.K., Japan

---

[1] For estimates of the positions of individual countries, see the study by Yeats (1979).

Table 10.1. Income level and trade barriers: Correlation coefficients (r)

Trade barrier	All goods (1)	Categories (5)–(8) (2)
(1) Nominal tariff, US	0.038	−0.036
(2) Nominal tariff, others	0.078	0.047
(3) Effective tariff, US	0.022	−0.109
(4) Effective tariff, others	−0.074	−0.222
(5) Index of NTB, US	−0.036	−0.149
(6) Index of NTB, others	−0.086	−0.104

None of the coefficients is significant at the 5% level.

and Canada (to be referred to henceforth as "other" developed countries). It is based on estimates carried out by the U.S. International Trade Commission, which refer to the post Kennedy-Round situation (that is, roughly, the late 1960s).[2] The source provides data classified by the SIC (Standard Industrial Classification), which have been transformed here into the SITC scheme. The method of transformation, as well as several other problems of concepts and methods, are discussed in the appendix to the present chapter. The appendix also records, in table 10.A.1, the detailed set of data thus constructed.[3]

If in general exports originating in low-income countries face relatively high barriers to trade, a negative correlation of the indexes of income level of exports and of the levels of barriers should be found. If, on the contrary, imports originating in low-income countries are admitted relatively more freely than other goods, the correlation of the two indexes should be positive. Such correlation provides, therefore, a test of the relationship of the levels of trade barriers to the levels of income of the countries from which the goods originate.

The correlation coefficients are shown in column (1) of table 10.1, for all (168) goods. It appears immediately that no relationship exists between the variables under consideration: all correlation coefficients are very low, with R^2's in the vicinity of zero (and are, of course, insignificant at any reasonable requirement of level of significance). The conclusion which must be drawn is that the existing structure of barriers to trade in the highly-developed countries – the levels of nominal tariffs, of effective tariffs and of non-tariff barriers – does not discriminate either in favor of or against the exports which originate primarily in LDC's.

[2] United States International Trade Commission (1975).
[3] Table 10.A.1 includes only 168 rather than 174 goods. For six items – 041, 212, 244, 267, 863 and 896 – data on trade barriers could not be compiled. The present investigation is confined, therefore, to the 168 goods listed in this table.

It might be argued that this apparent absence of discrimination in the system implies, in effect, some measure of discrimination *against* exports originating in LDC's in the *relevant range* of goods. Exports of LDC's, the argument would run, consist largely of primary goods – foodstuffs and raw materials. These goods, particularly the latter group, usually face little competition from domestic production in the highly-developed countries, and are thus unlikely to raise much demand for import barriers in the latter. Moreover, low tariff levels on intermediate goods are commonly used, in the universally prevalent system of escalated tariffs, to provide high effective protection for later stages of production. Hence, a low level of trade barriers on imports of primary goods may be anticipated. Had such goods been excluded, leaving only categories of goods in which substitution between imports and local production is likely to be meaningfully high, the system of barriers would then show discrimination against the goods exported relatively heavily by low-income countries.

To test this presumption, correlation coefficients have been calculated between the respective measures of trade barriers and the index of income level of exports not of all goods, but only of the (99) goods which are classified in the SITC major categories (5) to (8) – excluding, that is, categories (0) to (4) which clearly constitute primary goods. These correlation coefficients are presented in column (2) of table 10.1, and the result which emerges from them is once more unmistakably clear. All correlation coefficients are close enough to zero (and insignificant) to justify an inference that the structure of the systems of barriers to trade is, on the whole, indifferent to the income level of the exporting countries – even when only categories of goods which include mostly manufactures are investigated.

The reason for this apparent absence of an impact of exclusion of primary goods on the outcome is that both components of the foregoing hypothesis seem to be invalid. One was a presumption that primary goods face, on average, relatively low trade barriers. In table 10.2 the (unweighted) means and the medians of the levels of trade barriers are presented by major SITC categories. It appears that while average levels of barriers (whether represented by the mean or by the median) do differ substantially among categories, no consistent difference appears between the categories of mainly primary goods ((0) to (4)) and the other categories. The second component was the presumption that low-income countries tend to concentrate their exports relatively heavily in the categories of primary goods. Although this presumption is usually taken as only too obvious, it seems to be refuted by the facts. It will be recalled from the discussion of chapter 6 that the income-level of exports is, in general, quite close in the categories (0) to (4) to its level in the other categories. Indeed, it appeared there that only category (7) – machinery and transport equipment – deviates materially from the rest, and could be classified as a high-income group, whereas all other categories do not differ much, on average, from each other. Thus, even if there were a relatively low level of trade barriers on flows of primary goods, it could not be expected to act – in

Table 10.2. Levels of trade barriers, by major SITC categories

	Trade barrier	SITC category								
		(0)	(1)	(2)	(3)	(4)	(5)	(6)	(7)	(8)
Average (unweighted)										
(1)	Nominal tariff, US (%)	6.0	16.9	4.3	2.2	4.5	6.1	8.2	6.0	11.6
(2)	Nominal tariff, others (%)	9.1	53.2	4.4	4.7	7.7	7.8	9.2	8.7	10.9
(3)	Effective tariff, US (%)	23.4	26.1	7.5	4.1	6.7	9.5	14.2	7.6	20.5
(4)	Effective tariff, others (%)	21.6	60.4	5.9	10.4	14.5	12.6	20.2	11.3	16.7
(5)	Index of NTB, US	3.3	0.6	0.4	1.7	0.2	0.1	0.3	0.2	0.7
(6)	Index of NTB, others	5.1	7.8	1.2	1.3	3.1	0.4	0.6	0.2	0.6
Median										
(1)	Nominal tariff, US (%)	5.3	19.4	3.2	2.8	3.3	5.3	6.5	5.5	11.3
(2)	Nominal tariff, others (%)	9.4	51.7	4.9	6.0	7.9	7.8	8.7	8.9	10.6
(3)	Effective tariff, US (%)	7.4	25.5	3.1	5.8	4.3	8.9	11.0	6.2	18.5
(4)	Effective tariff, others (%)	20.6	58.2	5.8	13.6	13.6	11.1	14.5	11.0	18.0
(5)	Index of NTB, US	1.9	1.2	0.9	2.0	0.2	0.1	0.3	0.4	0.6
(6)	Index of NTB, others	4.7	8.5	0.3	0.8	3.0	0.2	0.3	0.3	0.3

general and *on average* – as a source of discrimination in favor of the exports of low-income countries.

2. Trade barriers and attributes of goods

By the assumption of uniform treatment of countries, applied here, any discrimination in the structure of trade barriers in favor of or against low-income countries could arise only from the *nature of* the *goods* these countries are exporting. And, although no overall discrimination in either direction has been found, it is worth exploring the relationships of the tariff structure to the attributes of goods – relationships which, if they do indeed exist, may have worked to offset each other in their overall impact on the degree of discrimination in the system. Indications of such relationships might possibly help to forecast the *future* course of discrimination, projecting some pattern of development of the trade structure of the LDC's.

One such relationship – the most obvious, perhaps – has just been explored: the distinction between primary goods and manufactures. We have seen that such a distinction would not lead to discrimination between the major classes of countries. A few other attributes suggest themselves as potential sources of discrimination.

One is the labor content, or labor ratio, in the production of goods. It is often suggested that high-income countries tend to establish particularly high trade barriers to the entry of goods whose labor content is high and, hence, whose import would lead to the displacement of relatively large amounts of labor in the importing country. It is presumed that the less-developed, low-income countries tend to export in relatively high degree goods whose labor content is high and capital content low. If this presumption holds, barriers on the trade of labor-intensive goods would have a particularly strong impact on the exports of low-income countries.

Another hypothesis worth testing is that it is the component of unskilled labor, rather than labor in general, which is the subject of protection. High-income countries may be expected to have a comparative advantage in industries in which relatively high skills are required, and a comparative disadvantage in goods which are intensive in unskilled labor. These countries may presumably be reluctant to admit freely imports of the latter goods. To the extent that high barriers are indeed erected against such goods, this would be a factor discriminating against the low-income countries, which presumably export only little of the high-skill goods.

Still another possible hypothesis is that countries tend to establish high barriers to trade in goods destined directly for final consumption, whereas they tend to admit relatively freely imports of goods which would need some transformation before being turned into consumer goods. Raw materials are an obvious case in point and have already been discussed. But final investment goods are another group of this nature.

The possible existence of such relationships is examined, again, through the use of the estimates of attributes developed by Hufbauer (1970), which have been applied earlier in this study on numerous occasions. Once more, a correlation analysis serves for the purpose. Table 10.3 presents the correlation coefficients of each of these possible explanatory variables – the capital/labor ratio involved in production of a good, the skilled-labor ratio (to total-labor input), and the ratio of sales for final consumption – with the six sets of indicators of trade barriers.

It appears, from column (1) of table 10.3, that the capital/labor ratio variable has no explanatory power at all as a determinant of the pattern of trade barriers: the correlation coefficients involved are all very low (R^2's around zero), and all but two are insignificant. It should be pointed out that the testing of this variable

Table 10.3. Attributes of goods and trade-barrier levels: Correlation coefficients (r)

	Trade barrier	Capital/labor ratio (1)	Skilled-labor ratio (2)	Proportion of sales for final consumption (3)
(1)	Nominal tariff, US	−0.217	−0.171	0.278
(2)	Nominal tariff, others	−0.146	−0.213	0.365
(3)	Effective tariff, US	−0.256	−0.290	0.270
(4)	Effective tariff, others	−0.177	−0.318	0.502
(5)	Index of NTB, US	−0.114	−0.365	0.487
(6)	Index of NTB, others	−0.114	−0.420	0.628

Underlined figures are significant at the 5% level.

has been carried out here because it is probably of interest in itself. Even, however, had a correlation (positive or negative) been found between the variable under consideration and the tariff structure, it would have been of no consequence to the immediate issue on hand, which is the possible reason for *a priori* expectation of tariff discrimination among goods by income level of exporters. The reason for this is that the widely-held presumption stated before, that low-income countries concentrate their exports on goods with a high labor/capital ratio, is apparently incorrect; it will be recalled, from chapter 7, that no general relationship is found between labor intensity in production of goods and the income level of exports of these goods.

The skill ratio, represented in column (2), appears to have some explanatory power, but it is a weak one. All but one of the indicators of trade barriers – the level of nominal tariffs in the US – appear to be significantly and negatively correlated with the variable at hand. And this variable is itself, we recall, positively correlated with the income level of exports of goods. Hence, this would be a factor working against the low-income countries, leading to a relatively higher level of barriers on their exports. But the size of the correlation coefficients would indicate that this factor is of only minor importance.

Of the variables tested, that of the proportion of sales for final consumption, represented in column (3), appears to be most relevant. All correlation coefficients of this explanatory variable with levels of trade barriers are significant, all are positive, and some seem to be high enough to indicate a substantial impact. This is true particularly with regard to the levels of non-tariff barriers, in both the US and in the "other" countries, and for the level of effective tariffs in the latter. In general, whatever the indicator of trade barrier tested (nominal tariffs, effective tariffs and NTB's), the relationship to the explanatory variables appears to be stronger in the group of "other" countries than it is in the US: the coefficients in rows (2), (4) and (6) are higher than those in rows (1), (3) and (5) respectively (this is true also for the skill-ratio variable, but is of lesser consequence there).

What inference does this finding indicate for the issue at hand? We recall, again, that contrary to some popularly-held notions, low-income countries tend to specialize, relatively to high-income countries, in goods which are primarily destined directly for final consumption. Hence, the finding points to the operation of a factor which tends to establish a degree of discrimination *against* the low-income countries in the structure of trade barriers, particularly in the system of non-tariff barriers, and more noticeably in the highly-developed countries other than the US.

While this factor may have been of only little consequence hitherto – hence the roughly neutral findings about discrimination in the present structure of trade barriers – it may be expected to assume much more significance in the future. Looking at the range of goods of which LDC's have tended recently to expand production and exports, particularly among manufactured goods, one would get the impression that these tend to be goods destined to a relatively large extent for final consumption. This impression, to be sure, is not sufficient evidence, and a more rigorous empirical verification would be desirable; even if found true, moreover, a projection of this tendency into the future would be still in the nature of conjecture. If this conjecture, however, is borne out, the present findings indicate that in the future the structure of trade barriers would tend increasingly to discriminate against the exports of the low-income countries. Put differently, while it seems that on average the present system is rather neutral, it is one which *at the margin* – that is, when related to trade *expansions* – tends to entail a degree of discrimination against exports of low-income countries. Thus, to come back to the hypothesis tested earlier, it seems likely that some discrimination against exports of LDC's does indeed exist in the *relevant* range of goods – although relevance is determined by criteria different from those presumed in the earlier test.

3. Conclusions

The main conclusions of this investigation are:

(i) The existing structure of trade barriers does not imply, on the whole, any degree of discrimination either in favor of or against exports of low-income countries. This is true for barriers both in the Unites States and in the group of other major highly-developed countries – the original EEC members, the United Kingdom, Canada and Japan – and it holds for the scales of nominal tariffs, of effective protection rates, and of non-tariff barriers.

(ii) The structure of trade barriers does not reveal any distinction between major categories of goods; likewise no overall tendency is found towards either high or low barriers on imports of labor-intensive goods. A slight tendency appears to increase the level of barriers with the increase in intensity of unskilled labor in the production of goods.

(iii) A clear tendency is revealed, on the other hand, for the level of trade barriers to increase with the extent to which a good is destined directly for final consumption. This implies the existence of a factor which works to raise the level of barriers on low-income exports (relative to other goods) – a factor which at present has probably only a minor effect on the average structure but which may have a more substantial impact on the future expansion of exports by LDC's.

Two policy implications, primarily, are suggested by these findings.

(a) Inasmuch as the highly-developed countries wish to lower the trade barriers faced by the exports of low-income countries (relative to the barriers to other trade flows) on a most-favored-nation basis, namely, by lowering barriers on imports of goods rather than on imports from specific countries, this could not be achieved by a favorable treatment of any *major category* of goods. Specifically, the lowering of barriers on exports of primary goods as a whole would not work in favor of the low-income countries.[4] A favorable treatment would have to involve a much more specific, narrowly defined range of goods.[5]

(b) The expansion of exports of LDC's seems likely to be concentrated in manufactures largely destined for final consumption. With the *existing* structure of trade barriers, this would imply that exports of LDC's would face an increasingly higher level of barriers, and would be increasingly discriminated against in relation to barriers on exports from other countries. For this to be avoided – that is, for the present absence of discrimination at least to remain intact – a relative lowering of barriers on trade in these particular goods would be called for.

Appendix: Sources and methods for data on trade barriers

As indicated in the text, the source of the raw data on tariffs and NTB's is the U.S. International Trade Commission publication (1975). Nominal tariff rates and indexes of NTB's are drawn from table 3 (pp. 44–49), as follows: U.S. nominal tariff – column (4); "other" countries nominal tariff – column (9); U.S. index of

---

[4] This statement is concerned, of course, with *relative* levels. The lowering of barriers on exports of primary goods without a compensating change in the barriers imposed on other goods (assuming that *effective* rates as well as nominal rates are not increased anywhere in the system) would constitute a lowering of the overall level of trade barriers and would presumably benefit low-income countries just as it would their high-income partners.

[5] It is certainly no accident that the main concrete result of the "generalized system of preferences" until now has been the specially favorable treatment granted to trade in tropical products. This segment of primary goods – mainly tea, coffee, cocoa, spices, sugar and tropical fruits – is distinctly the sector of exports with the lowest income levels. It would be much more difficult to define any similar *group* of goods with a markedly low income level (as opposed to *individual* goods – such as, for instance, jute).

Table 10.A.1. Levels of trade barriers

	Nominal tariffs (%)		Effective tariffs (%)		Non-tariff barriers	
SITC code	US (1)	EEC, Canada Japan, UK (2)	US (3)	EEC, Canada Japan, UK (4)	US (5)	EEC, Canada Japan, UK (6)
001	5.4	4.5	16.7	10.1	1.6	2.3
011	5.2	9.4	5.5	36.3	1.9	5.3
012	5.2	9.4	5.5	36.3	1.9	5.3
013	5.2	9.4	5.5	36.3	1.9	5.3
022	6.6	11.9	93.9	25.6	7.7	11.1
023	12.6	11.1	271.7	15.1	13.3	12.1
024	14.3	15.5	65.0	37.8	20.0	10.8
025	5.9	7.5	15.7	26.8	1.5	4.9
031	1.4	9.5	0.6	18.4	0.9	2.4
032	2.9	10.6	4.5	22.8	0.6	2.9
042	4.5	5.6	8.0	17.9	2.6	6.3
043	4.6	4.7	7.4	6.6	1.9	5.9
044	4.6	4.7	7.4	6.6	1.9	5.9
045	4.6	4.7	7.4	6.6	1.9	5.9
046	6.1	7.3	14.7	20.5	4.1	6.2
047	6.1	7.3	14.7	20.5	4.1	6.2
048	3.3	10.4	3.3	27.1	1.7	5.4
051	5.7	8.8	8.0	—	0.8	4.6
052	10.7	10.8	24.4	21.4	0.2	3.9
053	9.2	10.3	19.7	21.5	0.4	4.6
054	8.0	7.7	13.5	13.3	0.8	4.6
055	10.5	10.3	23.1	20.1	0.6	4.0
061	4.6	20.2	4.0	51.6	6.7	3.9
062	6.1	9.5	13.5	15.2	5.5	3.6
071	2.8	10.2	1.1	44.7	1.2	3.7
072	3.7	8.0	3.3	6.7	1.4	3.1
073	1.8	7.3	−1.3	6.7	2.1	1.7
074	7.9	4.9	11.9	5.8	0.9	2.4
075	5.2	6.0	7.3	7.1	0.7	3.0
081	3.2	9.7	−1.7	18.0	2.5	3.2
091	22.9	12.0	—	61.7	3.3	4.0
099	8.0	11.6	14.0	34.4	1.1	2.6
111	0.5	6.5	−3.9	8.3	0.0	4.4
112	16.3	23.5	24.7	35.9	2.4	9.8
121	28.3	102.9	57.2	80.4	0.0	8.8
122	22.4	79.8	26.3	117.0	0.0	8.2
211	4.7	5.0	5.4	17.6	1.2	2.6
221	2.6	6.7	4.6	7.0	1.0	4.1
231	1.8	6.2	−0.5	7.2	0.0	0.2
241	0.0	3.1	−0.9	4.0	0.0	0.0
242	0.5	2.5	−1.6	−3.8	0.0	0.0
243	1.7	5.9	2.7	9.8	0.1	0.1
251	0.0	1.8	−3.1	−0.6	0.0	0.0

Table 10.A.1. (*Continued*)

SITC code	Nominal tariffs (%)		Effective tariffs (%)		Non-tariff barriers	
	US (1)	EEC, Canada Japan, UK (2)	US (3)	EEC, Canada Japan, UK (4)	US (5)	EEC, Canada Japan, UK (6)
261	13.9	9.8	30.9	22.8	1.0	0.7
262	14.0	3.7	52.8	4.1	0.0	0.1
263	4.8	1.7	9.3	1.4	1.7	2.9
264	7.9	4.9	11.9	5.8	0.9	2.4
265	7.9	4.9	11.9	5.8	0.9	2.4
266	13.5	8.3	30.7	13.9	0.4	0.2
271	1.0	2.3	−5.1	−2.4	0.0	0.1
273	2.0	5.7	1.6	6.2	0.0	0.1
274	3.2	2.8	3.1	2.3	0.0	0.5
275	2.3	5.7	1.8	6.4	0.0	0.1
276	3.2	4.7	3.6	3.8	0.0	0.3
281	2.4	1.0	2.5	−0.1	0.0	0.0
282	2.4	1.0	2.5	−0.1	0.0	0.0
283	3.4	1.8	3.8	0.6	0.0	0.0
284	6.1	5.5	12.7	11.1	0.0	0.2
285	1.5	2.3	0.7	1.0	0.0	0.2
291	3.4	6.1	3.5	14.6	1.3	2.8
292	1.9	7.8	1.2	9.8	0.3	2.1
321	0.0	0.6	−1.5	−0.9	0.0	3.8
331	3.1	6.2	6.4	15.4	2.8	0.7
332	2.5	5.8	5.0	11.7	1.2	0.0
341	3.1	6.2	6.4	15.4	2.8	0.7
411	2.2	6.8	1.7	8.7	0.1	1.6
421	9.1	8.0	16.4	22.2	0.0	4.8
422	3.0	8.3	4.3	17.2	0.2	4.4
431	3.6	7.7	4.2	9.9	0.2	1.5
512	5.0	8.9	7.5	15.5	0.3	0.1
513	3.0	5.2	2.4	6.2	0.0	0.1
514	5.3	7.5	6.8	10.9	0.0	0.1
515	4.3	4.9	5.5	5.6	0.0	0.2
521	5.8	7.8	8.9	12.8	0.2	0.4
531	7.2	7.5	10.4	10.2	0.1	0.3
532	5.3	6.2	9.9	8.5	0.3	0.1
533	4.1	7.6	3.0	10.7	0.0	0.1
541	7.0	8.6	10.1	12.0	0.1	0.1
551	11.0	9.4	19.5	11.1	0.3	1.7
553	8.6	13.0	27.6	44.1	0.0	0.0
554	5.3	9.3	8.8	16.7	0.1	0.0
561	2.6	3.6	−1.2	0.7	0.0	0.2
571	8.8	9.7	11.9	12.9	0.0	0.0
581	8.3	7.8	12.3	10.4	0.1	0.1
599	5.0	7.7	7.8	13.3	0.3	0.5

Table 10.A.1. (*Continued*)

SITC code	Nominal tariffs (%) US (1)	Nominal tariffs (%) EEC, Canada Japan, UK (2)	Effective tariffs (%) US (3)	Effective tariffs (%) EEC, Canada Japan, UK (4)	Non-tariff barriers US (5)	Non-tariff barriers EEC, Canada Japan, UK (6)
611	4.0	10.4	5.5	23.5	0.0	0.0
612	4.5	12.4	4.3	19.7	0.0	0.0
613	24.6	15.0	43.1	20.5	3.0	2.0
621	5.3	6.2	7.9	8.1	0.1	0.0
629	5.2	9.4	5.0	13.2	0.2	0.0
631	4.3	7.6	9.2	14.7	0.1	0.2
632	5.3	7.9	11.2	15.1	0.0	0.3
633	5.3	7.9	11.2	15.1	0.0	0.3
641	6.0	11.1	9.0	19.7	0.0	0.0
642	6.9	11.6	12.2	18.5	0.0	0.2
651	12.2	8.6	24.1	15.4	0.9	0.4
652	12.2	9.2	27.9	20.7	2.0	1.6
653	15.1	11.0	38.4	25.7	1.8	1.4
654	14.0	11.5	27.2	25.8	1.7	2.2
655	13.9	11.5	30.8	27.5	2.1	2.0
656	14.3	13.3	24.6	33.1	2.3	2.7
657	8.6	13.7	8.9	40.6	1.1	0.7
661	4.8	5.4	8.5	7.4	0.0	0.0
662	8.0	8.4	12.9	12.0	0.1	0.3
663	5.1	8.1	8.3	11.2	0.0	0.0
664	10.9	9.7	16.7	13.2	0.0	0.4
665	13.2	11.5	22.1	16.1	0.0	2.5
666	13.2	11.5	22.1	16.1	0.0	2.5
667	11.3	9.4	26.7	16.1	0.0	0.7
671	5.0	7.3	7.7	12.1	0.1	0.2
672	5.8	7.8	8.9	12.8	0.2	0.4
673	7.0	8.1	10.7	11.4	0.0	0.4
674	7.1	7.8	11.6	10.2	0.0	0.5
675	7.1	8.0	11.0	11.4	0.0	0.5
676	5.8	7.8	8.9	12.8	0.2	0.4
677	7.1	8.0	11.0	11.4	0.0	0.5
678	6.5	9.0	9.8	13.6	0.0	0.1
679	5.0	9.5	5.7	13.9	0.0	0.0
681	6.4	6.1	11.7	10.3	0.0	0.1
682	5.6	8.3	9.4	18.5	0.0	0.0
683	6.1	7.5	8.2	10.5	0.0	0.2
684	6.2	7.3	11.5	14.5	0.0	0.0
685	4.8	6.4	4.8	10.6	0.0	0.2
686	7.4	6.5	16.0	11.2	0.0	0.3
687	6.3	6.5	10.8	10.4	0.0	0.1
689	6.4	5.6	11.1	7.1	0.0	0.1
691	6.3	8.4	8.5	10.8	0.0	0.1
692	6.5	9.9	11.3	16.0	0.3	0.0
693	6.6	10.4	9.4	18.1	0.0	0.1

Table 10.A.1. (*Continued*)

SITC code	Nominal tariffs (%) US (1)	Nominal tariffs (%) EEC, Canada Japan, UK (2)	Effective tariffs (%) US (3)	Effective tariffs (%) EEC, Canada Japan, UK (4)	Non-tariff barriers US (5)	Non-tariff barriers EEC, Canada Japan, UK (6)
694	5.2	10.0	5.5	14.4	0.0	0.0
695	6.4	8.5	7.6	10.2	0.0	0.1
696	17.6	12.3	43.6	23.9	0.0	0.4
697	7.3	10.1	12.3	17.8	0.0	0.3
698	7.1	10.0	10.2	15.8	0.0	0.1
711	4.6	8.9	5.0	10.6	0.3	0.3
712	3.1	8.4	0.3	10.9	0.0	0.4
714	4.6	8.7	5.0	10.5	0.0	0.2
715	7.3	9.4	9.3	12.4	0.0	0.0
717	6.3	8.1	8.6	10.1	0.0	0.8
718	5.1	7.3	5.3	8.2	0.0	0.0
719	5.2	8.0	5.6	9.5	0.0	0.1
722	8.8	9.8	12.7	12.4	0.0	0.2
723	9.2	9.7	13.5	12.7	0.0	0.3
724	5.4	9.0	5.7	11.1	0.0	0.4
725	6.0	8.8	7.7	11.8	0.0	0.0
726	2.7	8.9	1.3	10.7	0.0	0.0
729	6.4	9.3	7.6	11.7	0.0	0.5
731	9.7	8.6	17.1	11.2	0.0	0.2
732	4.2	11.3	5.3	20.9	0.0	1.4
733	7.3	10.5	13.5	18.3	0.0	0.6
734	4.9	8.6	5.6	10.4	0.5	0.2
735	5.6	3.4	6.7	−0.6	3.3	0.3
812	9.4	9.0	18.6	10.3	0.7	0.4
821	8.6	11.8	16.0	23.0	0.7	0.9
831	13.2	12.8	24.2	19.7	0.0	0.2
841	21.7	15.5	35.3	28.6	2.4	2.3
842	24.6	15.0	43.1	20.5	3.0	2.0
851	11.5	13.8	16.8	20.2	0.0	0.1
861	11.4	9.6	18.2	13.0	0.1	0.2
862	7.9	10.3	10.0	13.1	0.2	0.3
864	13.6	10.9	27.7	17.3	0.0	0.3
891	5.3	8.7	5.2	12.3	0.0	0.2
892	2.0	4.4	1.3	4.0	2.0	0.4
893	7.1	9.1	7.9	12.2	0.5	0.0
894	11.2	11.7	19.7	18.5	0.6	0.6
895	11.4	10.0	18.2	13.8	0.1	0.1
897	16.6	12.0	37.4	21.1	0.0	0.9
899	9.8	9.8	24.8	91.6	0.2	0.2

NTB's – column (11); and "other" countries index of NTB's – column (16). Effective tariff rates are drawn from table 10 (pp. 91–96): The U.S. – column (7); and "other" countries – column (12).

The original data used in the U.S.I.T.C. publication were partly compiled by it and partly taken from GATT compilations. It was originally drawn up by various forms of classification, and converted, using concordance schedules, into the classification of IO-SIC (Input–Output Standard Industrial Classification). Averaging of individual items into the IO-SIC commodities was carried out, in the U.S.I.T.C. work, in alternative ways; using import shares (those of the U.S., or of the "others", as the case may be) for weighting, or calculating simple (unweighted) averages. I have selected the simple-average calculation, which seems preferable for the present purpose. The problems involved in the interpretation of averages of tariff levels weighted by import shares are well known, and are compounded in comparisons of tariff scales of various countries. Simple unweighted averages too have a problem of interpretation, and could at worst be of little meaning, but they are free of biases. It should be noted, though, that the rank correlations of the alternative schedules of barriers (import-shares-weighted vs. simple averages), are given in the source and indicate a strong similarity. Overall results and generalizations would thus not be much affected by use of the alternative schedules.

The index of NTB is explained on pp. 16–17 of the source. It is designed to measure the frequency of appearances of various forms of NTB in the imports of each good. The *absolute* level of the index is devoid of meaning; at best, it is an ordinal measure, not a cardinal one and even then, it is probably less reliable than the measures of tariff levels.

In the present study, all data are classified by the (3-digit) SITC (Standard International Trade Classification). To convert the data from the IO-SIC, as they appear in the source, to the SITC, I have constructed a concordance schedule. This is based partly on a concordance list in Lary (1968), but mostly on appendix A (pp. A.1–A.8) in the U.S.I.T.C. publication, which presents the concordance relating the 5-digit SITC items to the IO-SIC. I have not adopted the latter fully, but made a selective list, according to the apparent content of each IO-SIC and SITC item – omitting SITC items which seem of little relevance to the IO-SIC item. Any such (remaining) SITC item was assumed to have the level of trade barrier of the IO-SIC item, a component of which it constitutes. The 5-digit SITC items were then aggregated into 3-digit SITC items by the use of simple, unweighted averages of the levels of trade barriers.

SYMBOLS AND INDEXES – A SUMMARY TABLE

1. Symbols

Q_{ij} = Production of good i in country j
A_{ij} = Availability of good i in country j
X_{ij} = Exports of good i by country j
$X_{.j}$ = Total exports of country j
$X_{i.}$ = World exports of good i
M_{ij} = Imports of good i by country j
$M_{.j}$ = Total imports of country j
$M_{i.}$ = World imports of good i
X_{kj} = Exports to country k by country j
M_{kj} = Imports from country k by country j
$X_{.k}$ = Total exports of country k
$M_{.k}$ = Total imports of country k
Y_k = Aggregate income of country k
$\tilde{Y}_k$ = Index of fluctuations of income of country k
$\hat{Y}_j$ = Aggregate income of country j
Y_j = Per-capita income of country j
$\hat{Y}_u$ = Aggregate U.S. income
Y_u = Per-capita U.S. income
$\hat{y}_j$ = $\hat{Y}_j / \hat{Y}_u$
y_j = Y_j / Y_u

2. Indexes

Weighted ratio of exports to product:

$$S_{jx} = \sum_i \frac{X_{ij}}{Q_{ij}} \frac{X_{ij}}{X_{.j}}$$

Weighted ratio of imports to availabilities:

$$S_{jm} = \sum_i \frac{M_{ij}}{A_{ij}} \frac{M_{ij}}{M_{.j}}$$

Commodity concentration of trade:
  Exports:

$$C_{jx} = \sqrt{\sum_i \left(\frac{X_{ij}}{X_{.j}} \right)^2}$$

  Imports:

$$C_{jm} = \sqrt{\sum_i \left(\frac{M_{ij}}{M_{.j}} \right)^2}$$

Geographic concentration of trade:
  Exports:

$$G_{jx} = \sqrt{\sum_k \left(\frac{X_{kj}}{X_{.j}} \right)^2}$$

  Imports:

$$G_{jm} = \sqrt{\sum_k \left(\frac{M_{kj}}{M_{.j}} \right)^2}$$

Commodity-weighted share in world trade:
  Exports:

$$W_{jx}^i = \sum_i \frac{X_{ij}}{X_{i.}} \frac{X_{ij}}{X_{.j}}$$

  Imports:

$$W_{jm}^i = \sum_i \frac{M_{ij}}{M_{i.}} \frac{M_{ij}}{M_{.j}}$$

Geographically-weighted share in world trade:
  Exports:

$$W_{jx}^k = \sum_k \frac{X_{kj}}{M_{.k}} \frac{X_{kj}}{X_{.j}}$$

  Imports:

$$W_{jm}^k = \sum_k \frac{M_{kj}}{X_{.k}} \frac{M_{kj}}{M_{.j}}$$

Weighted ratio of trade to partners' income:
   Exports:

$$W_{jx}^y = \sum_k \frac{X_{kj}}{Y_k} \frac{X_{ki}}{X_{\cdot j}}$$

   Imports:

$$W_{jm}^y = \sum_k \frac{M_{kj}}{Y_k} \frac{M_{kj}}{M_{\cdot j}}$$

Country concentration in world market:
   Exports:

$$C_{ix} = \sqrt{\sum_j \left(\frac{X_{ij}}{X_{i\cdot}}\right)^2}$$

   Imports:

$$C_{im} = \sqrt{\sum_j \left(\frac{M_{ij}}{M_{i\cdot}}\right)^2}$$

Monopsonistic position facing a country's exports:

$$PS_{jx} = \sum_i C_{im} \frac{X_{ij}}{X_{\cdot j}}$$

Monopolistic position facing a country's imports:

$$PO_{jm} = \sum_i C_{ix} \frac{M_{ij}}{M_{\cdot j}}$$

Instability of incomes of trade partners:
   Export customers:

$$F_{jx} = \sum_k \tilde{Y}_k \frac{X_{kj}}{X_{\cdot j}}$$

   Import suppliers:

$$F_{jm} = \sum_k \tilde{Y}_k \frac{M_{kj}}{M_{\cdot j}}$$

Per capita income level of trade in good:
   Exports:

$$y_{ix} = \sum_j y_j \frac{X_{ij}}{X_{\cdot j}}$$

Imports:

$$y_{im} = \sum_j y_j \frac{M_{ij}}{M_{\cdot j}}$$

Aggregate income level of trade in good:
  Exports:

$$\hat{y}_{ix} = \sum_j \hat{y}_j \frac{X_{ij}}{X_{\cdot j}}$$

Imports:

$$\hat{y}_{im} = \sum_j \hat{y}_j \frac{M_{ij}}{M_{\cdot j}}$$

Income level of a country's trade:
  Exports:

$$y_{jx} = \sum_i y_{ix} \frac{X_{ij}}{X_{\cdot j}}$$

Imports:

$$y_{jm} = \sum_i y_{im} \frac{M_{ij}}{M_{\cdot j}}$$

THE STANDARD INTERNATIONAL TRADE CLASSIFICATION (1960 REVISION, 3-DIGIT LEVEL)

Code	Description
0	Food and live animals
001	Live animals
011	Meat – fresh, chilled, frozen
012	Meat – dried, salted, smoked
013	Meat – canned or prepared
022	Milk and cream
023	Butter
024	Cheese and curd
025	Eggs
031	Fresh fish
032	Canned or prepared fish
041	Unmilled wheat
042	Rice
043	Unmilled barley
044	Unmilled maize
045	Unmilled cereals, n.e.s.
046	Wheatmeal or flour
047	Non-wheatmeal or flour
048	Cereal preparations
051	Fresh fruit and nuts
052	Dried fruit
053	Preserved or prepared fruit
054	Fresh vegetables
055	Preserved or prepared vegetables
061	Sugar and honey
062	Sugar preparations
071	Coffee
072	Cocoa

Code	Description
073	Chocolate
074	Tea
075	Spices
081	Animal feeding stuff
091	Margarine, shortening
099	Food preparations, n.e.s.
1	Beverages and tobacco
111	Non-alcoholic beverages, n.e.s.
112	Alcoholic beverages
121	Tobacco, unmanufactured
122	Tobacco manufactures
2	Crude materials, inedible, except fuel
211	Hides and skins
212	Fur skins
221	Oil seeds, nuts, kernels
231	Crude synthetic rubber
241	Fuel wood and charcoal
242	Rough wood
243	Shaped wood
244	Raw cork and waste
251	Pulp and waste paper
261	Silk
262	Wool and animal hair
263	Cotton
264	Jute
265	Vegetable fibers, excluding cotton and jute
266	Synthetic, regenerated fiber
267	Waste of textile fabrics
271	Crude fertilizers
273	Stone, sand and gravel
274	Sulphur
275	Natural abrasives
276	Other crude minerals
281	Iron ore, concentrates
282	Iron and steel scrap
283	Non-ferrous base metal ore, concentrates
284	Non-ferrous metal scrap
285	Silver and platinum ores
291	Crude animal materials, n.e.s.

Code	Description
292	Crude vegetable materials, n.e.s.
3	Mineral fuels, lubricants, related materials
321	Coal, coke, briquettes
331	Crude petroleum
332	Petroleum products
341	Natural gas and manufactures
4	Animal and vegetable oils and fats
411	Animal oil and fats
421	Fixed vegetable oils, soft
422	Fixed vegetable oils, non-soft
431	Processed animal and vegetable oils
5	Organic chemicals
512	Organic chemicals
513	Inorganic elements, oxides, etc.
514	Other inorganic elements
515	Radioactive and associated elements
521	Coal, petroleum etc. chemicals
531	Synthetic organic dyestuffs, etc.
532	Dyes n.e.s., tanning products
533	Pigments, prints, etc.
541	Medical and pharmaceutical products
551	Essential oil, perfumes, etc.
553	Cosmetics, etc.
554	Soaps and cleaning preparations
561	Manufactured fertilizers
571	Explosive and pyrotechnic products
581	Plastic materials, etc.
599	Chemicals n.e.s.
6	Manufactured goods classified by material
611	Leather
612	Leather manufactures
613	Fur skins, tanned or dressed
621	Rubber materials
629	Rubber articles, n.e.s.
631	Veneers, plywood, etc.
632	Wood manufactures, n.e.s.
633	Cork manufactures

Code	Description
641	Paper and paperboard
642	Paper articles
651	Textile yarn and thread
652	Woven cotton fabrics
653	Woven non-cotton fabrics
654	Lace, ribbons, tulle, etc.
655	Special textile products
656	Textile products n.e.s.
657	Floor coverings, tapestry, etc.
661	Cement building products
662	Clay building products
663	Other non-metal mineral manufactures
664	Glass
665	Glassware
666	Pottery
667	Pearls, precious and semi-precious stones
671	Pig iron
672	Ingots of iron and steel
673	Iron and steel shapes
674	Universals, plates and sheets of iron and steel
675	Hoop and strip of iron and steel
676	Rails and other track materials of steel
677	Iron and steel wire, excluding rod
678	Iron and steel tubes, pipes, etc.
679	Iron and steel castings, unworked
681	Silver, platinum, etc.
682	Copper
683	Nickel
684	Aluminium
685	Lead
686	Zinc
687	Tin
689	Non-ferrous base metals, n.e.s.
691	Structures and parts n.e.s.
692	Metal containers
693	Non-electric wire products
694	Nails, screws, etc., of iron, steel or copper
695	Tools
696	Cutlery
697	Base-metal household equipment
698	Metal manufactures, n.e.s.

Code	Description
7	Machinery and transport equipment
711	Non-electric power machinery
712	Agricultural machinery
714	Office machines
715	Metal-working machinery
717	Textile and leather machinery
718	Machines for special industries
719	Non-electric machines, n.e.s.
722	Electric-power machinery switches
723	Equipment for distributing electricity
724	Telecommunications equipment
725	Domestic electric equipment
726	Electromedical, X-ray equipment
729	Electric machinery, n.e.s.
731	Railway vehicles
732	Road motor vehicles
733	Road non-motor vehicles
734	Aircraft
735	Ships and boats
8	Miscellaneous manufactured articles
812	Plumbing, heating and lighting fixtures
821	Furniture
831	Travel goods, handbags
841	Clothing, except fur
842	Fur clothing
851	Footwear
861	Scientific instruments and apparatus
862	Photographic and cinematographic supplies
863	Developed cinema film
864	Watches and clocks
891	Musical instruments, recorders, etc.
892	Printed matter
893	Plastic articles, n.e.s.
894	Toys, sporting goods, etc.
895	Office supplies, n.e.s.
896	Works of art, etc.
897	Gold and silver ware, jewelry
899	Other manufactured goods

REFERENCES

Branson, William H. and Nikolaos Monoyios (1977), "Factor Inputs in US Trade", *Journal of International Economics*, Vol. 7, 111–131.

Chenery, Hollis B. and Lance Taylor (1968), "Development Patterns: Among Countries and Over Time", *Review of Economics and Statistics*, Vol. L, 391–416.

Cooper, Richard N. (1964), "Growth and Trade: Some Hypotheses about Long-Term Trends", *Journal of Economic History*, XXIV, 609–628.

Deutsch, Karl W. and Alexander Eckstein (1961), "National Industrialization and the Declining Share of the International Economic Sector, 1890–1959", *World Politics*, XIII, 267–299.

Emmanuel, Arghiri (1972), *Unequal Exchange: A Study of the Imperialism of Trade*. New York and London: Monthly Review Press.

Findlay, Ronald (1980), "The Fundamental Determinants of the Terms of Trade", in S. Grassman and E. Lundberg (editors), *The World Economic Order: Past and Prospects*. London: The Macmillan Press, 425–457.

Grassman, Sven (1980), "Long-Term Trends in Openness of National Economies", *Oxford Economic Papers*, Vol. 32, 123–133.

Helpman, Elhanan (1981), "International Trade in the Presence of Product Differentiation, Economies of Scale and Monopolistic Competition: A Chamberlin-Heckscher-Ohlin Approach", *Journal of International Economics*, Vol. 11, 305–340.

Hirschman, Albert O. (1945), *National Power and the Structure of Foreign Trade*. Berkeley and Los Angeles: University of California Press.

Hufbauer, G. C. (1970), "The Impact of National Characteristics and Technology on the Commodity Composition of Trade in Manufactured Goods", in R. Vernon (editor), *The Technology Factor in International Trade*. New York: Columbia University Press for the National Bureau of Economic Research, 145–231.

Keesing, Donald B. (1965), "Labor Skills and International Trade: Evaluating Many Trade Flows with a Single Measuring Device", *Review of Economics and Statistics*, Vol. 47, 287–294.

Keesing, Donald B. (1971), "Different Countries' Labor Skill Coefficient and the Skill Intensity of International Trade Flows", *Journal of International Economics*, Vol. 1, 443–452.

Kindleberger, Charles P. (1962), *Foreign Trade and the National Economy*. New Haven and London: Yale University Press.

Knorr, Klaus (1975), *The Power of Nations*. New York: Basic Books.

Kravis, Irving B. (1956), "Wages and Foreign Trade", *Review of Economics and Statistics*, Vol. 38, 14–30.

Kravis, Irving B. (1970), "Trade as a Handmaiden of Growth: Similarities between the Nineteenth and Twentieth Centuries", *Economic Journal*, LXXX, 850–872.

Kravis, Irving B. and Robert E. Lipsey (1971), *Price Competitiveness in World Trade*. New York: Columbia University Press for the National Bureau of Economic Research.

Kuznets, Simon (1959), *Six Lectures on Economic Growth*. Glencoe, Illinois: The Free Press.

Kuznets, Simon (1967), "Quantitative Aspects of the Economic Growth of Nations: X. Level and Structure of Foreign Trade: Long-Term Trends", supplement to *Economic Development and Cultural Change*, Vol. 15, No. 2, Part II, 1–140.

Lancaster, Kelvin (1980), "Intra-Industry Trade under Perfect Monopolistic Competition", *Journal of International Economics*, Vol. 10, 151–175.

Lary, Hal B. (1968), *Imports of Manufactures from Less-Developed Countries*. New York: Columbia University Press for the National Bureau of Economic Research.

Lewis, W. Arthur (1952), "World Production, Prices and Trade, 1870–1920", *Manchester School of Economic and Social Studies*, Vol. XX, 105–138.

Lewis, W. Arthur (1954), "Economic Development with Unlimited Supplies of Labour", *Manchester School of Economic and Social Studies*, Vol. XXII, 139–191.

Linder, Staffan Burenstam (1961), *An Essay on Trade and Transformation*. New York: John Wiley and Sons.

Lipsey, Robert E. (1963), *Price and Quantity Trends in the Foreign Trade of the United States*. New York: Columbia University Press for the National Bureau of Economic Research.

Michaely, Michael (1958), "Concentration of Exports and Imports: An International Comparison", *Economic Journal*, Vol. LXVIII, 722–736.

Michaely, Michael (1960), "The Shares of Countries in World Trade", *Review of Economics and Statistics*, Vol. XLII, 307–317.

Michaely, Michael (1962a), *Concentration in International Trade*. Amsterdam: North-Holland.

Michaely, Michael (1962b), "Multilateral Balancing in International Trade", *American Economic Review*, Vol. LII, 685–702.

Michaely, Michael (1981), "Foreign Aid, Economic Structure and Dependence", *Journal of Development Economics*, Vol. 9, 313–330.

Posner, M. V. (1961), "International Trade and Technical Change", *Oxford Economic Papers*, Vol. 13, 323–341.

Prebisch, R. (1950), "The Economic Development of Latin America and Its Principal Problems", *Economic Bulletin for Latin America*, Vol. 7, 1–22.

Robinson, E. A. G. (editor) (1960), *Economic Consequences of the Size of Nations*. London: The Macmillan Press.

Singer, H. W. (1950), "The Distribution of Gains between Investing and Borrowing Countries", *American Economic Review*, Vol. XL, 473–485.

Spraos, John (1980), "The Statistical Debate on the Net Barter Terms of Trade between Primary Commodities and Manufactures", *Economic Journal*, Vol. 90, 107–128.

Tuong, Dac and Alexander J. Yeats (1976), "A Note on the Measurement of Trade Concentration", *Oxford Bulletin of Economics and Statistics*, 38, 299–309.

Vernon, Raymond (1966), "International Investment and International Trade in the Product Cycle", *Quarterly Journal of Economics*, Vol. LXXX, 190–207.

Yeats, Alexander J. (1979), *Trade Barriers Facing Developing Countries*. London: The Macmillan Press.

Primary statistical sources

International Monetary Fund (1980), *International Financial Statistics*, Yearbook.

United Nations, *Direction of International Trade*, various issues.

United Nations, *Statistical Yearbook*, various issues.

United Nations, *Yearbook of International Trade Statistics*, various issues.

United Nations, *Yearbook of National Accounts Statistics*, various issues.

United Nations (1977), *Standardized Input–Output Tables of ECE Countries for Years around 1965*.

United States International Trade Commission (1975), *Protection in Major Trading Countries*.

World Bank, *Atlas*, various issues.

INDEX